Fire in the Canyon

Fire in the Canyon

Religion, Migration, and the Mexican Dream

LEAH SARAT

NEW YORK UNIVERSITY PRESS
New York and London

NEW YORK UNIVERSITY PRESS
New York and London
www.nyupress.org

© 2013 by New York University
All rights reserved

References to Internet websites (URLs) were accurate at the time of writing.
Neither the author nor New York University Press is responsible for URLs that
may have expired or changed since the manuscript was prepared.

For Library of Congress Cataloging-in-publication data,
please contact the Library of Congress

ISBN: 978-0-8147-5937-0 (cl.)
ISBN: 978-1-5836-7315-7 (pbk.)

New York University Press books are printed on acid-free paper,
and their binding materials are chosen for strength and durability.
We strive to use environmentally responsible suppliers and materials
to the greatest extent possible in publishing our books.

Manufactured in the United States of America
10 9 8 7 6 5 4 3 2 1

Also available as an ebook

*For those whose friendship
has stretched my mind, humbled my spirit, and enlivened my heart*

CONTENTS

Acknowledgments	ix
Introduction	1
PART I	
1. Fire from Heaven	29
2. Living Crosses	54
3. I Lift Up My Eyes to the North	68
PART II	
4. Send Us Power	87
5. To Crush the Devil's Head	102
6. Shielded by the Blood of Christ	122
PART III	
7. The Night Hike	145
8. The Mexican Dream	168
Conclusion	191
Glossary of Spanish and Hñähñu Terms	209
Notes	213
Bibliography	221
Index	231
About the Author	241

ACKNOWLEDGMENTS

Although those of us in academia often work under the illusion of individualism, I am deeply aware that this book is a social product that could not have come into being without the vision, inspiration, and support of many, both within and outside of the university setting. Above all, I would like to extend my gratitude to the members of the community of El Alberto, on both sides of the border, who have contributed to this work in diverse ways. I thank those who offered their stories and wisdom in interviews, as well as those who extended hospitality, friendship, and support during my visits to the town and during my time in Phoenix. I offer this work in the hope that it will contribute toward the community's larger goal of deepening public understandings of migration. Special thanks go to the Bautista, Santiago, and Moran families, as well as to the pastors and congregations of Templo Bethel in El Alberto and Bethel Centro Familiar Cristiano in Phoenix.

I extend a heartfelt thanks to Manuel Vásquez and Robin Wright in the Department of Religion at the University of Florida for their mentorship and feedback on the manuscript, as well as to Philip Williams and Pablo Vila for their careful reading and insightful comments. I thank the other graduate faculty of Religion at the University of Florida, especially David Hackett, whose kind advice taught me to distinguish between "necessary and unnecessary suffering," and Anna Peterson, whose graduate seminar on Religion and Social Change helped lay the theoretical foundations for this project. I extend thanks to Anne Newman and Ronald Ozbun for their practical support, to the faculty and staff at the University of Florida Center for Latin American Studies, and to the Tinker Foundation for the grant that financed my first research visit to El Alberto. I thank Tom Peterson for passing along a fascination for the study of ritual in his excellent seminars at Alfred University, and I thank my mentors at Wilfrid Laurier University, especially Ron Grimes, Carol Duncan, and Janet McClellan.

My colleagues at Arizona State University have provided a supportive and stimulating intellectual environment as I have worked to complete this project. I extend special thanks to Joel Gereboff, Tracy Fessenden, Carlos Vélez-Ibáñez, and Cecilia Menjívar for their advice and insight. I am grateful to Stephanie Bilinksy and Martha Hernández for their research and transcription assistance, and I extend my appreciation to Bradley DeBiase, Eric Breault, Michael Broyles, Derek Schuttpelz, Alana Vehaba, Matthew Wilson, and Shawn Worden for their illuminating comments in my "Religion, Migration, and Mobility in the Americas" graduate seminar at ASU.

A fellowship through the Institute for Humanities Research at ASU provided invaluable support for this project during the 2011–2012 academic year. I am grateful to IHR Director Sally Kitch and Assistant Director Kathy Holladay, as well as to IHR fellows Andrea Ballestero, Wei Li, Franscoise Mirguet, Yajaira Padilla, Claudia Sadowski-Smith, and Sujey Vega for providing a supportive intellectual environment as I worked through many of the ideas contained within this book. I also received valuable feedback from colleagues Evelyn Cruz, Jennifer Glick, Luis Plascencia, Carlos Santos, and Marie Provine, who were involved in an Immigration Research Cluster made possible by support from the Institute for Humanities Research at ASU.

I extend my thanks to colleagues outsides of ASU who have commented upon chapter drafts, as well as those who have shaped the book's direction through conversations about religion, life, death, the U.S.-Mexico border, and everything in between. I thank Robinson Herrera, Richard Ramsay, Ella Schmidt, David Charles Wright Carr, Tex Sample, Andrew Paxman, and Rose Caraway for reading and responding to chapter drafts. I extend a special thanks to Rose Caraway and Robin Globus for their continued friendship and for the many insights our conversations about religion have helped to uncover over the years. Thanks to Eleanor Finnegan, Greg McElwain, and my other colleagues at the University of Florida, and thanks to the many people outside of the academy whose challenging questions and creative insights have expanded this project, including Purificación Álvarez, Laura Basualdo, Margarito Blancas, Julie Cruse, Raymundo Martin, Alfonso Martínez, and Chris Zurheide.

I am grateful to Jennifer Hammer, my editor at New York University Press, for her consistently prompt and insightful guidance. I also extend thanks to fellow researcher Guadalupe Rivera Garay and to the staff at Hmunts'a Hem'i in Ixmiquilpan, who have offered valuable research support, and to Yolanda Lastra, Verónica Kugel, and the other organizers of the Colloquio Sobre Otopames for providing a supportive intellectual community in Mexico.

Throughout the writing process I have had the privilege to share my intellectual journey with those who are engaged first-hand in the struggle for immigrant rights at the U.S.-Mexico border and in the United States. To the good folks at Annunciation House, the Gainesville Catholic Worker, the Restoration Project, Puente, and the Arizona Interfaith Alliance for Worker Justice, I owe heartfelt thanks for the reminder that the best knowledge is that which is applied toward fostering spaces of loving community and justice in the world. Finally, I am deeply grateful for the support and understanding of my family. My mother, Melissa Sarat, has passed along a spirit of creativity and a deep appreciation for the art of storytelling, and my father, Frank Sarat, has shared his love of writing and adventurous spirit. I thank my sister, Evangeline Sarat, for setting a fearless example of how to put one's dreams into action, and I thank my extended family, especially Yheva, Saul, and the Blackburn, Martin, and Taylor families, for their ongoing love and support.

Introduction

On a spring night in 2008, hundreds of people in the Mexican state of Hidalgo pressed into the base of a canyon ablaze with torches. So palpable was the shared shock and grief, people later said, that neither pastor nor priest was needed. The place was El Alberto, an Otomí community located several hours north of Mexico City, in the region known as the Valle del Mezquital. The event was a memorial service for one of their own who had died in the desert of southern Arizona, shortly after an attempted border passage. Earlier that evening, several young men from this community of about two thousand people had climbed steep, rocky trails to light giant luminaries upon the canyon walls. As families arrived by the carload, the smell of kerosene and the flicker of torchlight cut through the growing darkness. It was nearly dawn by the time the remains of the deceased arrived. The event marked the first time a migrant from El Alberto had died at the U.S.-Mexico border. It was not the first time the torches had been lit.

Since 2004, residents of El Alberto have produced the torch show once a week. They do so as part of the Caminata Nocturna, a U.S.-Mexico border crossing simulation that invites tourists—the majority of them young professionals from Mexico City—to step into the shoes of an undocumented migrant for a night. The border simulation is the main attraction within Parque EcoAlberto, the ecotourism park that is owned and operated by the members of the community. The majority of the actors in the Caminata are former U.S. migrants who have returned to El Alberto to give a year of unpaid service to their hometown. Since the program's inception, thousands of Mexican citizens and scores of international reporters have muddied their clothes, bruised their ankles, and at times been moved to tears in this rigorous, four- to five-hour nighttime hike. Contrary to expectations, the border enactment does not end with a simulated arrival to the United States. Rather, the Caminata closes with a display of torches representing those who have died en route, as was done during the outdoor memorial service in 2008. Gathered below this stark reminder of lives lost, tourists join one another in a rousing chorus of the Mexican national anthem.

By staging the Caminata Nocturna each week, residents of El Alberto bring much-needed economic resources to their town. Yet they also seek to spark a shift in national consciousness. After catching tourists' attention through the rigorous exertion of the border simulation, they urge participants to join them in pursuing the "Mexican Dream." In contrast to the individualism and consumerism associated with the American Dream, the Mexican Dream is a vision of a sustainable future in which Mexico's citizens will be no longer be compelled to leave the country in search of work. What tourists do not know is that well over half of El Alberto's residents—including several key visionaries behind the border simulation—are Pentecostal, and that the religion is deeply intertwined with the daily challenges of migration to the United States. Indeed, the influence of Pentecostalism within the town's collective imagination is so strong that a survivor of the 2008 border passage accident emerged from a coma to tell of a near-death encounter with God that prompted his born-again salvation experience. While the Caminata Nocturna has been featured by media outlets as wide-reaching as National Geographic and 60 Minutes, this book examines the relationship between religion, migration, and collective organizing in the town behind the headlines.

Moving beyond "push-pull" economic explanations, scholars of migration have called attention to the role of social networks in shaping people's migration choices. According to social network theory, migrants do not make decisions simply as individual, rationally calculating actors. Rather, the decision to migrate and the success of the journey largely depend upon the social relationships in which a person is embedded. Yet social network approaches alone cannot fully explain how people grapple with the possibility of death while crossing an increasingly militarized U.S.-Mexico border. As Jacqueline Hagan argues, today the risks and uncertainties involved in undocumented U.S. migration are such that even the resources provided by social networks are no longer enough. Rather, people turn increasingly to religion before, during, and after the undocumented journey, seeking the spiritual strength and vision necessary to complete the ordeal when all other resources are exhausted.[1] Building upon Hagan's findings, the starting assumption of this book is that the act of undocumented U.S.-Mexico border passage is far more than a social, economic, or political phenomenon. Crossing the border is also a deeply religious matter. The journey confronts people with hard-hitting questions about life, death, and the limits of human power. Migration challenges those who travel, those who live in receiving countries, and those who remain behind to reexamine the authority upon which earthly governments rest. Religions are especially relevant within the context of migration, for they provide lenses through which people chart out their places in the cosmos and make sense of suffering.[2] They connect physical, flesh-and-blood experiences with collective representations of ultimate reality. Since religions are embedded in everyday, social experience, they are also tied to people's semi-conscious desires and notions of the possible.[3] As Peggy Levitt rightly claims, "we miss the boat by insisting that religion and culture stop at the nation's borders."[4] Likewise, we miss the mark if we neglect to recognize the role of religion in the migration process. Yet this book is more than a story of immigrants turning to religion as they cross the U.S.-Mexico border in pursuit of a better life. The reality is more complex.

This book makes two arguments. First, Pentecostalism in El Alberto is deeply intertwined not only with the challenges of the undocumented journey, but also with the daily fabric of cross-border life. The religion's combined arsenal of faith healing and prosperity theology resonates with the promises and perils of pursuing income in the United

States. At the same time, Pentecostal salvation and spiritual warfare offer a sense of protection to those whose bodies must cross through dangerous physical and spiritual spaces in search of work. Over the past decade, however, the undocumented journey has become more deadly than ever, and so the second argument is that even religion is no longer enough to help potential migrants navigate the complex choices they face. Poised between life-threatening danger at the border, life-sapping marginalization in the United States, and grueling unemployment at home, members of El Alberto's Pentecostal majority continue to pursue individual salvation. Yet they are also rolling up their sleeves and joining their non-evangelical neighbors in this-worldly, collective efforts to draw attention to the root causes of migration and demand an alternate future. As they participate in the Caminata project and call for the "Mexican Dream," Pentecostals in El Alberto do not leave their faith behind. Rather, keeping their sights on heaven and earth alike, they draw upon all of the resources at their disposal to expand their range of options on the local and international scene.

Religion, Migration, and the Caminata Nocturna

My interest in religion and migration first emerged in 2001 when I began a position as a full-time volunteer at a migrant women's shelter in Ciudad Juárez, Chihuahua. By November of that year, the effects of post-9/11 immigration enforcement were clearly visible upon the local landscape. Wait times at the El Paso ports of entry had tripled. Helicopters had become a common presence in the region's skyline. In 2003, Immigration and Naturalization Services was placed under the authority of the Department of Homeland Security. The transfer was accompanied by a shift in ideology that increasingly associated undocumented immigration with terrorism. I witnessed the effects of this shift first-hand when a nineteen-year-old guest at Annunciation House, our organization's sister shelter in El Paso, was shot and killed by Border Patrol agents when he was taking out the trash in the shelter parking lot one afternoon. As another volunteer and I drove Juan Patricio's parents from the Juárez airport to El Paso for the memorial service, his father asked us, "Why did they kill my son?" We had no response.

Juan Patricio's death was but one of the effects of border militarization that I witnessed in El Paso and Juárez. In El Paso, a sixteen-year-old shelter guest lost her legs while attempting to hop a train headed deeper into the United States. Immigration checkpoints on the highways leading out of town had become so heavily attended that she dared not travel by road. In Juárez, I met women who had traveled not only from southern Mexico but also through the entire migration corridor through Honduras, El Salvador, and Guatemala. Some were brought to our door by Mexican immigration officials after failed border crossing attempts. One woman from Honduras had been raped by her *coyote*, the guide whom she had paid thousands of dollars to lead her across the border. On several occasions I mistakenly assumed that the new arrivals suffered from mental illness, so shaken, hungry, and exhausted they were when they arrived at our door.

While the situation for migrant women in Juárez was dire, I also witnessed multiple ways in which they generated the resilience necessary to go on. In particular, I observed the effectiveness of narrative in helping women to process their experiences. At times women told of their travels throughout Mexico and across the border with the same intensity with which one might recount the birth of a child or the death of a loved one. The migration journey was, for these women, a life crisis.[5] As described in ritual studies theory, a life crisis is a transition in human life, such as birth, death, or coming of age, which stirs such fundamental questions about physical experience and identity into view that people inscribe collective meaning into the event through ritual action. As I listened to scores of women tell their stories, I noticed that religious faith often made the difference between action and paralysis, between hope and despair. A woman who had survived domestic violence at the hands of a prominent member of a drug cartel, for example, drew upon her Catholic faith as she gradually worked out a plan while telling and retelling her story. I also witnessed the psychological benefits of performance as the shelter guests danced, joked, and processed their memories as a community. One afternoon as we sorted piles of donations, the woman who had survived rape at the border donned a pair of mustached Groucho Marx glasses and an oversized T-shirt and galloped around the house, transforming the energy of the horrors she had endured into cathartic laughter. I remember a young boy who had traveled the length of Mexico with his mother as they sought to escape domestic violence. A natural entertainer, Jesús would chant and sway as he acted out stories invented on the spot.

The women and children I met in Juárez used creative action to transform their individual migration experiences into something that could be collectively shared. Yet the process was relatively ad hoc and spontaneous. If religious narrative and performance were so effective in helping these women to chart out plans of action in the face of severely limited options, I wondered how communities throughout Mexico and Central America might be using religion to respond to migration on a collective level. After leaving Ciudad Juárez, I scanned the literature on religion and immigration to find cases in which people have used collective action to make sense of the border and respond to the migration journey. I learned of the Posada Sin Fronteras, an annual protest ritual in which migrants, activists, and faith workers gather to celebrate mass through the chain-link fence at the Tijuana–San Diego border.[6] I learned of the rich tradition of migration-related *retablos*, devotional paintings left at Catholic shrines in thanksgiving for miracles performed during the journey and throughout the trials of working in the United States.[7] I learned of makeshift shrines that migrants in transit have constructed in the desert using found materials.[8] And, echoing my experience in Juárez, I learned of the extensive role of faith workers in responding to the needs of people in motion throughout Central America, Mexico, and the United States.[9] Some faith leaders have even taken steps to develop a "theology of migration" that takes migrant experience as the starting point for religious reflection.[10] I was most interested, however, in learning about the steps migrants themselves have taken to reflect upon and make collective sense out of their lived realities. Jacqueline Hagan's study of Pentecostal Maya migrants from the Totonicapán region of Guatemala[11] became a key inspiration for my research. Hagan finds that potential migrants draw upon fasting, prophecy, and prayer as they make the initial decision to travel to the United States. Relatives and fellow worshippers then pray for migrants in their absence and welcome them after their arrival, thus spinning the fibers of enduring transnational religious bonds.

When I came across a news article about the Caminata Nocturna in the winter of 2007,[12] I was taken aback, almost offended. I pictured a theme park complete with plastic cacti and oversized sombreros. Rumors circulated that the border simulation served as a training-ground for would-be migrants.[13] After reading further, I soon found that the project is a sincere, grass-roots effort through which the members of a community strained by migration have come together to convey the hardship of border passage to their well-heeled fellow citizens. They have taken the ugliness of the undocumented journey—the dull ache of thirst, the threat of death, the violence and indignity of encounters with Border Patrol agents—and transformed it into something new. The tourist cabin in which I spent my first night at Parque EcoAlberto was the product of such alchemy. Thick stone walls, a sturdy roof of agave leaves, pillowcases embroidered with vivid birds: the cabin was stunning. Its design was the product of two unlikely sources. It drew inspiration from the humble, cactus-walled dwellings that were common in years past when poverty was dire and food sparse. And it also drew inspiration from the early twenty-first century housing boom in the U.S. Southwest. Migrants from El Alberto who have honed their construction skills building houses and hotels in Las Vegas, Phoenix, and Salt Lake City, have learned something of tourism, as well.

My initial research plan was to investigate the Caminata Nocturna alone, interpreting the tourist reenactment in light of ritual and performance theory. Although the Caminata is not overtly religious, it is a form of creative performance that shares much common ground with religious practice. Like religion, the Caminata helps people to establish places of belonging in space and time.[14] It also facilitates passage across physical and temporal borders.[15] Like religious practice, the Caminata Nocturna proposes ways for people to locate themselves in the cosmos and redefine their relationships with one another. The Caminata serves, like ritual, as "a mode of paying attention,"[16] using imagined border space to direct people's gazes toward new possibilities as the presence of glowing torches evokes the souls of those departed.

The first time I donned my sneakers to join in the Caminata Nocturna, I had come straight from the *clausura*, a festival marking the closing of the school year. Hundreds of the town's residents had gathered to watch their children and their neighbors' children, dressed in suits and satin gowns, dance in solemn, choreographed rows and sing the Mexican national anthem. The children's relatives and neighbors clapped modestly at the teachers' urging. Weeks later I would stand in a Pentecostal church with many of the same people as they clapped until their hands burned. "*Y me quema y me quema y me quema!*" ("and it burns me and it burns me and it burns me!") they sang, invoking the fire of the Holy Spirit as the pastor pounded out music on the electric keyboard. That first night, however, I was unaware of the strong presence of Pentecostalism in El Alberto. I was led past the school basketball court and toward a classroom-turned-banquet hall. I sat at a table crowded with local dignitaries and was served barbecued goat and rich broth with wedges of lime. Outside, the basketball court-turned-stage made a second metamorphosis into a dance floor. Tunes and announcements spiraled out through amplifiers to ricochet off of the surrounding hills.

"This one's going out to the cute girls sitting at the corner—someone get up and dance with them!"

A few couples braved the floor.

"And here's a greeting for my *compadre* Miguel who's about to go to the Union Americana—*buen viaje!*" said the DJ, reading off messages. "And 'hello' to Lupe, in Las Vegas—that's from her man, José!"

The festival that night was intimately local yet shot through with transnational elements. The event's planning committee had worked for months to ensure nothing would be lacking. The day before, a dozen men from the town had butchered half a dozen goats and prepared the underground pits where they would be roasted between agave leaves and over hot stones through the night. Women made tortillas by the hundred. Parents, grandparents, aunts, uncles, and neighbors joined together to show support for their youth. Yet the DJ's stream of greetings to and from the United States provided a gripping reminder of those not present, while at the same time suggesting that El Alberto is part of a "transnational social field"[17] that extends well into the United States.

I would soon find that the same sense of separation that was so palpable during the school closing festival also pervades Pentecostal worship. On Saturday nights, when the Caminata Nocturna's sirens and simulated gunshots sound through the riverbanks and cornfields of El Alberto, they mingle with songs, handclapping, and prayers spilling forth from the windows of the town's two Pentecostal churches. Many of those prayers are for relatives and loved ones in the United States.

Pentecostalism was present in the Valle del Mezquital by the early 1930s, yet it was not until the 1960s that the religion reached El Alberto. Contrary to popular assumptions about Protestant presence in Latin America, in this case the key agents of religious transmission were not U.S. missionaries but rather a few men from the region who had returned home after working as *braceros*[18] (temporary contract laborers) in the United States.

The emergence of Pentecostalism can be traced to 1901, when a group of seminary students in Topeka, Kansas, began speaking in tongues. While glossolalia was not new to Christianity, the students interpreted the phenomenon in a new light. They saw it as a sign that the spiritual gifts described in the New Testament had been restored to the church and the world was entering the final days before Christ's Second Coming. The movement soon spread to Los Angeles and gave rise to the famous Azusa Street revival. There, participants prayed, spoke in tongues, and conducted divine healings in a fervor that extended from weeks to months to years. The revival was uniquely interracial, drawing energy from the social ferment of a newly expanding American West.[19]

Since American Pentecostals hailed mostly from among the working classes, the new religion lacked the resources and institutional structure necessary to sustain centrally organized missionary activity.[20] But that did not stop its growth. Pentecostalism spread, as its adherents describe, like "fire" at the grassroots level, transmitted from pastor to pastor and from worker to worker across the American Southwest and into Mexico. The religion's popularity can be explained in part by its emphasis on the immediate, embodied workings of the Holy Spirit. Within Pentecostalism, physical and spiritual states are closely intertwined. Just as bodies can fall ill from spiritual causes, so they can be healed through the presence of the Holy Spirit. This non-dualistic approach to illness and healing resonates with *curanderismo*, or traditional Mexican folk healing. It would not be long before newly formed Mexican Pentecostal organizations began sending missionaries of their own to the United States.[21] The religion was thus transnational from the start, following the paths of myriad workers from Kansas to Los Angeles, Hidalgo to Texas, and Arizona to Mexico City.

When Pentecostalism reached El Alberto in the 1960s, religious change coincided with a wave of socioeconomic development that greatly transformed life in the region. As new converts sought spiritual salvation, they also sought salvation from the poverty and social marginalization they had endured for too long. Pentecostals in El Alberto state that the new religion "opened their eyes" and caused them to think of the future. Nevertheless, the community's material problems were not over. After the initial wave of conversion, El Alberto's members began traveling out in ever-widening spheres in search of work. U.S. migration eventually led to hardships of its own, thus providing an impetus for continued religious change. Before we turn to that story, however, it is necessary to provide contextual background about the community and the surrounding region.

El Alberto

El Alberto is located several hours north of Mexico City, in the Central Mexican state of Hidalgo. The community belongs to the municipality of Ixmiquilpan, a nearby city of about 34,000 people.[22] Due to high levels of migration to the United States, the exact population of El Alberto is difficult to ascertain. The 2010 Mexican census lists 834 inhabitants, with a higher percentage of women than men, suggesting high levels of emigration.[23] However, this source includes only those who were living in El Alberto at the time the information was gathered and does not account for those who dwell across the border yet are considered full members or "citizens" of the community. Thus, according to town authorities, El Alberto has a population of about 2,000 people, half of whom live in the United States. The majority of the people in the community speak Otomí, an indigenous language with over 230,000 speakers over the age of four in Mexico. Over half of the Otomí speakers in El Alberto are also bilingual in Spanish.[24]

As a *comunidad,* or legally recognized indigenous community, El Alberto contains a combination of both private and collectively managed lands, and individuals within the town cannot sell land to outsiders.[25] Several thousand of the community's shared acres form the basis of Parque EcoAlberto. The ecotourism park is divided into two main sites: the "Gran Cañón," named after the Grand Canyon in the United States, and the *balneario,* or swimming pool area. The canyon surrounds the Tula River, and the *balneario* makes use of natural hot springs. The surrounding Valle del Mezquital spans 2,782 square miles within the Central Mexican Highlands.[26] The region, which falls mostly within the state of Hidalgo, is not a single valley but rather a collection of seven valleys and the mountains that surround them.[27] Known as "Mbonthi" in Otomí, the region's name refers to the mesquite trees that are a common sight throughout.[28]

In the Mexican national imagination, the Valle del Mezquital was long known as an arid region, home to an impoverished and socially isolated indigenous population.[29] Despite their proximity to the Tula River, residents of El Alberto once struggled to produce food, given the sparse rains and poor soil of the area. Since the introduction of irrigation in the mid-1970s, however, much of the valley's terrain has been transformed into arable land. At the same time, the benefits of irrigation have not come without a cost, for the region is now irrigated with treated wastewater from Mexico City which has introduced new contaminants to the soil.

The Valle del Mezquital remains a concentrated center of indigenous population. Along with the Sierra Otomí, who occupy the mountainous region at the boundary of the states of Puebla, Hidalgo, and Veracruz, the Otomí of the Valle del Mezquital belong to the larger Otomí language group. Since the term "Otomí" derives from the language of the Nahua-speaking people who conquered Otomí lands during the pre-colonial era, today the endonym "hñähñu" is the preferred term of self-reference within the Valle del Mezquital.[30] In keeping with this preference, the word "hñähñu" rather than "Otomí" will be used throughout this book. The ethnic group rose to power after the fall of the Toltec capital of Tula in the twelfth century CE. Their kingdom was based in Xaltocan, near present-day Mexico City.[31] When Xaltocan fell at the end of the thirteenth century, the Otomí dispersed, giving rise to the regional distinctions that exist today. By some accounts, the hñähñu were already present in the Valle del Mezquital as early as 250 CE.[32] Other accounts estimate their arrival approximately four hundred years later.[33]

Early sources state that the hñähñu of the Valle del Mezquital lived in small, isolated groupings because the natural resources of the region were not amenable to concentrated settlement.[34] After coming under the control of the Aztec Triple Alliance and later Spanish colonizers, the hñähñu retreated to the most remote regions of the Valle del Mezquital and developed a tradition of resistance that continues to the present day.[35] The residents of El Alberto, like many hñähñu speakers throughout the Valle del Mezquital, continue to identify as survivors deeply committed to maintaining autonomy in the face of external political and economic manipulations. Originally known as "Santa Cruz El Alberto," the community was largely isolated from the surrounding region until the mid-twentieth century, for it was accessible only by foot and the residents were almost entirely monolingual. Despite their relative isolation, communities within the Valle del Mezquital differed markedly at the time. Some consisted almost entirely of people employed in the region's mining industry. Others enjoyed a greater economic independence by producing artisan goods and marketing them directly to the public.[36]

Beginning in the 1950s, however, the communities of the region underwent significant change due to the formation of the Patrimonio Indígena del Valle del Mezquital, a government agency that sought to alleviate the region's poverty through Western-style education and development.[37] By 1970, the organization had begun to bring schools, electricity, roads, and water into communities in the region, including El Alberto. This process of development was closely intertwined with religious change. As communities responded to the organizational demands of development, young, bilingual individuals took on greater leadership roles. In doing so, they challenged the authority of traditional civil-religious hierarchies, in which political influence is reserved for those who have undertaken the costly burdens of Catholic festival sponsorship. Meanwhile, evangelical Protestantism began to gain a hold in the region. The origins of the Pachuca, Hidalgo-based Iglesia Cristiana Independiente Pentecostés (ICIP), the movement from which El Alberto's two Pentecostal churches derive, lie with Mexican migrants who had witnessed the beginnings of Pentecostalism in the United States and returned in the 1930s to plant churches in Mexico. ICIP churches soon spread from Pachuca and the Valle del Mezquital to other parts of Mexico and, later, to the United States. Today, ICIP has about eight thousand churches worldwide. It was in the early 1960s that the organization made inroads into El Alberto. The town's first Pentecostal church was founded a decade later, and subsequently divided due to a leadership conflict. El Alberto's two Pentecostal churches, Bethel and Sinaí, reflect organizational divisions in the ICIP organization as a whole. Among these, Bethel has stronger transnational connections, with over 150 churches in the Valle del Mezquital as well as churches in sixteen U.S. states and parts of Central America.

In a recent census, three hundred of the town's members identified as Catholic. Over five hundred identified as Protestant or as belonging to other biblical religions, and twenty stated that they had no religion. My research revealed that the town contains a small number of Jehovah's Witnesses and Latter-day Saints, along with a handful of Spiritualists whose worship practice is centered mostly within one extended family. The prominence of Pentecostalism in El Alberto is not representative of the municipality of Ixmiquilpan as a whole, which has a Catholic majority.[38] A frequent refrain among Catholics and Pentecostals in El Alberto is that their community has passed through an era of religious conflict and now enjoys a considerable degree of harmony. Despite their religious differences, the town's residents are united by their participation in the town's system of collective labor. That system is grounded in ties of kinship and ethnicity that are in some ways stronger than the bonds of religious affiliation. But El Alberto's interreligious harmony is not shared by all indigenous communities in the Valle del Mezquital. Some towns remain largely Catholic, some are almost entirely Pentecostal, and others are bitterly divided. Nevertheless, all have been affected on some level by the presence of evangelical Protestantism.

The religious change that El Alberto has witnessed is part of a larger wave of Protestant conversion that is transforming the religious landscape of Latin America today. Over 15 percent of Latin America's population is evangelical Protestant,[39] and the numbers are growing. The percentage in Mexico is somewhat lower than in other parts of Latin America. Nevertheless, Mexico experienced a concentrated period of Protestant growth between 1970 and 1990, and the numbers have continued to climb. By 2010, there were over eight million Protestants in Mexico, representing over 7 percent of the country's total population.[40] During the period of intensive growth, the Protestant population of Hidalgo rose at a rate slightly higher than the national average.[41] Conversion has been higher in areas with large indigenous populations, partly because the radical shift in identity involved in evangelical conversion helps to redefine social categories that have long relegated indigenous people to an inferior status within Mexico.

Members of the Mexican public tend to recognize much less denominational difference within Protestantism than do their North American counterparts. Given the prominent historical presence of Roman Catholicism within the society, Mexicans often simply distinguish between *católicos,* on the one hand, and *cristianos* or *evangélicos* on the other, thus gathering Pentecostals, other evangelical Protestants, and mainline Protestants under a single *cristiano* umbrella. While the country has a small presence of mainline Protestants, evangelicals are by far the largest Protestant presence in the country, constituting seven and a half million of the country's roughly eight million Protestants.[42] In turn, about three-quarters of Mexican evangelicals are Pentecostal.[43] For the purpose of simplicity, and to more accurately reflect the ways in which Pentecostals in El Alberto self-identify, I use the words "Pentecostal," "evangelical," and *cristiano* interchangeably throughout the book.

Although residents of El Alberto began converting to Pentecostalism in large numbers in the 1960s and 1970s, they did not begin to migrate to the United States until the 1980s. U.S. migration was well established by the mid-1990s. While the earliest migrants from El Alberto found work in Texas, they later gravitated toward the Southwest cities of Phoenix, Las Vegas, and Salt Lake City. El Alberto's migration patterns reflect a growing trend of indigenous migration to the United States, as well as changing migration patterns among Mexicans as a whole.

As the town's residents traveled to the United States in the 1980s and 1990s, they took part in a "new geography of Mexican immigration"[44] that arose in the aftermath of the 1986 Immigration Reform and Control Act. Until the mid-1980s, most Mexican migrants to the United States traveled to states such as California, Texas, and Arizona. By the mid-1990s, the growing militarization of the border, combined with an increasingly nativist political climate in California, had driven immigrants to seek opportunities in other parts of the country.[45] In just a few years, Mexico-U.S. migration transformed from a regional to a nationwide phenomenon.[46] Not only did Mexican immigrants settle in new states such as Nevada, Florida, and North Carolina, but they also gravitated toward new urban centers, including El Alberto's prime destinations of Las Vegas and Phoenix.[47]

As Mexico-U.S. migration became more geographically diverse in the 1980s and 1990s, it also began to involve a broader portion of the country's indigenous population. For years, the Mexican government looked upon the rural poor as a surplus population that would best serve the national economy by leaving the countryside.[48] In the mid-1990s, policy-makers actually predicted that the implementation of the North American Free Trade Agreement (NAFTA), combined with cuts to agricultural subsidies, would cause the rural poor to move to cities for industrial jobs, thus reducing the country's rural population by about half in a few short decades.[49] While the prediction did not entirely come true, NAFTA did contribute toward the migration of large numbers of people from rural communities, including El Alberto, to the United States. Indigenous migration had largely been an internal, regional phenomenon until the 1980s, but by the 1990s, increasing numbers of indigenous people began crossing the U.S.-Mexico border in search of work. By the year 2000, the state of Hidalgo had the second highest emigration growth rate in the country.[50] Whereas migrants from El Alberto gravitated toward the U.S. Southwest, other hñähñu-speaking migrants from Hidalgo have traveled to Florida, North Carolina, and Georgia.[51] Migrants from the city of Ixmiquilpan, for example, have settled overwhelmingly in the tourist town of Clearwater, Florida.

Often treated as second-class citizens in Mexico, indigenous migrants face unique challenges but also draw upon unique cultural resources once they arrive in the United States.[52] In some cases mobility and dislocation serve to strengthen ethnic identity as they come to see themselves as belonging to social units that extend beyond their towns of origin. Indigenous migrants in the United States have developed a wide range of transnational political and civic self-help organizations, some of them pan-ethnic and pan-regional in nature.[53] Hñähñu migrants in Florida, for example, have established the Consejo Mexicano de la Bahía de Tampa, or Mexican Council of Tampa Bay, a transnational organization that was initially created to provide financial and logistical support to hñähñu speakers in Mexico who were seeking to transport home the bodies of relatives who had died in the United States.

Research across Borders

The material gathered in this book is drawn from a combination of qualitative, semi-structured interviews, informal conversations, and extensive participant observation in El Alberto as well as in Phoenix, Arizona. I first visited El Alberto for five weeks during the summer of 2007, and have visited the town at least once a year ever since. My longest stay in the town was for period of approximately nine weeks in the summer of 2009. Since accepting a position at Arizona State University in 2010, I have had the opportunity to form close friendships with several families from El Alberto who live in Phoenix. By attending services at Bethel's Phoenix congregation, I have gained valuable insight on the transnational dimensions of Pentecostal practice, as well as the daily challenges facing congregation members in the United States.

As noted above, I originally traveled to El Alberto intending to conduct a short-term investigation of the Caminata project. I sought to better understand the effects of U.S.-Mexico border militarization upon the members of this community by exploring which aspects of the migration journey they have chosen to reproduce for tourists, and why. I also sought to understand how tourists, in turn, perceive the Caminata's reinvented border space. While formulating my questions, I drew upon the literature of U.S.-Mexico border militarization.[54] I also drew upon ritual and performance theory[55] to examine the Caminata as a form of entertainment that crosses into the realm of efficacious performance for actors and participants alike. I would later learn of the parallel efforts of Tamara Underiner, who examines the Caminata Nocturna in light of other indigenous performances throughout Mexico.[56] Insights from the anthropology of tourism as well as comparative approaches to tourism and pilgrimage[57] also influenced the formative stages of the project.

During my first summer in El Alberto, I participated in the Caminata five times, both with tourists and from the perspective of the Border Patrol actors. I carried a voice recorder to note the sequence of action, and gathered tourists' reactions through semi-structured, recorded interviews each day following. I observed the Caminata again in the summers of 2009 and 2011. These additional observations allowed me to note how the event had shifted to incorporate new dangers, such as the heightened presence of drug-related violence in the border zone. On one occasion, the costumed Border Patrol agents invited me to join their ranks by speaking on a megaphone to the tourist "migrants" hiding in the bushes. Participants later concluded that my American accent was realistic, but I "should have made my voice meaner"—I sounded much too nice.

After the first visit to El Alberto, I soon realized that the Caminata Nocturna had to do with much more than the act of crossing the U.S.-Mexico border. The simulation also posed larger questions about work, consumption, and desire, about what it means to live well with others, and about what counts as a good and satisfying life. I expanded my research in order to better understand the origins of migration in El Alberto, as well as the evolving vision of the Mexican Dream that underlies the simulation. As the local people began to tell me about the period of religious conversion that had so deeply affected the collective life of their community, I also broadened my focus to explore that wave of conversion and to examine the role of Pentecostalism within today's migration practices.

Early on in my research, I considered giving equal weight to Pentecostal and Catholic perspectives on migration, and spending an equal amount of time in both the Bethel and Sinaí churches. However, I found it virtually impossible to divide my time equally among El Alberto's three churches. I first accompanied the members of my host family to services at Templo Bethel during my stay in El Alberto in the summer of 2007. The conventions of religious participation in the town were such that I then found it difficult to gain an equally welcome footing in the other congregations. The pastor of Sinaí put it quite clearly: while I was free to attend services at his church, I would be best advised to choose one congregation and stay there.

When residents of El Alberto asked about my own religious background, I explained that I was raised in a liberal Protestant tradition that shares some common ground with but also differs considerably from Pentecostalism. I also explained that I have strong ecumenical convictions and thus do not look upon Catholic practices as mistaken or idolatrous. In practice, however, my identity as a non-Catholic from the United States, coupled with the popular tendency to use the terms *cristiano* and *evangélico* interchangeably, often resulted in my being categorized as evangelical. I found that although this classification closed some doors to me, it also opened others. On the one hand, Catholic perspectives are underrepresented at this book, since I was not always able to achieve the same level of rapport among Catholic informants as was the case among Pentecostals. However, consistent participation at a single congregation allowed me to obtain a greater level of trust among Pentecostal worshippers than would have otherwise been possible. One key evangelical informant who had declined being interviewed by a Catholic researcher actually introduced himself to me and offered an interview without my asking.

I also had specific scholarly reasons for focusing on Pentecostalism. Not only is Pentecostalism the most widely practiced religion in the town, but its entry into the region helped lay the groundwork for U.S. migration. Highlighting the stories of Pentecostal migrants allows me to challenge popular North American assumptions that Mexico is a monolithically Catholic nation. It also allows me to bring a new layer of complexity to the immigration debate by presenting readers with the reality of undocumented evangelicals who embrace the proverbial "Protestant origins" of the very country that denies them access. Finally, whereas the presence of evangelical Protestantism in Latin America is often associated with apolitical, otherworldly orientations, the case of El Alberto challenges us to understand evangelicals as multidimensional religious actors who engage in civic and religious life in complex and overlapping ways. Focusing on Templo Bethel rather than on both Pentecostal churches has allowed me to obtain valuable insight on transnational processes, as the church has strong denominational ties to congregations in the United States. The pastor himself is a transnational figure who regularly travels across the border, connecting geographically dispersed worshippers through his greetings, sermons, and prayers.

Throughout the course of my research I attended approximately thirty worship events at Templo Bethel, including regular evening services, special services held at congregation members' homes, group fasts, and two large retreats attended by U.S. missionaries. I also had the opportunity to attend the Bethel's annual festival, which is held in late December and attracts hundreds of people from Mexico and the United States. In addition, I attended several worship services and a youth Bible class at Templo Sinaí, along with Sinaí's annual fiesta. I found it interesting that members of all three churches—Catholics and Protestants alike—attend these anniversary celebrations. Despite denominational differences, the fiestas provide opportunities for relatives and neighbors to *convivir,* or to spend close time together. I attended two masses and one evening prayer session at the Catholic church, as well as a meeting of the Catholic youth group. The academic calendar prevented me from attending the Catholic patron saint festival, the fiesta of San Alberto, which is held annually in November. However, I was able to attend a similar festival in the neighboring community of El Dadho, and observed planning sessions for the anniversary of the Caminata Nocturna, a large-scale celebration attracting thousands of attendants and national media presence.

During my first trip to El Alberto, I sought interviews primarily among tourists who had participated in the Caminata, former U.S. migrants in El Alberto who were serving as actors in the simulation, and town leaders who had been instrumental in bringing about the project. As I broadened my focus, I sought interviews with a diverse range of individuals who could comment on their use of religion in the migration process. I also sought key informants who, due their status in the community or to their close association with leading figures in the past, could offer insight on the process of social and religious change that occurred as evangelical Christianity first made an entrance in the community. Altogether, I conducted thirty-seven semi-structured interviews with residents of El Alberto. The majority of the interviews were recorded. I also interviewed two priests based in Ixmiquilpan, a Catholic religious worker who had been active in El Alberto in the past, and a Pentecostal pastor from the United States who was visiting El Alberto as part of a mission trip in 2009. Finally, I conducted recorded, semi-structured interviews with approximately thirty tourists. With several exceptions, most of the names used within the text are pseudonyms. A few people requested that I use their actual names; I thus have provided notes within the text to indicate which names remain unchanged.

While the majority of this book focuses on observations gathered within El Alberto, my time in Phoenix has opened my eyes to the crucial role of religion in people's lives across the border. This time has also challenged and humbled me in my role as a researcher and friend. When I arrived in Phoenix in July of 2010, the political climate in the state was as intense as the triple-digit heat. Earlier that spring, Governor Jan Brewer had signed into law S.B. 1070, which greatly expanded the role of local law enforcement agents in matters of immigration. The most controversial portion of the bill required local police to inquire about the immigration status of those whom they suspected of being in the country without documents. By the time the law took effect, the damage had been done: undocumented immigrants had received a clear message that they were not wanted. Meanwhile, heightened collaboration between state and federal officials resulted in increased detentions and deportations. As the pastor of Bethel's affiliated church in Phoenix preached of an imminent end of days when the righteous would be taken and the unrepentant left to perish, his words mirrored an earthly reality that was nearly as apocalyptic. One day, a fellow worshipper would be at one's side in a service. The next day, he or she might be in the county jail, in a detention facility, or across the border in Nogales. Family separation was painfully frequent.

While religious and civic activities seem to exert equal influence upon people's lives within El Alberto, in the United States the church becomes central,[58] for churches offer an alternate arena in which people are able to recreate the close-knit sense of community they have left behind. Especially for those who are undocumented, the church offers a space of belonging amidst an external social and political climate that is often quite hostile.[59] Doing "fieldwork" within my own city of residence has also led to new challenges and revealed new insights about the ethnographic process. When I travel from Phoenix to El Alberto, I no longer travel as a lone researcher. Rather, I travel laden with letters and packages, sometimes carrying the clothing and belongings of recent deportees. Then, when I return to Phoenix, I carry gifts, food, and greetings from those in Mexico to their relatives in the United States. Living in Phoenix has also caused me to stop using the term "the field" in my work. Unless we are studying prairie dogs or meadow grasses, there is no "field" to speak of, only the places that human beings call home. Since I began living in Phoenix, I have also become aware of racial and linguistic segregation in the United States as never before. The greater Phoenix metropolitan area is a strange phenomenon. A desert realm that attracts retirees and upper middle-class transplants seeking to escape the snow and cold, it has neighborhood names like "Sun City," "Paradise Valley," and "Carefree," and yet the bulk of the construction, gardening, and housecleaning work in these neighborhoods is done by immigrants, including those from El Alberto.

After my first year in Phoenix, I found that I could not sustain the same level of participation observation with Bethel's affiliated Pentecostal church as I had with the church in El Alberto. The pressures of attendance in Phoenix were so strong that it was nearly impossible to maintain the perspective of a detached observer on a long-term basis. Nevertheless, I have now had the opportunity to experience first-hand the strength with which residents of El Alberto maintain ties and social solidarities across religious divides. Research relationships are a two-way street, and during the past few years people from El Alberto living in Phoenix have accompanied me through challenges of my own. In November of 2011, as I was preparing this book for publication, my father suffered a severe rock climbing accident outside of Monterrey, Mexico. He fell twenty feet after accidentally rappelling off the end of his rope, and suffered temporary but distressing frontal lobe damage. As I boarded the flight from Phoenix to Monterrey, I sent a text message to a friend at the Pentecostal church in Phoenix. Despite my agnostic qualms, I knew that he and the other *hermanos* at Bethel would pray for my father, and I was grateful.

When I arrived at the understaffed hospital in Monterrey, I found my father disoriented and broken. As my family and I accompanied him through the acute stages of injury and recovery, we saw how he struggled for sanity on the brink of chaos, struggled for a sense of self and wholeness in the face of a close scrape with death. My father's accident was preventable—the result of a miscalculation during the practice of a high-risk sport. And yet many people face the boundary between life and death as rote necessity, as they cross the U.S.-Mexico border in search of work. Some state that at times there is a thrill to the journey. It is fraught with adrenaline, a high-risk game—a dimension that the Caminata Nocturna seizes upon and transforms. After sitting with my father as his mind struggled to piece itself together anew, I gained greater insight onto the experiences of those who have come face to face with death after finding themselves with little choice but to participate in border passage. And I am more vividly aware of the ways government policies help create and sustain unnecessary suffering. More than a political line, the southern boundary of the United States is a barrier that thousands of people each year call upon the power of God to transcend even as it pushes them to the brink of death and, sometimes, beyond.

Overview of the Book

The book is divided into three parts. The first takes a step into El Alberto's past to chart the intertwining processes of social, religious, and material change that laid the groundwork for current migration patterns; the second explores the relationship between Pentecostalism and U.S. migration today; and the final part examines the Caminata Nocturna project and the Mexican Dream that drives it. Several themes are interlaced throughout all parts of the book. One centers on the enduring influence of indigenous religiosity within Pentecostalism. I find that Pentecostalism in many ways entails a continuation of rather than a radical break with indigenous cosmologies. Pentecostalism's non-dualistic approach to the body resonates with traditional hñähñu conceptions of illness and healing, just as indigenous notions of personhood and agency continue to play out within Pentecostal spiritual warfare. A second, overlapping theme concerns the connections among embodiment, performance, and lived religion. I examine how Pentecostal practices are intertwined with the physical dimensions of the migration experience, and I explore how the Caminata Nocturna, in turn, recreates the embodied experiences that migrants encounter within the border space.

While the book as a whole follows these related threads, chapter 1 sets the stage by outlining the arrival of Pentecostalism to El Alberto. There, I argue that early conversion, which began in the 1960s, coincided with a process of socioeconomic development that drastically altered the material circumstances of people's day-to-day lives. As material changes fueled religious transformation, Pentecostalism in turn introduced a narrative of progress that instilled the socioeconomic development process with a sense of higher purpose. The changing conceptions of work, self, and community that emerged continue to inform today's migration dynamics. In contrast to this chapter's focus on development and religious change as seen through Pentecostal eyes, chapter 2 looks at Catholic perspectives. Unlike evangelicals, Catholics do not attribute their town's material progress to spiritual causes. For Catholics, the period of intensive evangelical conversion in El Alberto was a time of trial, as the loss of congregation members threatened to dissolve the fabric of the traditional *fiesta* system. Yet the solidarity-building function of the traditional festivals was not lost. Rather, that function was transferred to the secular realm, as the town's system of collective labor came to provide an infrastructure for community projects like the Caminata Nocturna. Today, Catholics and Pentecostals alike agree that despite their religious differences, El Alberto is "*un pueblo unido*," a united town.

Despite evangelical claims, the wave of religious and socioeconomic change that swept El Alberto in the 1960s and 1970s was not enough to lift people out of poverty. Thus, chapter 3 outlines the ensuing rise of migration to the United States. Beginning with internal migration in the 1960s and continuing with U.S. migration in the late 1980s, residents of El Alberto left home in growing numbers in search of work. Chapter 3 tells the stories of women who left home as children to work as domestic servants within Mexico, and men who left home as teenagers to work in Mexico City, Texas, and beyond. At first, religion receded into the background of these early migration narratives. It would not be long, however, before the hardships of migration would inspire religious responses of their own.

While the first part of the book provides a historical context for today's migration, the following part examines the relationship between migration and Pentecostalism in the present day. In chapter 4, I focus on the religious practices of those who remain in El Alberto—the relatives of emigrants who endure uncertainty as they wait for news of loved ones en route and deal with income fluctuations by supplementing migrant remittances with piecemeal work. Drawing upon aspects of prosperity theology, Pentecostals seamlessly combine daily efforts to make ends meet with fasts and prayers aimed at supporting the physical, spiritual, and financial wellbeing of relatives in the United States. After this discussion of "health-and-wealth" doctrine within U.S. migration, chapter 5 examines another dimension of Pentecostalism: spiritual warfare. Pentecostals describe Satan as a divisive force who mobilizes multiple demonic agents to attack individuals and destroy family unity.

Using spiritual warfare, Pentecostals seek to control the dangerous effects of mobility and globalization upon the bodies of the faithful and, especially, the youth. As they do so, they draw upon understandings of spiritual agency that resonate with traditional hñähñu religion.

While chapters 4 and 5 examine the broader migration context, chapter 6 centers upon Pentecostal interpretations of the undocumented journey itself. There, I argue that changes in U.S. border enforcement over the last few decades have led to an increasingly dangerous border situation that is sparking new theological reflection and even, in some cases, religious conversion. The chapter examines practices through which Pentecostals prepare migrants for departure, as well as evangelical reflections on how the act of migration has impacted their faith. The chapter closes with an analysis of the narratives and practices surrounding one man's near-death accident at the U.S.-Mexico border.

Even as Pentecostalism has become deeply intertwined with all facets of the migration journey, the rise in border danger over the last decade has also prompted residents of El Alberto to seek solutions outside of the religious sphere. In the final section of the book, I turn the reader's gaze to the Caminata Nocturna and the underlying Mexican Dream it seeks to promote. Chapter 7 provides an in-depth description of the border simulation along with the vision and planning process behind it. I argue that the project does not simply protest the trend of U.S. border militarization that has rendered undocumented passage increasingly difficult. Rather, the simulation also unlocks the creative potential of the undocumented journey and channels it toward new ends. *Coyotes* become tricksters, Border Patrol actors become catalysts of suspense, and death becomes a symbol of sacrifice as the Caminata calls not only for an end to migrant deaths at the U.S.-Mexico border, but also for a transformation in the international migration system as a whole. Then, chapter 8 looks behind the scenes of the Caminata Nocturna to examine the collective vision that drives it, showing how residents of El Alberto are finding within their ethnic heritage a tradition of endurance and collective survival that bridges religious divides and offers an antidote to the individualism and materialism of American life. Through the Caminata Nocturna, residents of El Alberto call upon one another to set their sights on their Mexican Dream of a future free of dependence on international migration. They critique the cycle of migration and consumption that is damaging their bodies and eroding their collective wellbeing, and they call for new solutions.

Week after week, year after year, residents of El Alberto carry out the Caminata Nocturna project in an effort to slow the tide of emigration from their town. Yet they recognize that the Mexican Dream is far on the horizon. In the meantime, the Pentecostal churches continue to brim with cries of the faithful as they accept the redeeming power of the Holy Spirit in anticipation of the fast-approaching end of days. The conclusion analyzes the relationship between the Caminata Nocturna and the religious beliefs of the many evangelicals who are striving to help make it a reality. I argue that, on the one hand, there are contradictions between Pentecostal doctrine and the vision of social change embodied in the Caminata Nocturna. While the Mexican Dream calls for collective, this-worldly action, Pentecostals highlight the importance of individual salvation above all earthly pursuits. Nevertheless, for some of the key architects of the Caminata Nocturna, it is the very promise of individual salvation that inspires them to give their time and efforts so that the generations who follow might have a better life. I argue that Pentecostalism and the Mexican Dream represent two interrelated calls for action in the face of migration's many challenges, and I offer some concluding observations on how the case of El Alberto can challenge us to rethink the metaphors we employ while examining the role of religion in the migration process.

Further Thoughts

After moving to Phoenix, I became friends with a woman from El Alberto whose parents had brought her to the United States as a teen. She and her husband, who is also from Mexico, once remarked on how surprised they had been when they met me. The husband explained that he had never imagined that he would one day meet a white, English-speaking American who could speak Spanish fluently and who would relate to him as an equal. I find it deeply troubling that the immigration climate in the United States is such that an undocumented person is surprised to receive from a U.S. citizen the same level of respect that all people deserve, and I write in the hope that one day no person in the United States should feel compelled to thank another person for basic human treatment.

As anthropologist Jonathan Xavier Inda tells us, current U.S. border policy is predicated on the assumption that some human lives are more worthy of protection than others.[60] This is the logic of biopower at work: in the name of preserving American life, the lives of outsiders are diminished, dismissed, and denied. For many U.S. citizens, mention of "illegal immigration" brings to mind images of drug cartels, human smugglers, and foreigners whose sheer numbers threaten to destroy the "American way of life." Seen in this light, immigrant deaths at the southern boundary of the United States are merely an unfortunate consequence of the necessary task of ensuring the safety and wellbeing of the nation. For undocumented migrants and their loved ones, meanwhile, the border has far different connotations. While this book is a scholarly investigation of the role of religion and collective action in the migration process, at its core it is an expression of something much more basic. Woven throughout these pages is the simple assertion that life, all life, is precious. Within El Alberto, the act of religious conversion, the rise of U.S. migration, and the development of the Caminata Nocturna all embody a fierce assertion of worth in the face of the pervasive societal message that the lives of migrants and indigenous people do not matter. Religious conversion and collective organizing alike represent efforts by members of this town to survive and flourish amidst the myriad forces that would restrict their mobility and devalue their existence.

PART I

1

Fire from Heaven

The word of God that came here—it changed us. This religion opened people's eyes. Those who thought of today, now think of tomorrow. So then that sense of organization began, of working together.
—Hermano Tomás

After evangelicalism arrived, the people began to multiply. Children were born. They didn't die anymore. . . . Now one can see the unity of the town.
—Hermano Roberto

A community study produced by El Alberto's health clinic in 2008 opens with a story about the town's past, describing it as a "savage town" where "nobody entered for fear of being killed." But in 1960, a man who had been working as a *bracero* in the United States brought back evangelical Christianity, "and from that day forward the town allowed people to enter, and their evolution began."[1] While the image of progression from savagery to civilization may appear extreme, the words echo a narrative of progress voiced, time and again, in interviews and informal conversations with the El Alberto's Pentecostal residents. These residents recall a past of bitter poverty and social isolation followed by a period from the late 1950s through the late 1970s when circumstances began to change. At a time when Mexico was experiencing unprecedented growth, the government made a concentrated effort to bring education and development projects to the Valle del Mezquital. El Alberto's first internal migrants traveled to Mexico City and beyond in search of work. As the town's residents learned Spanish, they engaged in greater interaction with the outside world and thereby found ways to bring schools, electricity, roads, and irrigation into the community.

It was during this time that Pentecostalism arose and flourished. While the reforms of Vatican II were taking effect, an undercover process of religious change that had begun in the early 1960s swept the town in a vigorous wave of conversion. The rise of Pentecostalism in El Alberto was thus tied to a process of development that began well before migration to the U.S. became commonplace.

This chapter explores the stories of Pentecostals in El Alberto who witnessed those crucial decades of development and religious change. While Catholics and Protestants alike recall a past of poverty and hardship, what sets evangelical accounts apart is the moral lens through which Pentecostals view their town's transformation. Pentecostals do not recall a mere lack of resources in the past. They recall a profound, debilitating lack of harmony. They speak of drunken brawls that ended in murder and of acts of sorcery that caused children to waste away and die. For them, the poverty of the past was a crisis in which moral and material wellbeing were inseparably intertwined. By extension, Pentecostals view religious conversion as the single most important change that El Alberto witnessed during the period of intensive development. They claim that evangelicalism made people stop drinking. It made them stop fighting. It made people think of "tomorrow," channeling their time and resources toward the common good. Even money from migration, many say, would have meant nothing had evangelicalism not given the people the sense to invest it well. Evangelicals state that once scarcely populated, the community has grown well into the thousands, with children and grandchildren on both sides of the border. Once a mere collection of cactus-walled huts, the town now contains scores of concrete houses and a thriving ecotourism business. I have been told, on more than one occasion, that El Alberto's material prosperity is a sign that the town has been "blessed by God."

I argue that Pentecostal narratives of the past have key implications for understanding today's migration dynamics. On the one hand, these narratives evoke the Protestant ethic described by Max Weber, in which this-worldly, material success is regarded as a sign of salvation. Pentecostals in El Alberto explain that the poverty their community once endured was a spiritual problem, and that the development process was divinely sanctioned. By extension, they imply that religious faith is an essential component of effective labor migration. We can also detect within these stories a hint of North American prosperity theology, or the "gospel of health and wealth" made infamous by scandal-prone televangelists who claim that God rewards the faithful with material goods. Yet we must be careful to avoid simplistic readings of the relationship between Protestantism and economic activity. Pentecostalism in El Alberto does bear some influence of prosperity theology, and the religion is intertwined with North American consumer capitalism in deep and at times disconcerting ways. But that is not the whole story. In order to fully understand the relationship between Pentecostalism, development, and migration in El Alberto, we must pay attention to indigenous motivations for conversion. A close look at conversion stories reveals something more basic than the desire for financial progress. Early conversions were rooted in a simple effort to overcome illness, restore harmony, and survive.

I draw here upon five formal conversion stories in addition to dozens of informal conversations gathered over the course of three summers in the town. Giving particular attention to the voice of El Alberto's first Pentecostal pastor, I also draw upon a historical study produced by the Iglesia Cristiana Independiente Pentecostés, the religious movement to which El Alberto's two evangelical churches trace their origins.

National Development in the Valle del Mezquital

In the classic Mexican anthropological literature, the Valle del Mezquital is a desert devoid of everything but cacti, mesquite trees, and indigenous people whose lives are fraught with tragedy.[2] Today, irrigation has transformed much of the landscape into lush farmland. Maize grows tall. Pomegranate trees line the roads, laden with fruit. But at the time when the stories from my interviews begin, in the mid-twentieth century, the situation in the Mezquital was dire.

The roots of poverty in the Valle del Mezquital date to before the Conquest. Early sources state that the hñähñu-speaking people of the region supported themselves by hunting and gathering. They lived in small, isolated groups, for the soil was too barren to support concentrated settlement.[3] By the time of the Conquest, the Triple Alliance had conquered the hñähñu and divided their territory into tributary provinces. The hñähñu retreated to the most marginal lands of the Mezquital as they sought to maintain autonomy in the face of Mexican and later Spanish domination. After Mexican Independence, the rugged nature of the landscape kept hñähñu-speaking people largely isolated from non-indigenous society. Even the Catholic Church had only marginal success in penetrating the region. Eighteenth- and nineteenth-century historical accounts are punctuated by tales of indigenous uprisings, most of them centered on efforts to defend territory against external encroachment. The situation began to change in the mid-twentieth century as the Mexican government made a systematic effort to develop and integrate the region.

From the 1940s to 1970s, Mexico underwent a period of unprecedented economic growth. The combined effects of high import tariffs along with national investment in agriculture, education, and transportation were so pronounced that the period is often referred to as the "Mexican Economic Miracle." In 1951, in an effort to bring the Valle del Mezquital "up to stride" with the rest of the nation, President Miguel Alemán called for the creation of the Patrimonio Indígena del Valle de Mezquital, or PIVM (Indigenous Patrimony of the Mezquital Valley). The program brought irrigation to the region, along with agricultural products suited to an arid climate. A cadre of bilingual teachers was sent forth to teach the population to read, write, and speak Spanish. Efforts were made to battle illness and to bring drinking water to the most remote villages. The program's efforts were momentarily slowed when the PIVM came under the control of local landed elites who did not have the best interests of the people in mind. By 1970, however, a change in leadership made it possible for the program to bring about genuine improvements in the lives of residents of the region.[4]

Early government documents outlining the development plan express a deep concern for the plight of the Mezquital's population. Yet the documents also express an awareness of social difference that borders on disgust. The documents describe the residents of the region as not merely poor, but destitute, competing with "the very beasts" by "sharing with them puddles stinking with semi-putrid water."[5] One document speaks of a typhus epidemic that festers amidst "the filth, the rot, and the lice-infested rags that half-cover the scrawny flesh of almost all of the natives."[6] Children stare from black-and-white photos with miserable eyes. One shows a family outside their home; the caption reads, "the dwelling: caves and dark hovels that don't even deserve to be called 'huts,' in which adults and children, people and animals are mixed together in revolting promiscuity."[7]

While government officials and development agents described the residents of the Valle del Mezquital as something less than human, a pitiable "other" to be uplifted, redeemed, and transformed, the hñähñu-speaking residents of the region had their own thoughts on the matter. In order to understand the conditions that spurred evangelical conversion and eventually drove residents of El Alberto to seek a better life in the United States, we must pay attention to their own stories about the past. As Cecilia Mariz claims, although poverty has large-scale, structural causes, we must look to the level of day-to-day experiences if we wish to understand what poverty means to people on the ground.[8] Poverty lies close to the skin, worked out in the fabric of personal relationships. And it is through everyday, culturally embedded practices that people cope with poverty and carve out possibilities for the future.[9]

Pentecostal Stories of the Past

Inside accounts suggest that there was indeed some truth in the PIVM's portrayal of life in the Mezquital. When asked about the past, El Alberto's oldest residents state, quite simply, that life was difficult. The soil was poor and rains were sparse. The people had "no food, no clothes." Children often died. The town had no electricity, no roads, and no schools. Scarcely anyone spoke Spanish. The people rarely ventured into Ixmiquilpan unless to sell the firewood they gathered or the baskets they wove from cactus fiber. Even the assertion that the people had to compete with "the very beasts" for survival is not far off the mark. Tomás, an evangelical man who now owns a landscaping company in Phoenix, recalls that as a child, his bed was a leveled-off cactus covered in boards, safe from the wild animals that roamed at night. Another man remembers being dressed as a child in clothes made of the rough cotton sacks that grain and sugar were sold in.

Although memories of extreme poverty are nearly universal among El Alberto's older residents, Pentecostal narratives of the past bring an additional element to the table. Pentecostals recall something worse than a simple lack of resources. They recall a profound and debilitating lack of harmony. They state that the past was fraught with conflict, and that alcohol often lay at the root of the problem.

In the past, when water was so hard to come by, young and old alike regularly consumed *pulque,* a mildly alcoholic drink made from fermented agave nectar. For a desert population whose only water was obtained through great exertion, the agave plant with its sweet *agua miel,* or "honey water," and strong, fibrous leaves was once, quite literally, a life-source. In small quantities the alcohol has little effect, but some people would drink up to twenty liters a day, the equivalent of more than fifteen pints of beer. While *pulque* consumption is an integral part of popular festivals in the region, Pentecostals reject the drink as they reject alcohol in general. Often Pentecostals describe Catholic saints' days as little more than excuses to "toss back a few cups." The trouble with drinking, they explain, is that it leads to conflict. While *fiestas* are supposed to foster harmony, Pentecostals state that in practice, they often have the opposite effect. As a Pentecostal man in his seventies put it, "[T]he thing about Catholic *fiestas* is that people would start drinking, and then they'd fight. Good friends, brother and brother, would start fighting."

If the people did not kill one another with knives and guns, evangelicals recall, they killed each other through what evangelicals considered to be witchcraft and sorcery. As Tomás, the man who describes sleeping on a leveled-off cactus as a young child, remembers, "My dad was Catholic, but I didn't know that Catholic church, no, no, no. . . . This town was drunk. Everyone, everyone used to kill one another. Lots of sorcery here." Tomás recalls stumbling upon acts of sorcery while pasturing his family's goats as a child. "'Get out of the way, kid,' they'd say, . . . and they'd have something here, carrying it, I don't know what they'd have, but they'd leave it up on the hilltop so that it would kill other people."

Traditional hñähñu religion recognizes a variety of ritual specialists, ranging from herbal healers to bonesetters to practitioners of shamanic healing. The nuances of these categories are largely lost within Pentecostalism due to a general distrust of traditional religion. Pentecostals use the terms *brujo/bruja* (witch) and *hechicero* (sorcerer) interchangeably to refer to healers and malevolent religious practitioners alike. They state that the town once contained many witches who were responsible for the deaths of infants and children. Due to the constant machinations of these malevolent beings, the town's population remained low. In the words of Don Cipriano, the "town was totally disorganized. Pure fighting. Here in El Dexthi [a neighborhood of El Alberto] there were just six people. Here in El Centro, there were seven houses. And in El Toxi, four little houses, that's all. In El Camino, there were just four houses, as well." Today children live and thrive, whether in El Alberto or in the town's immigrant settlements in the United States. While improved nutrition and medical care have much to do with today's lower child mortality rate, Pentecostals explain that deaths have declined because the arrival of evangelicalism has reduced the presence of witchcraft.

Don Cipriano was one of El Alberto's first converts and served as the first Pentecostal pastor in the town. In his view, drunkenness, sorcery, and internal conflict were not the only problems plaguing El Alberto in the past. Cipriano recalls that the town was once bound in submission to external, non-indigenous authorities. In his understanding, the Catholic *fiesta* system played a key role in the people's subjugation.

When Cipriano was a young child in the late 1940s, El Alberto's four neighborhoods functioned more independently than they do today. Each had a *mayordomo,* or Catholic festival sponsor, who was responsible for making a contribution to the town's *fiestas.* One supplied the music; another, the mass; and another, the carved wax decorations. The fourth would provide the "castle," an elaborate tower frame wired with colorful explosives. Such castles, or *castillos*, are in common use today, a high point of the entertainment during Catholic festivals. Fireworks shoot from the top and sides or spin out in wheels, sending thunderous booms across the night to neighboring towns.

"But the saddest thing about it," Cipriano remembers, "is that there was pure injustice. If someone–for example I'm a *mayordomo.* For lack of money, if I don't fulfill what the town calls me to do . . . the authorities would have to come and tie me up!" If the person in charge of the *castillo* failed to generate the necessary funds, he would be tied to a tree all night in punishment. And if the person in charge of the music failed to provide it, he would be tied near the *castillo.* When the fireworks began to explode, the unfortunate individual's family members would lay a wet cloth on him to protect his skin from the sparks.

While Catholic *fiestas* are often explained as means of generating *communitas*,[10] in Cipriano's memory, a central symbol of the fiesta—the colorful and celebratory castle—was a torture device. While speaking of the *fiesta*, Cipriano recalls not conviviality but coercion, not voluntary sacrifice but enforced compliance to repressive ritual obligations. Interestingly, he remembers the external, secular government as the driving force behind the punishment. Cipriano states that in those days, the municipal government based in Ixmiquilpan was not concerned with indigenous people's needs. "Just traditional fiestas, just traditional fiestas," he recalls, "and so this community—we didn't even have a road. Or light. Or water. Or—or a school!"

When public education finally arrived in El Alberto, the teachers did not hesitate to use physical punishment. If one didn't write what the teacher told one to write on the board, Cipriano continues, "the teacher would take out a knife, saying 'bring a stick from outside.'" And they'd hit you, "and *órale!* Until there was nothing left of the stick." Another punishment was to kneel on the ground until recess, holding a stone in each hand. "If you let a hand down, they'd knock you over."

The realm of the market was no gentler than that of the school. Before the arrival of irrigation, it was nearly impossible to grow enough food to support a family. People in El Alberto worked by collecting and selling firewood, or by making baskets and extracting agave fiber for rope and coarsely woven cloth. They would leave before dawn to carry a load of goods three hours or so over rough terrain to Ixmiquilpan to sell, and would return late at night with corn and other staples. Municipal authorities demanded a tax on every load of items sold in Ixmiquilpan. Those who did not pay risked having their wares confiscated, and those who complained were thrown in jail. "And it was hardest for the family," Cipriano remembers. "Waiting and waiting, when will the man or woman come back home; well, how are they going to come home if they're imprisoned? So the people [at home] were dying of hunger."

Cipriano recalls Catholicism as an integral part of the structural injustices of the past. As alcohol kept people's minds fogged, the *fiesta* system kept their energies bound in needless activity, preventing them for pressing for material change. Indeed, anti-Catholic sentiment among evangelicals at times assumes a distinctly anti-colonial form. As Tomás puts it, "this religion, this Catholic religion, the Spaniards brought it as a way to deceive a lot of people. I could tell you a little bit about that." The Virgin of Guadalupe, he said, was a scheme to keep indigenous people bound under Spanish authority. The arrival of Protestantism, however, "opened people's eyes," in a conversion dynamic similar to that described by progressive Catholics in other parts of Latin America.[11]

Isolated, destitute, and conflict-ridden, bound into submission and ignorance by alcohol and an onerous *fiesta* system: this was the situation in which, as evangelicals tell it, the flames of the Pentecostal "fire from heaven" found ample fodder beginning in the early 1960s. Fueled by the national spirit of development expressed in the Patrimonio Indígena del Valle del Mezquital, Pentecostal conversion was both a practical response to the poverty that the residents of El Alberto had endured for centuries and a spiritual response to the disharmony they believed underlay that poverty. Before exploring inside accounts of the conversion process, however, it is necessary to examine the larger context of Protestantism in Mexico, with particular attention to the origins of the Iglesia Cristiana Independiente Pentecostés, the movement to which El Alberto's two evangelical churches trace their roots.

Protestantism in Mexico

Often, Protestant presence in Latin America is assumed to be the result of aggressive North American missionary activity. In Mexico, however, internal church-state dynamics helped lay the foundations for Protestant growth.[12] Late-nineteenth-century liberal reformers looked to Protestant missionaries as allies who could help weaken the national presence of the Catholic Church and thus pave the way for foreign investment. As mines, factories, and railroads emerged throughout the Porfiriato, a string of Methodist schools and churches followed in their wake. These Methodist institutions helped instill the sense of discipline suited to an emerging labor class, in a dynamic similar to the process E. P. Thompson has described in nineteenth-century England.[13] Some North American missionaries of the time even claimed that without the transformative effect of Protestantism upon the individual character, development and modernization would be for naught and capitalism would be unable to take hold in the country.[14] As is often the case, however, religion contained the seeds of revolution. The same Protestant institutions that helped forge a disciplined, submissive work force in the late nineteenth century also trained a new generation of leaders who would help put an end to the Porfiriato.[15]

The religion that reached El Alberto decades later was a migrant religion, introduced by men who had converted while working as *braceros* in the United States. Yet the events of the nineteenth and twentieth centuries had helped fertilize the soil in which the religion would take root and flourish. Before Pentecostalism arrived in El Alberto, several government actors had forged alliances with Protestant missionaries in the region. One such figure was Moisés Sáenz. A native of the Valle del Mezquital, Sáenz became Mexico's Undersecretary of Education in 1924 and helped establish the country's National Indigenous Institute. Sáenz's education philosophy reflects his Presbyterian roots, for he used education to spread a "Protestant ethic" of individualism and self-control among students.[16] Sáenz's efforts to promote bilingual education coincided with a new wave of religiously conservative Protestant missionary organizations. Prominent among these was the Summer Institute of Linguistics (SIL), or Wycliffe Bible Translators. The movement was driven by the philosophy that the key to lifting indigenous Latin Americans out of poverty was to teach them to read the Bible in their own languages. Once indigenous people had direct access to God's word, they could sustain their own churches and would no longer fall prey to exploitation by *mestizo* authorities or to the costly burdens of the Catholic *fiesta* system.

Although they were not the sole carriers of Protestantism to Mexico, SIL missionaries had a notable presence in the Valle del Mezquital in the mid-twentieth century and provided resources and guidance for newly emerging churches. Each time I ventured to speak a few words of hñähñu during my time in El Alberto, people would tell me of an elderly woman from the United States who spoke hñähñu perfectly and had even translated parts of the Bible into the language. This woman was the much-respected *hermana* Nancy, an SIL missionary who lived and worked in the region for decades. When people spoke of Sister Nancy, they would often venture into their houses to bring out the fruits of her efforts: hñähñu-language Bibles, bilingual hymnals, and cassette tapes of songs and Bible verses read in hñähñu. As this example suggests, SIL efforts to spread the Christian message through native languages struck a chord with the residents of El Alberto. Recall Cipriano's words about the oppressive social system, in which municipal leaders meted out harsh punishment to those who did not comply with their tax demands and the Catholic *fiesta* system kept people bound in ignorance and submission. Within such a context, the message of a hñähñu-speaking woman who told of a new kind of Christianity, distinct from that of the oppressors, fell upon on ready ears. Pentecostals in El Alberto remember *hermana* Nancy as someone who spoke to them as equals rather than as peons in the rigidly defined caste system of indigenous and *mestizo* society. The original spark for Pentecostalism, however, came not from missionaries but from relatives and friends in Ixmiquilpan and neighboring towns. By the 1950s, early U.S.-Mexico migration was underway, bringing new cultural and religious forms to the Valle del Mezquital.

From Arizona to Hidalgo: The Iglesia Cristiana Independiente Pentecostés

Pentecostalism first reached El Alberto by way of the Iglesia Cristiana Independiente Pentecostés (ICIP), one of Mexico's largest Pentecostal denominations.[17] Based in Pachuca, Hidalgo, the organization was founded by Mexican migrants who encountered evangelical Protestantism while working in the United States in the early 1900s. The story of ICIP's origins, as recounted by a former movement leader,[18] sheds light on the relationship between migration, capitalism, and religious change in early twentieth-century Mexican society.

The tale begins with Andrés Ornelas, a man who picked up an evangelical pamphlet while working in Arizona in 1919. Months later, after returning to his home state of Jalisco, Andrés found himself under great emotional distress. Upon reading the pamphlet, he was deeply affected and sent away for more reading materials. Seized by a profound desire to read the Bible, he began a school in his home community to teach others to read and write. At one point Andrés returned to Arizona to raise funds for the school. Meanwhile, his brother Silvestre fell ill with silicosis from working in the mines. Knowing that Silvestre, under the influence of "Bolshevik" doctrine, was plotting to kill the mining company owners, Andrés wrote to him:

Silvestre! You and I have aspired to combat the empire of the rich who gathered their fortunes with the sweat of the workers, and without a doubt some of our children will continue dragging the chain of hateful slavery. You have exhausted your energies in the rough work of the mines to increase the company's treasure, and I too go following your example, and within a short time I will be sick like you are now. You, with the scant savings of your work, bought a pistol of the best German brand, and with it you've taken 300 bullets with the goal of using it against the rich . . . now my brother, I invite you to accompany me in the new business that God has entrusted to me, and I desire with all my soul that you and I should unite our forces and resources to bring down another empire more harmful than that of the capitalists. This empire is the power of Rome that has invaded the whole world with its horrendous idolatry.[19]

Silvestre converted, and his lungs healed. The two brothers eventually sought work in the mining city of Pachuca, Hidalgo, where they began to attend a Methodist church. At a prayer meeting in a private home, they came into contact with Raymundo Nieto, a man who had worked in Kansas during the early stirrings of Pentecostalism in Kansas. Nieto taught the brothers about divine healing, glossolalia, and baptism of the Holy Spirit. Invigorated by these teachings, the three men founded the first church of what would become the Iglesia Cristiana Independiente Pentecostés.[20]

The ICIP movement was born of the sweat of migrants whose labor enriched the mining companies in Mexico and the U.S. Southwest, and whose travels brought them into contact with the flames of Pentecostalism in the early years of the twentieth century. As we see in Andrés's letter, the religion found enthusiastic reception among workers disillusioned by capitalist exploitation. It would not be difficult to make a Marxist analysis of the brothers' conversion. Their lungs literally blackened by the soot of the mines, the brothers began to cry out in protest, but in the final moment channeled their woes into a new religion that allowed them to cry out in unknown languages and to call upon the power of a spirit that heals. The brothers were well aware of the injustice of the economy they found themselves working in. As Andrés grimly accepts, "without a doubt, some of our children will continue dragging the chain of hateful slavery."[21] But rather than fight the powers of exploitation, they turned their aggression toward what they saw as a more formidable enemy, the Catholic Church. Their message would find a ready audience among the hñähñu-speaking residents of the Valle del Mezquital, who would come to associate their stark history of poverty with the oppressive grip of Catholicism.

In the 1930s, a man from Ixmiquilpan by the name of Prudencio Esquivel came into contact with Raymundo Nieto and the Ornelas brothers. Esquivel, like the others, had been exposed to Protestantism while working in the United States. After holding services in private homes, he went on to become pastor of Ixmiquilpan's first Pentecostal church. Soon converts began to arrive from surrounding villages, often traveling in secrecy due to the hostility they faced in their home communities. Some relocated to Ixmiquilpan. A new Protestant neighborhood, the "Colonia Cristiana del Calvario," came into being at the edge of the city.[22]

Fueled by the populist spirit of the 1930s, members of El Calvario brought indigenous communitarian values together with Protestantism in a new experiment in collective living.[23] The Colonia drew heavily upon the tradition of collective labor. For example, members used *faenas,* or traditional work parties, to build houses for new families. At the same time, a theme of progress infuses inside accounts of the settlement's early years.[24] Recall the words of the founders of the Patrimonio Indigena del Valle del Mezquital, who described the indigenous residents of the Valle del Mezquital as dwelling in "caves and dark hovels that don't even deserve to be called 'huts.'"[25] To members of El Calvario, the transforming power of Christ "was immediately visible, for in place of the agave-leaf huts they once had, they were building houses with cement blocks and concrete roofs."[26] Members viewed organized, productive labor and modern-style houses as signs of divine agency, in ways that foreshadowed similar attitudes in El Alberto today.

"This Religion Opened Our Eyes"

The Colonia Cristiana del Calvario had been established in Ixmiquilpan for several decades before Pentecostalism would make its entrance to

El Alberto. First the religion emerged in the neighborhood of El Dexthi, brought by a migrant who had recently returned from the United States. A church was built and the neighborhood became a Protestant stronghold. El Dexthi later separated from El Alberto when the distant collection of families managed to establish their own primary school and government. Reports vary as to when exactly Protestantism arrived in El Alberto proper. The process was a gradual one that began undercover, escalated through the 1960s, and came into the open with the establishment of the town's first Protestant church in the 1970s.

El Alberto's earliest converts first learned of Pentecostalism not from foreign missionaries but rather from relatives, neighbors, and friends. Conversion largely followed lines of kinship and other close associations. After gradually absorbing new ideas through contact with Pentecostal relatives, a given individual would convert when a crisis he or she experienced could not be resolved through traditional means.[27] In most cases, the chain of conversion can be traced back to a person who had worked in the United States at some point in time. Tomás relates that his uncle became Pentecostal after getting to know an Ixmiquilpan-based evangelical who had been "living there in the U.S., I don't know what part, but the important thing is that he went to the U.S., he brought back the word of God."

The earliest conversion story I gathered is that of Cipriano, the retired pastor who shared his childhood memories of the Catholic *fiesta* system in the late 1940s. The tale begins when he was a young father in the early 1960s. At this time, no one from El Alberto had yet ventured to the United States in search of work, and internal migration to Mexico City was not yet fully established.

One day Cipriano's year-and-a-half-old daughter fell ill. "And in that time," he remembers, "there weren't so many doctors as there are now. There were only doctors who used traditional medicine. Or natural medicine, from plants. And then, the sad thing is, there were lots of sorcerers. So the girl fell ill, and I went here, there, everywhere, looking for medicine. And I never found any. The moment arrived when the girl died for three days. Just her little heart—it kind of jumped. But her eyes were completely closed. And then one day I said to my late wife, 'What are we going to do with the girl? She's already dead.'"

"I didn't know what to do," Cipriano continues, "where I could go for this girl, it made me sad to think that she would die, because her heart still jumped, jumped." One day, however, Cipriano's brother-in-law passed by on his way to El Dexthi.

"'And if I bring the girl there with the evangelicals, do you believe that she will be healed?'" Cipriano asked. The brother-in-law didn't answer, for he knew that Cipriano had a strong personality, and was afraid to anger him. Cipriano's brother-in-law took him directly to El Dexthi. Knowing Cipriano's reputation, the *hermanos* offered him *pulque* (an alcoholic drink made of agave nectar) as a trick, hoping to convince him to attend their service later that evening. "But they didn't know that I was there for that very reason!" he recalls. The hour of the service arrived, and Cipriano accepted the Pentecostals' invitation. Although the *hermanos* sang, prayed, preached, and even applauded him for attending the service, Cipriano did not tell them why he had come. Afterwards, however, he told his sister of the child's predicament.

"'And why didn't you say anything in the service?!'" Cipriano's sister exclaimed. She promptly sent out word, and soon "everyone arrived. Even those who hadn't been at the service came. To see me. They started to pray." During the first prayer, the girl remained deathly still. During the second prayer, however, "the girl opened her eyes. And she was looking at all those who were praying." After about four prayers, the *hermanos* left, promising to return first thing the next day.

"And at about four in the morning," Cipriano remembers, "the girl started to cry. She cried. But now she was speaking. I said, 'What's the matter, daughter?' 'I'm hungry,' she says. And then my sister, hearing her crying, got up. . . . Well, my sister quickly warmed up some tortillas and some broth, and the girl ate perfectly well. And from then on I began to see the wonders that the Lord worked."

Cipriano's conversion sparked a religious conflict that came to a head in a confrontation with the village priest. While previous Pentecostals had attempted to keep their worship secret, Cipriano boldly invited the *hermanos* and the pastor from El Dexthi to his house for a prayer service. His relatives were the first to find out. If Cipriano wished to become evangelical, they told him, he might as well leave town. A group of people went to the priest to complain.

"So they called me to a meeting," Cipriano remembers. "Everyone was there, from the youngest to the oldest. Each with a stick in hand. Wanting to kill me. But I said I wanted to speak with the priest." The father, who was from Mexico City, asked Cipriano why he had converted. Cipriano turned the tables on the priest by asking him how long he had been in service to the church.

"Twelve years," the father answered.

"And in those twelve years, how many liars, how many drunks, how many malcontents, and how many people have you changed?" Cipriano asked.

"Not a single one," the priest replied. "You, for example, you used to come here all the time—you'd just come here and drink and you never wanted to enter the church. Just as you did, many people are doing. They don't want to come inside."

Cipriano proceeded to tell the priest about the changes God was working in his life. The priest congratulated Cipriano, saying that he himself would convert if what Cipriano said were true. But the town's members were incensed by the priest's laxity toward religious dissent. They chased the Catholic leader away, saying, "We don't want to see him here, because he's going to contaminate our church!"

Ricardo,[28] another Protestant who would have been a young child at the time, remembers things differently. Ricardo recalls that the town chased the priest away not because he was too soft on Protestantism, but rather because the people resented having an external authority dictate their religious choices. In this version, the priest vengefully seized the church's statues as he fled. Multiple sources confirm that some of the church's most ancient and valuable artifacts have been lost.

However they may differ, each version of the story draws attention to El Alberto residents' commitment to taking matters of governance into their own hands. Protestants and Catholics alike recall that the period of religious conflict was a bitter test from which the town emerged stronger and more united. The town's civil-religious hierarchy was restructured into a committee-based government system in which Catholics and Protestants served side by side on common projects. It was decided that the new town government would set aside an equal amount of funds for each church's annual festival.

As Cipriano tells it, the benefits of Protestant thrift and organization became increasingly apparent in El Alberto as religious conflict was overcome and as evangelicals gained a foothold in local politics. Peace did not come immediately, however. The people initially blamed Cipriano for the priest's departure and plotted to have him killed. Cipriano's potential assassin found him one day when he was walking in a remote canyon. The man had come to kill him, he said, to prevent him from "infecting everyone else" with evangelicalism.

"I had a pistol," Cipriano remembers, "and I had a Bible that someone had given me. I took out the Bible in my hand, and I took out the pistol. And then—'Which do you prefer?'" Cipriano's attacker begged him to spare him his life. Cipriano sent four warning shots in the air. The assassin left, trembling. "And from then on, I defeated the enemy," Cipriano concludes. Time passed, Cipriano's cousin became *delegado*, and his position began to improve within the town. Not long after, Cipriano went on to pastor El Alberto's first Pentecostal church.

A narrative of progress drives Cipriano's tale of his first years as a pastor. The new role required that he attend pastoral meetings outside of town. Through these meetings he forged connections between his home congregation and a growing Protestant network that offered an alternative to traditional religious and political hierarchies.

"There were about twenty-five churches," he remembers, "that were really far away. And I had to go on foot. But one day I began to pray with my wife, I tell her 'you know what, help me pray. Hopefully one day I'll get money to buy at least a bicycle.'" Eventually a fellow *hermano* in the nearby city of Progreso gave Cipriano a bike, saying, "If it's for God, *hermano*, . . . there's no problem. Choose the bike you want, and take it."

Cipriano continued on with the bicycle for some time. He would leave home at five in the morning and arrive at the meetings by ten. Each meeting would be followed by a worship service ending as late as eleven at night. Following the services, Cipriano would begin the long ride home, often arriving after four in the morning. Later he managed to buy a horse, and eventually, a car.

Cipriano tells of slowly getting ahead through perseverance, personal connections, and prayer. His efforts extended into civic and political spheres. As he puts it, "When the people saw that I was concerned with the things of the town, and not just the things of God . . . they started to respect me." Cipriano claims that becoming Protestant helped him to establish strategic alliances with outsiders. First, he befriended the municipal president. Later, he worked with a friend who was involved with the Patrimonio Indígena del Valle del Mezquital and had connections with the governor of the state. The friend trusted Cipriano, he said, because he was Protestant and didn't drink. He took Cipriano to Mexico City to meet with government officials and solicit funds for projects. "So we start to work, I started to organize the people, I say, 'You know what, stop drinking, we're going to work.' And from then on we began, little by little."

Pastor Isaías, the current pastor of El Alberto's other Pentecostal church, Sinaí, tells a slightly different version of El Alberto's development process. At first, he notes, Protestant converts were brutally threatened by some Catholics in the town. The evangelicals appealed to the municipal government in Ixmiquilpan for help, and the municipality stood behind them. When the Catholics did not succeed in kicking out the evangelicals, they decided, out of spite, to appoint a Protestant as *delegado,* or town leader, each year. The move was originally intended as a leveling mechanism, for the leadership position demands a year of unpaid work. Once in charge, however, the Protestants turned punishment into opportunity by soliciting development projects from the state.

Protestants note that they did not do away with the old governing system altogether. Rather, they transformed it from within and redefined its priorities. Protestantism did not simply replace an old, communal ethos with a new ethic of individualism and progress. The traditional ethic of self-sacrifice to the group remained strong, but was taken in new directions. As Pastor Isaías explains, Protestants did not oppose making contributions to the common good. They opposed what they considered the superfluous expense of Catholic *fiestas*, and they chose to redirect collective resources toward "practical" efforts. Today, collective efforts once applied to Catholic festivals are now applied toward the town's ecotourism projects. As has occurred in other indigenous communities in Latin America, Protestants have harnessed the discourse of universal Christian salvation in ways that contribute to the preservation of local, indigenous traditions.[29] We will see in the next chapter that Catholics have their own perspective on the process of change that occurred during this period. Yet Protestants and Catholics agree that their community has survived and overcome the period of acute conflict. The case of El Alberto meshes with Peter Cahn's findings in the community of Tzintzuntzan, Michoacán, in which evangelicals and Catholics have managed to overlook theological disagreements in pursuit of the common goal of community stability.[30]

The religious and political transformations that El Alberto experienced during the 1960s and 1970s coincided with the efforts of the Patrimonio Indígena del Valle del Mezquital. By the late 1960s, the agency's efforts had produced tangible change in the Ixmiquilpan region. It is no coincidence that people sought Protestant salvation just as the promise of material change came tantalizingly close within reach. Needs that had been endured for centuries now stood the chance of being met. Government offices could be visited, funds could be sought, and projects could be designed that would begin to lift the residents of the region out of their desperate state. At the same time, greater exposure to urban, non-indigenous society produced a deepening awareness of lack among those who had not yet reaped the benefits of modernization. Yet hope was appearing in new ways upon the horizon. While Protestant conversion was partly driven by material change, the new religion, in turn, offered a legitimating narrative for development. Pastor Isaías states that the changes that we see today in El Alberto would not have been possible without the arrival of Protestantism. Even U.S. migration would have done little to improve the town's material circumstances had Protestant thrift and sobriety not guided people to invest their wages well. As Tomás puts it, "The changes are because of religion. The word of God that came here—it changed us." Protestantism "opened people's eyes. Those who thought of today, now think of tomorrow. So then that sense of organization began, of working together."

Religious Transformation and Social Change

It would be difficult to discuss the relationship between religion and development in El Alberto without paying heed to Max Weber's thesis on Protestantism and the rise of capitalism in Western Europe.[31] According to Weber, early Calvinists' doubts about salvation led them to experience tremendous inner anxiety. As a result, they began to look for signs of their own salvation in the material world, viewing self-discipline and frugality as possible signs of divine favor. Wealth, though not a virtue in its own sake, was considered the acceptable by-product of a morally upstanding life.[32] While the rise of Protestantism did not directly cause the rise of capitalism, Weber maintained that certain features of the religion favored capitalist development, and capitalism in turn reinforced Protestant growth.

Whether they view religion as a cause of or a response to social change, most scholars of Protestantism in Latin America have engaged with Weber's thesis at some level. Emilio Willems, for one, has argued that Pentecostalism is a progressive force, for it helps people adapt to the social changes brought about by industrialization, urbanization, and capitalist growth.[33] More recently, David Martin has argued that Protestant growth has been flourishing in Latin America as Catholicism loses its monopolistic hold on society.[34] Rushing in to fill the "free social space" left by a faltering Catholic hierarchy, Martin maintains, Protestantism helps to generate "new concepts of self and new models of initiative and voluntary organization" that are amenable to capitalist development.[35]

We must use caution when applying Weber's thesis to Latin America, however. Protestantism emerged in mid-twentieth century Mexico under very different circumstances than those facing Western Europeans during the period Weber described. We must also be wary of overly simplistic interpretations of Weber, especially those that apply his insights as prescriptions for rather than descriptions of social change. In the case of Mexico, it is perhaps more accurate to say that Protestantism has served as a convenient medium for expressing tensions already present within the society. In some cases those tensions have centered on economic change. In indigenous communities, Protestantism challenges the moral authority of the Mesoamerican *cargo* system. The religion appeals to those who feel that the burdens of festival sponsorship impede personal and collective economic advancement.[36] In the case of El Alberto, evangelical converts came to associate their deep-seated economic frustrations with oppression by the Catholic Church. Early converts describe struggling within a social system that was too limiting and coercive to allow change. As the PIVM introduced development projects into the region, new leaders, including bilingual teachers, began to challenge the authority of the Catholic civil-religious hierarchies in the town.[37] By helping to "overthrow orthodoxy rooted in the colonial past," Protestantism facilitated new types of engagement with the changing economic system.[38] Thus, while Protestantism is not intrinsically and necessarily a force for change, when people see it and embrace it as such, it can be. Today, Pentecostals in El Alberto claim that Protestant conversion was the single most important factor driving the development and modernization that coursed through their town in the mid-twentieth century. Government agents and missionaries helped spread a narrative of progress, yet Pentecostals in El Alberto have embraced that narrative as their own and tailored it to their own circumstances.

As sociologist David Smilde has argued, evangelical salvation narratives play a key role in proselytization and conversion.[39] Such narratives work by amplifying people's internal psychological conflicts and then redefining these conflicts as struggles between supernatural agents over the fate of the individual soul. In cases where an internal struggle is not present, evangelical narrative works to produce such struggle by "actively 'dividing' the self."[40] In El Alberto, this narrative dynamic is at work on a collective level. Pentecostals cast the history of their town into the same dramatically bifurcated narrative structure that they use to make sense of their individual experience. As they tell it, religious conversion brought not only salvation to individuals' lives; it also brought harmony to the town as a whole. Religious conversion helped bring the community out of isolation and poverty and into a new state of prosperity and engagement with the outside world.

Evangelical Protestant narratives arrived in El Alberto at a critical juncture, when centuries of gruelling poverty came face-to-face with a new sense of possibility fostered by a rapidly modernizing Mexico. Protestant salvation narratives became intertwined the process of development, as the new religion offered a source of moral authority that challenged traditional power structures. But there is more to the story. The earliest conversions involved not a radical break with communal values, but rather a subtler redefinition of the relationship between the individual and the larger social group. In order to fully understand this shift, we must take a closer look at the role of embodied experience within the early conversion stories. Conversion was initially about something much more basic than development and modernization. Conversion was initially about survival.

Embodied Conversions

Many early conversion stories in El Alberto center on illness and healing. In these stories, a person becomes sick, often as a result of witchcraft. The family exhausts all available means to save the individual, including herbal remedies, traditional healers, and Western medicine. As a last resort, the desperate family seeks help from the *hermanos* who, they have heard, know of a new and powerful way to heal. The patient and often the patient's family members convert when Pentecostal prayer and worship prove to be an effective form of healing. As conversions spark resentment and social conflict, the conflict contributes to additional cases of illness, and the chain of conversion continues. Tomás remembers that as the number of Protestants grew in the 1970s, "the others wanted to kill us, the people here didn't like evangelicalism. . . . Because they said we were demons, because we were speaking the word of God." Tomás's father wanted to kill his newly converted Protestant cousin. But when Tomás's father himself fell ill, his family brought him to the evangelicals. "And my dad was healed. He was healed, and there he is to this day. He's 80, 87 years old, and you'd never know it." Other conversions center on overcoming alcoholism. One Pentecostal man in his late fifties recalls attending mass as a young adult with a group of friends who used to drink all night long. Out of curiosity, the group began to attend the evangelical church. At first they would arrive drunk, but when the evangelical message resonated with this informant, he quit drinking and continued on in earnest.

As these stories indicate, early conversion was a practical effort driven by the basic desire to survive and to live a better life. To fully understand indigenous conversion to evangelical Protestantism, we must recognize that, within much indigenous thought, moral change happens in and through the body.[41] Conversion involves a shift in what one eats and drinks and how one carries oneself. This does not mean that beliefs and morals are irrelevant, but rather that morality is located in and expressed through physical experience.[42] The body is a social product, shaped and molded in ongoing ways from birth.[43] When one changes religions, it is thus not only the mind and soul, but also the body that is converted. To recall the work of Cecilia Mariz, religions help people cope with the daily hardships of poverty.[44] The residents of El Alberto who converted to Pentecostalism sought to overcome the hardship of poverty by making concrete changes in their daily habits. They gave up drinking. They adopted new healing practices.

In traditional Mesoamerican thought, physical decline and death are often traceable to breaches in respect toward and reciprocity with other living beings. A slighted neighbor might enlist the help of a ritual specialist to inflict harm on the one who did her wrong. An ancestor or spirit might send illness to the man who has neglected to show proper respect. Supernatural causes for illness are possible because the body is permeable to external, spiritual forces. Bodies can fall ill both through "soul loss" and through the intrusion of foreign objects, such as a dart or a stone, sent through magic by the wronged party.[45] Among hñähñu speakers, health is restored when the ritual specialist identifies the source of the illness and prescribes the actions necessary to set the relationship right.

As early converts in El Alberto sought out Pentecostal faith healing, they reinterpreted indigenous notions of illness through a Christian lens. Thus, for example, Consuelo, who was in her late eighties at the time of the interview, converted in her late sixties when her evangelical relatives' prayers eased the symptoms of a disease that left her nearly crippled. The *hermanos* held a group prayer and shared their testimonies with her. Some fasted on a mountaintop in attempt to restore Consuelo to health. That night, Consuelo dreamed that she, too, was on a mountaintop. She dreamed that a white hog was chasing her, trying to bite her feet. The animal, she explains now, represented Satan. Consuelo awoke to share her story with the *hermanos* and converted shortly thereafter. At that time, Consuelo's son was already Protestant, but her husband was not. Not long after her conversion, Consuelo had another dream. She related the dream to me in hñähñu, which her son translated as follows:

> She had a dream here, here where [a neighbor's] land is. . . . She was up there standing like this, and my father was pulling her down, and I was

pulling her hand . . . like I wouldn't let her fall downward. Like when one doesn't believe in God entirely. One agrees, the other doesn't agree. That's when one is balancing. Balancing. And then once everyone believes in God equally, the sick are healed quickly. It's like having a single plan, one single hope. When the whole household loves God.

Harmony emerges as a tangible and efficacious force within Consuelo's narrative. We have already seen the power of unity in Cipriano's story of his daughter's recovery. Cipriano tells us that when he asked the evangelicals to pray for his child, "everyone arrived. Even those who hadn't been at the service came. To see me." Nothing could heal the girl but the power of the *hermanos*' united efforts to invite the Holy Spirit into their midst.

These healing stories suggest that the earliest converts responded to the same visceral desire to restore harmony that had driven their parents' and grandparents' religious rites. However, they responded to that need in a new way. They replaced a multitude of diverse, morally ambiguous supernatural agents with the simple binary of good and evil. Pentecostals determined that illness is caused not by slighted neighbors or angry ancestors but by the ultimate source of disharmony, Satan. They determined that health is restored not through careful negotiation with multiple non-human beings, but through direct communication with the ultimate source of wellbeing, God. They sought to achieve harmony by pursuing the "single path" of Protestant salvation.

Just as individual conversion transforms one's way of being in the world, El Alberto's collective "conversion" has, in evangelical eyes, transformed the town's way of being. From the rampant conflict and drunkenness of the past, evangelicals claim, the town has emerged enlightened, forward thinking, and free of the coercive obligations of the Catholic *fiesta* system. As we move on to explore the relationship between Protestantism and migration, we must remember that religious change, like migration, emerged out of a basic effort to survive. Conversion was initially a practical matter, as practical as taking medicine for an illness or feeding broth to a hungry child. As migration to the United States arose years later, the quest for dollars would introduce new patterns of consumption, along with a new set of spiritual challenges. At the same time, however, the core concerns expressed within these conversion stories—concerns about how to survive and live well and in harmony with others—have not been lost. Today, these same concerns have inspired Pentecostals to join their neighbors in staging the Caminata Nocturna and calling for the Mexican Dream. Yet the evangelical perspective on development and religious change is not the only tale to be told. El Alberto's Catholics have their own story about those crucial years of social transformation, and I turn now to their voices.

2

Living Crosses

We live in harmony together . . . the religions that exist in this community. There is no distinction. We are the same, the same brothers and sisters. We are all human. We are all flesh and blood. And we have been born into one single cradle, because we're in the same community.
—Don Agustín

Catholics and Protestants alike frequently say that El Alberto is a harmonious town. Despite religious differences, they insist, they are bound together by their common heritage and by their strong tradition of collective labor. So pervasive is this notion of harmony that at first I had difficulty gathering Catholic stories about religious change. The first Catholic perspective on the past that I managed to gain came not from a resident of El Alberto, but rather from Lucita, a hñähñu cultural promoter who had participated in pastoral outreach efforts in El Alberto in the 1980s. By Lucita's account, evangelicals did not simply abandon the Catholic faith as they embraced the new religion. Rather, they actively condemned Catholics and made a mockery of their practices. At first, Catholics reacted negatively to Pentecostal conversions. Yet the evangelicals responded with aggression of their own by attacking the Catholics' sacred images and interfering with their rites. During the *fiesta* of the Santa Cruz, El Alberto's former patron saint festival, evangelicals followed behind Catholics and taunted them as they carried large, wooden crosses through the town. A representative of El Alberto's Catholic church later confirmed this report by stating that one person even went so far as to burn a cross used in the festival. He mentioned this detail briefly, as though not wishing to stir up bitterness about a conflict that lay well in the past.

This chapter looks beyond the evangelical storyline to examine Catholic perspectives on religious and material change in El Alberto's past. I pay particular attention to the transformation of the town's patron saint festival and the emergence of the collective labor system that exists today. I argue that although Catholics agree that their town's economic situation has improved, they do not identify religion as the driving force of change. Rather, Catholics and other non-evangelicals in El Alberto attribute socioeconomic development to a diverse combination of political and material causes, including the dedicated efforts of a few key community leaders. Catholics describe the early period of religious change as a time of trial. As increasing numbers of people converted to Pentecostalism or left for the United States, a moment arrived when it was no longer possible to keep the patron saint festival afloat. Yet the collective fabric of the community did not unravel. As Catholics changed the *fiesta* system to accommodate religious pluralism, they joined Pentecostals in strengthening the tradition of collective labor that now forms the infrastructure of the Caminata Nocturna. Today, Catholics and other non-evangelicals share with Pentecostals the conviction that, despite religious differences, El Alberto is *un pueblo unido*—a united town.

La Santa Cruz

During a visit to El Alberto in the summer of 2011, I was confronted on the road by a man from the community. "You've gotten it all wrong!" he exclaimed. I had traveled to El Alberto that summer to share the news about the publication of this book. When I presented a chapter summary to the town leaders, they had voiced no objections. Yet Raúl, a Catholic, was not convinced by the Pentecostal accounts of the past recounted in the previous chapter. He insisted that El Alberto is not an evangelical town, and that the community has an important Catholic and pre-Catholic history that must be told. I recalled that Raúl had met me at the entrance of the town's Catholic church when I attended mass two years earlier. He had pointed to a small, weathered figure carved into stone in the outer wall near the doorway: a sun with a human face, surrounded by two crescent swirls. The sun was male and the moon female, he explained.

I would later learn the celestial bodies' association with Zidada and Zinana, the Father and Mother deities of hñähñu tradition who denote the sun and moon and have also come to represent the Christian God and the Virgin of Guadalupe. I sensed that the stories embodied in these small stone figures were merely the tip of a rich religious heritage that members of El Alberto's non-evangelical minority may, with good reason, be hesitant to share with outsiders. The figures called to mind the alluring tale told in paint in the sixteenth-century Church of San Miguel Arcángel in downtown Ixmiquilpan. Indigenous artisans forced into labor by Spanish friars crafted a dramatic battle scene, replete with jaguar-skin clad warriors, into the plaster walls that encircle the sanctuary. The iconography surrounding a decapitated Tezcatlipoca indicates the death and resurrection of Christ,[1] and in place of blood, a blue fluid substance whirls outward from the wounds of warriors, interlacing with an omnipresent leaf-like motif. Scholars have speculated that the substance refers to the life force known as *tonalli* among Nahua-speaking cultures throughout Mesoamerica, its blue color indicating the exchange of blood for the life-giving power of rain through the act of human sacrifice.[2]

While the local Catholic authorities say that the church mural symbolizes the triumph of Christianity over the "pagan" religions of the past, the image is indicative of continuing indigenous religious influences within various expressions of Catholicism in the surrounding region today. During one visit to El Alberto, I found myself at the side of a woman in her eighties who spoke scarcely spoke a word of Spanish. I had been waiting to interview her daughter, Silvia, a member of El Alberto's Catholic Church. Yet when I greeted the elderly woman in hñähñu, she took my faltering words for fluency, and a torrent of stories spilled from her lips. I recognized the words for God, for Jesus Christ, and for the earth. Silvia came and sat beside us. When God created the world, Silvia translated, the Lord Jesus sent the first man to go and see his *milpa* (plot of land). The man said that he was afraid to go alone, so God created a female companion for him by removing one of his ribs. But this was not the first time that people had roamed the earth. Our race was preceded by a group of beings so small that God found them unsuitable, and later by beings so tall that "where they fall, they don't get up again." Both races perished in floods. Since we human beings have existed, however, there has been no more destruction. Our continued life is a sign that God is happy with our existence.

This woman's stories blend biblical accounts of the creation and the flood with local references. The first man treads not through paradise but through his *milpa,* the Mesoamerican term for a small plot of farmland. The beings that preceded humans are the mythical dwarf and giant beings whose bones appear as small stones in fields today and whose bodies formed the mountains that now tower over the region.[3] While my observations of Catholic and indigenous religious practices in El Alberto are far more limited than my observations of Pentecostal practices, fleeting ethnographic moments such as this encounter with Silvia and her mother point to an underlying religious tradition that is grounded in a unique sense of place and deeply intertwined with the natural world.

Before evangelical Christianity entered the scene, religion among the hñähñu of the Valle del Mezquital consisted of a blend of popular Catholicism and traditional Mesoamerican religious practices. Like members of other indigenous communities throughout Mexico, residents of El Alberto use the term *costumbre,* or "custom," to refer to indigenous ritual practices that are not officially recognized by the Catholic Church but nevertheless play a vital role in the life of the community. Until better transportation became available in the mid-twentieth century, clerical presence in El Alberto was scarce. Typically, residents of small villages in the Valle del Mezquital had contact with a priest once every few months at most. While priests officiated at functions such as weddings and baptisms, the people were largely left to themselves in their day-to-day religious practices. The dates of the Catholic *fiestas* were closely tied to the pre-Columbian agricultural cycle.

While El Alberto's first Pentecostal pastor remembers an onerous and coercive Catholic *fiesta* system, Catholics remember the festivals of the past as part of a rich cultural heritage that is being lost. Agustín, the Catholic man whose words form the epigraph for this chapter, remembers that in the past, "people put on four or five *fiestas* a year . . . and it was nice. They'd bring a band . . . or trios! And yes, there was a lot of atmosphere, people celebrated a lot of things . . . they do now too, but it's not like before." Today, as a result of religious change, "the culture doesn't work like it worked before." Although each of the town's neighborhoods was responsible for staging a *fiesta*, the most important event of the year was the patron saint festival.

The green-robed image of San Alberto Magno, or Saint Alberto the Great, who sits in El Alberto's Catholic church today was not always the patron saint of the town. Until about 1970, that role was fulfilled by La Santa Cruz, or the Holy Cross. At first I had difficulty gathering information about the festival of the Santa Cruz. I heard in passing from elderly residents of the town that the festival was good for "bringing the rain." Later, an elderly Catholic man confirmed these stories. This man asked to be identified simply as a representative of the Catholic church. For the sake of clarity, I will refer to him here as Marcos. Marcos is not a priest, yet he serves as something of a "pastor" of the town's Catholic church by leading prayer services and overseeing religious festivals. Marcos explained that during the celebration of the Santa Cruz, people would bring a cross to a nearby hilltop and then bring it down after a few days. "I believe it was very good," he explains, "because they say that it rained a lot. Every time they brought it down it rained, and now—now it doesn't rain."

It may seem strange for the function of a patron saint to be fulfilled by such a "non-person" as the cross. In Mesoamerican societies, a Catholic patron saint typically serves as a guiding figure who offers the members of a town protection in exchange for collective devotion. In an agrarian context, people have often turned to patron saints for pragmatic reasons such as the need for agricultural fertility. The Santa Cruz was able to fulfill this role for El Alberto because, within hñähñu popular Catholicism, the cross is a living entity. It is at once a "tree of life" and a "god of rain, health, and sustenance" whose form embodies and signifies the four directions.[4] Today, these connotations are interlaced with Christian references to the death and resurrection of Christ. A member of the nearby town of El Maye explains that the original cross was a tree that was made not by human hands, but by God.[5]

More than a symbol, the Santa Cruz in hñähñu popular Catholicism serves as a living being with the power to connect human beings with other parts of the cosmos. The cross's role can be better understood if we recognize that indigenous religions in the Americas do not make a sharp distinction between society and the natural world. The type of social relations that exist among humans also extend to non-human "persons" such as plants, animals, and bodies of water.[6] Traditional hñähñu *costumbre* involves placing offerings of flowers, candles, incense, and food at springs, caves, and mountain shrines to appease non-human beings and to ensure the necessary flow of rain and agricultural fertility to their fields. Rites also emphasize the four directions, and nighttime ceremonies often include the use of fire or torches.[7] Although such rites continue in some communities, they have receded in places with an evangelical majority.

While the festival of the Santa Cruz is no longer practiced in El Alberto, it has a continued presence in other communities near Ixmiquilpan. At the beginning of the festival, people carry three crosses to the summit of a nearby mountain and place them at an altar with stones piled at the base. These crosses, two large and one small, embody God, the Virgin Mary, and the child Jesus. In the hybridity typical of popular Catholicism, the two larger crosses also embody Zidada and Zinana, the Father and Mother deities of hñähñu tradition. The smaller cross is dressed in cloth, as though it is in fact a living child.[8]

The festival of the Santa Cruz occurs at the beginning of May, just as the start of the rainy season brings sparse but much-needed storms to the region. The mountaintop location is significant, for in this arid region mountains are traditionally viewed as sources of water.[9] After raising the crosses, worshippers hold masses and make offerings on the mountaintops to ask for rain and good health.[10] Individual families may place small offerings of candles, incense, flowers, and food at the crosses' base. In some communities, the festival includes a practice of lighting scores of small fires on the hillside to form giant, cross-shaped luminaries. According to one informant in a neighboring town, these fiery figures serve as landing guides for arriving rainstorms.[11] Although I have not heard explicit mention of this tradition of lighting luminaries during my time in El Alberto, it is highly likely that it is the inspiration for the closing torch scene in the Caminata Nocturna.

Marcos explains that the *fiesta* to the Santa Cruz lost strength as people began to convert to Pentecostalism. While he recounts many of the same details told by Cipriano, he interprets people's motives for conversion quite differently. Marcos confirms Cipriano's memory that the demands of Catholic festival sponsorship were onerous. He also confirms that those who did not fulfill their duties as festival sponsors were punished by being tied up, and he agrees that *fiestas* often did lead to drinking and violence. Yet Marcos is much less condemning of the situation. He states that the people who left Catholicism were those who failed to grasp the true meaning of the faith. If the post–Vatican II shift toward worship in the vernacular had come sooner, he explains, more people would have understood Catholic doctrine and would not have been so easily led astray by Protestant teachings. Marcos's emphasis on belief is worthy of note. While it is often suggested that the suppression of traditional devotional practices after Vatican II caused Catholics to seek more fulfilling religious experience elsewhere, in Marcos's view, people left the church because those changes had not come soon enough. He interprets evangelical conversion as a reaction to a genuine need for change within the Catholic Church, albeit a reaction that was premature and misguided. By the early 1970s, so many people had either converted or emigrated that there were no longer enough people to fund the *castillo,* the music, and the decorations. "Half of the people had already left," he explains; "everyone, everyone."

While Pentecostals recall that their conversions sparked opposition from Catholics, Catholics, in turn, recall that the newly converted evangelicals derided them and desecrated their sacred objects. Such interreligious conflicts continue to rage bitterly in some communities of the region today. In the town of San Nicolás, for example, members of the Catholic majority recently went so far as to deny a deceased evangelical woman's family the right to bury her body in the village cemetery, sparking a conflict that required the intervention of municipal authorities.[12] In order to understand the emotional depth of these conflicts, we must remember that popular Catholicism emerged in rural Mexico at a time when bonds of solidarity between neighbors were essential for survival. As anthropologist Kristin Norget points out, popular Catholic *fiestas* embody a "sacrificial, reciprocal economics" that runs counter to the ethic of individual advancement embraced by capitalist societies.[13] Members of indigenous communities often distrust Protestantism because it threatens to undermine the solidarity-building functions of religious *fiestas* and unravel the fabric of the *cargo* system. Through the *cargo* system, a socio-religious structure common throughout Mesoamerica, individuals alternate between positions of civil leadership and festival sponsorship. In exchange for the significant outlays of time, energy, and material resources that festival sponsorship demands, participants gain respect and prestige among their neighbors. Thus, struggle between Protestants and Catholics in El Alberto was not simply a struggle over religion, but rather a struggle over the structure and function of the community itself. In addition, an ecological shift—a shift in the relationship between the town's members and their natural environment—was also underway.

A *Fiesta* Transformed

I received a revealing insight about the decline in the festival of the Santa Cruz one evening in a conversation with an elderly evangelical man. "Yes, [the people] said they did it to bring the rain," he explained. "But it wasn't true, because only God brings the rain." At a time when development projects were making headway into the Valle del Mezquital, converts to Pentecostalism shunned the festival of the Santa Cruz as an idolatrous practice that perpetuated a mistaken understanding of the relationship between divine power and material reality. They rejected Catholic ritual because, as they saw it, evangelical prayer had proved to be a more effective way to ensure survival.

Ricardo, an evangelical man in his fifties, explained to me in no uncertain terms that the arrival of irrigation during the 1970s helped convince him of the truth and efficacy of evangelical faith. In the early years of conversion, he explains, people began to pray. They prayed for water, for irrigation. They prayed for electricity and roads. They prayed and they fasted on the same mountaintops where they had once brought offerings to nature-based deities and where they had once carried the Santa Cruz to ask for rain. All along, they backed up their prayers with action by organizing and soliciting funds for development projects. About five years later, irrigation became a reality, roads were introduced, and people began to have electricity in their homes. God had answered their prayers.

For Ricardo, the arrival of irrigation in El Alberto was proof that Pentecostal worship worked, and that it worked better than popular

Catholicism. I asked him whether the physical improvements in El Alberto today result more from religion or from the town's system of collective labor. Without hesitation, he answered, "Religion. Religion, because of the things I've seen—I've seen things that you can't explain in any other way." The arrival of irrigation helped make it apparent to Ricardo and other evangelicals that there was no longer any need for crosses on mountains or for offerings of flowers and incense and chocolate and bread. In their view, the Santa Cruz was not a living being. It was a lifeless piece of wood.

For me, a minor incident that occurred one summer helped drive home the earnestness of Pentecostals' anti-idolatry. I had bought a small, wooden cross pendant at a fair in Ixmiquilpan and placed it on a string around my neck. The grandmother within my host family spotted the string and asked me what it was. When I showed her the pendant, she chided me. "Those are for Catholics," she said. On another occasion, a Pentecostal woman had told me that "believers" have no need of wooden crosses. Human bodies, with arms outstretched, naturally contain the form of a cross, as a vivid indication of the Holy Spirit's ability to enter and dwell within human flesh.

For Pentecostals, the years of adoration of the Santa Cruz were years of going hungry and carrying water barefoot and losing siblings to disease. Pentecostals state that things began to change when people tapped into their own power to access the divine source of all water and health and blessings. For Catholics, meanwhile, the decline in *fiesta* participation was deeply troubling. The patron saint festival eventually ended when excessive emigration and religious conversion caused the town to lose the critical mass of Catholics necessary to keep the event afloat. Thus, termination of the *fiesta* also signaled a loss of a collective way of life.

Lucita recalls that some Catholics were so disheartened by religious division that they fell ill. They became "spiritually sick," their bodies weakened by discouragement. Note the parallel to the instances of illness described in the last chapter. Pentecostals state that sorcery-induced illness once ran rampant in El Alberto and, in many cases, prompted their conversion to evangelicalism. In this Catholic account, the cause of illness was not sorcery but rather the discouragement brought about by religious division. Not all Catholics, however, sought healing through evangelical conversion. Lucita recalls that a concerned priest sent for a team of doctors and missionaries from Mexico City. A set of rooms was built near the Catholic church to house them as they administered to the people and provided educational outreach. The missionaries "came and went, came and went," and the Catholics began to regain their morale. There was even a small presence of *comunidades eclesiales de base* (base ecclesial communities, or CEBs) in the town in the 1970s and 1980s, although the groups eventually lost steam due to inconsistent involvement from the outside.

The few Catholics who remained in El Alberto decided to consolidate their efforts by celebrating only one *fiesta*, the festival to the Virgin of Guadalupe. A priest who was active in the community in the past suggested that the Catholics may have chosen the Virgin's feast day because it falls during the month of December, when the largest numbers of migrants were able to make the journey home. The decision to "celebrate the Virgin" was a survival measure designed to optimize the dwindling presence of Catholics in the town. The adoption of Guadalupe may have also had something to do with her unifying power as a religious figure with tremendous popularity throughout Mexico as a whole. By about the year 2000, a new priest began working in El Alberto. He insisted that the community needed its own unique patron saint. Too many other towns celebrated the Virgin's feast day. The priest suggested that the town's members either return to celebrating the Santa Cruz or adopt Saint Alberto the Great, after the name of their town. Marcos sent a letter to the Catholics who were working in the United States to ask for their input. At first the migrants were hesitant to make a change. Perhaps out of the wish to leave the conflict surrounding the Santa Cruz in the past and make a fresh start, Catholics on both sides of the border eventually agreed upon San Alberto. Gradually, with the financial help of the migrants, the Catholics bought an image of the saint and began to celebrate his festival on November 15.

The process of decision-making surrounding the fiesta indicates a strong transnational Catholic presence, well before the use of cell phones and digital communication technology became commonplace. Today, funds from migration and a generally improved standard of living make it possible for Catholics to host a larger and more elaborate *fiesta* than they did in years past. The structure of that festival, however, has changed. The event is no longer hosted by rotating *mayordomos* who sacrifice large sums of money in exchange for personal prestige. Rather, the event is funded by contributions from community members, earnings from the town's ecotourism project, and outside funders. Today, evangelicals attend Catholic *fiestas*, and vice versa. As Agustín explains, about 120 Catholics from El Alberto actively plan and participate in the *fiesta*. But "the *hermanitos* also visit us, and we visit them, as well."

The significance of the new patron saint may not, at first glance, appear to run very deep for Catholics in El Alberto. The saint's image has inhabited the church for less than a generation, and the timing of his festival has no apparent correlation to the agricultural cycle. However, the adoption of San Alberto does make sense in light of growing internal and external pressures upon the community to package its group identity for profit. "Alberto" has become part of a brand name, from the title "Parque EcoAlberto" used for the town's ecotourism park to the label "Agua EcoAlberto" adopted by the town's budding water purification business. Today, residents of El Alberto bring in revenue by selling aquatic recreation to the tourists who visit the town each weekend. Soon, they will make money by selling purified drinking water at a discounted rate to other residents of the Valle del Mezquital. While the saint might not have the power to interact with natural forces and bring the rain, he helps bring sustenance to the town's members by contributing to the brand identity that helps them more efficiently utilize and profit from the natural resources of their land.

"Un Pueblo Unido"

Today El Alberto's Catholics share with Pentecostals the refrain that, despite religious differences, their town is harmonious and united. While the town is certainly not immune to internal conflict, its members present a strikingly unified face to researchers, members of the media, and other outsiders. I cannot count the number of times that residents of El Alberto have stressed, without any prompting on my part, that theirs is *"un pueblo unido"* whose members value harmony, cooperation, and respect. Joined by common ethnicity and a shared commitment to self-governance, the town's members have reached beyond religious difference to find in their system of collective labor the social-leveling and solidarity-building functions once fulfilled by Catholic *fiestas*.

Although Catholics and Protestants agree that their town is now a place of harmony, the morally charged narrative of progress that so infuses Pentecostal stories is almost entirely absent in Catholic accounts. Indeed, Catholic stories emerged more slowly in interviews than in the Pentecostal versions, and proved more difficult to piece together into a common narrative. This difference is likely due to the fact that Catholics do not share the act of "bearing witness" that is common within evangelical Protestantism. In interviews, Catholic informants did not appear to draw upon a common story structure. Rather, their speaking style reflected the mood of a group prayer service that I observed one evening at the Catholic church. Speaking mostly in hñähñu, Marcos led a discussion among the dozen or so people gathered. He spoke quietly and reflectively, and invited participation from all gathered. While not indicative of Latin American Catholicism per se, this leadership style reflects the participatory, consensus-driven nature of indigenous town meetings, and also reflects the post-Vatican II initiative of encouraging greater lay involvement in the Church.

Catholics are wary of evangelical salvation narratives that cast individuals' past and present lives into strongly bifurcated terms. While Catholic informants were careful not to be openly critical, they did occasionally assert that evangelicals are mistaken in the belief that being saved makes a person "clean" or free of sin. One's sins cannot be washed away in a single moment. Rather, the effort to live correctly is a lifetime balancing act. As Marcos put it, if one sins and then confesses, "hopefully God forgives me. But to say 'I'm already clean'—not even the clothing is clean!" Marcos's critique of evangelical logic extends to his view of the town as a whole. He states that in the past, El Alberto was not any more backward or "superstitious" than any other town. Rather, "many communities, many towns believed in" such things as the evil eye. Although "in truth, the people were very poor," Marcos does not regard erroneous religious practice as the cause of poverty. And although it is true that adult evangelicals do not drink, he states that many of their teenaged and young adult children do so "in secret," and that they are the ones who end up causing the most trouble in *fiestas* and dances in neighboring communities today.

Catholics and other non-evangelicals thus do not identify religion as the saving force that brought their town out of poverty and into a state of harmony and wellbeing. Instead, they explain that improvements have been driven by a combination of material and political changes both within El Alberto and in the surrounding society. Marcos notes that the dominant political party in the past "didn't help at all. They treated people like slaves, like animals." Then, during Luis Echeverría's presidency from 1970 to 1976, roads were built, schools were established, and electricity and irrigation were introduced to the town.

According to Agustín, improvements came as migration brought new resources to the community. In the past, the people "didn't work in such a unified way as they do now," for they simply did not have enough money to fund collective projects. While migration is often associated with introducing new inequalities, in this case migrant earnings helped bring about the basic level of material wellbeing necessary for cooperation. The most crucial change that Agustín remembers, however, came through the organizing efforts of a now-deceased community member by the name of Eulogio Barrera.[14] When Barrera became Representative of Public Goods in the early 1970s, Agustín explains, he transformed the way land and labor were managed. El Alberto's residents had worked together in the past, but only in their respective neighborhoods. Yet Barrera "had a lot of courage, a great deal of concern for the community." During his three-year position, he "lifted up the community! Yes, it cost him work to do it. But yes, he managed to unite the people."

Today Eulogio Barrera is survived by his brother Leonardo, who does not identify as either Catholic or Protestant. Well-respected in El Alberto for his service to the community, Leonardo attributes his efforts to their father's legacy. As one of the earliest people in El Alberto to learn Spanish, Leonardo explains, his father helped townspeople by serving as a translator for their dealings with the outside world. Later, Leonardo's brother Eulogio took up the torch. As Leonardo puts it, "from 1970 and before, there was no authority to unite people . . . there was no electricity, no roads, no school, nothing! . . . So he organized the people, and started to visit government offices to ask for services, and through all of that, united people . . . evangelicals, Catholics, everyone." By 1982, the town's members called a general assembly, transformed the town government from a civil-religious *cargo* system to a secularized system of committees, and compiled the internal community rules that are still in operation today. In an ironic challenge to Pentecostal narratives, the much-esteemed leader was a Catholic who turned to Spiritualism later in life. He managed to bring about monumental changes even as his own drinking brought him to a premature death.

Catholics and other non-evangelicals state that it was Barrera's leadership, along with the changing material and political circumstances described above, that allowed them to tap into their potential for collective organizing. Although the "culture" of the town may not function in the same way as it did before, Agustín states, today collective labor brings people together. "When there's work in the community," he explains, "we work together, across the board." As Agustín observes in the epigraph that opens this chapter, belonging to the community is like being "born into one single cradle." Pentecostals express similar sentiments. One of El Alberto's Pentecostal pastors states that he often advises potential U.S. migrants not to forget their community, for the community "is like our home." He states that the love and respect people share for one another are stronger than religious divides. This assertion is worthy of note. While official Pentecostal doctrine stresses the importance of individual salvation above all other concerns, Pentecostals in El Alberto also exhibit a fierce loyalty to their hometown. The ethic of collective participation runs deep, for it is grounded in ties of kinship.

Today, it is this very ethic of collective participation that serves as a vehicle for cooperation between Catholics and Protestants as they join together to generate alternatives to migration. That story, however, is reserved for the final chapters of this book. The next chapter outlines the rise of U.S. migration from El Alberto. Regardless of how Catholics or Pentecostals describe their past, the transformations brought about by development, religious conversion, and political change in the 1960s and 1970s were not sufficient to lift them out of the poverty they had long endured. Decades later, the same gripping hardship that first drove many of El Alberto's residents to seek evangelical salvation drove them to seek a better life in the North.

3

I Lift Up My Eyes to the North

Migration had been a good thing for her family, Cecilia explained as we chatted outside her house one afternoon in 2009. Four young children hung in the doorway listening. Cecilia said that it was thanks to her husband's time in the United States that the family now had a place to live. Their house once looked like the outdoor kitchen—she pointed to a spindly structure made of wooden poles. Cecilia said that she and her husband used to cover their children with plastic when the water came pouring in when it rained. She held up a scrap of plastic sheeting to demonstrate. For beds they would prop cactus stumps on cement blocks, out of reach of the water.

Javier, a Pentecostal man in his mid-forties, describes similar hardships. He recalls accompanying his mother from the market in Ixmiquilpan as a young boy in order to carry home the two bottles of lamp oil the family used to light the house. His mother had no room for them on her back, laden as she was with a sack of maize and with a baby in tow. Javier's feet would be bleeding by the time they reached El Alberto. Their home, he said, "wasn't even a house," but a single room where the entire family slept together. The children would huddle under one of their mother's old skirts or a cloth sack to keep warm at night. The place flooded when it rained.

Javier would have been a child in the 1970s; Cecilia and her husband were just beginning to raise children by the mid-1990s. That these individuals remember such difficult conditions so recently is evidence that development and religion were not sufficient, and did not benefit all families equally. Javier's and Cecilia's stories reveal a variety of strategies through which families made ends meet, from enlisting the labor of the youngest to help transport necessary supplies, to using scraps of found materials to protect children from the cold. Labor migration was a natural extension of such basic household efforts to survive.

Today, due to income from migration, Cecilia's family has not only a solid house but also clothing and food. She states that they no longer depend on the weed-and-cactus diet of lamb's quarters, purslane, and prickly pears that was so common in the past. They need no longer dress in *ropa de manta*, the rough, hand-sewn cotton cloth that was never enough to keep the children warm in winter. In a similar vein, Paula, a Pentecostal woman who now has children and grandchildren in the United States, explains that as a result of migration

> The children began to eat much better; they started to dress much better, above all, wearing shoes. . . . Because before, children really did go around barefoot. They didn't have clothes, they'd wear something but it was the same little piece of clothing, day after day. . . . Parents go to the U.S., although they run a great a deal of risk, but at least their children don't go hungry.

As evangelical fire swept the town with its promise to alleviate misery, and as development in the region improved access to transportation, people also began to seek a better life outside of El Alberto. Both evangelical conversion and migration initially emerged out of the desire to live well and to raise children who would survive into adulthood. As people turned to Pentecostal prayer and faith healing to strengthen their bodies and purge sorcery-induced illnesses from their midst, they also traveled to nearby cities in search of work. Before cross-border migration became commonplace, a pattern of circular, internal migration had emerged. Throughout the decades that followed, the town's members gradually ventured further and further from home in search of work, eventually becoming firmly embedded in a pattern of transnational migration to the United States. This chapter seeks to tell that story, focusing on the experiences of Pentecostal migrants.

In contrast to the poignant evangelical narrative about El Alberto's "salvation" and development, there is no widespread evangelical story about the town's early years of migration. Despite their occasional identification with the Pilgrims—those proverbial first North American settlers who traveled in search of religious freedom—El Alberto's Pentecostals do not generally cast their early migration stories into religious terms. I argue that at first, the material changes brought about by U.S. earnings were so pronounced that religious concerns could momentarily be put aside. Migration, for the time being, was its own form of salvation. However, what these early migration stories also reveal are changing gender relations and new forms of subjectivity that would later provide fertile ground for continued evangelical growth.

To Mexico City and Beyond

For years, language barriers and a lack of employment opportunities prevented people in El Alberto from venturing beyond Ixmiquilpan in search of work. By the mid-1950s, however, some of the town's members managed to find wage labor in other parts of the state. "But not just anywhere," remembers Cipriano, the retired pastor cited in chapter 1. Some found work harvesting crops in Progreso, a city about an hour from El Alberto. "How much did they pay those who managed to fill up those big containers? Fifty *centavos*. And the kids, like this one here," Cipriano said, pointing to a ten-year-old boy, "ten or twenty *centavos*."

Later on, the town's members began seeking work in Mexico City. Evaristo, a man in his mid-forties, remembers that he first worked there when he was seventeen. At that time virtually "the whole town, all of the adults" would go. Women worked as maids, while men found work in construction. The men would stay in Mexico City for a week at a time, leaving home each Monday and returning on Saturday nights. Women would remain away for longer periods of time, for their employers provided room and board. This pattern of internal migration was well established by the 1970s and continued through the 1990s.

It may seem contradictory that the period of economic growth known as the "Mexican Miracle" was accompanied by a rise in migration. However, for residents of El Alberto in the 1970s, such migration was not so much a response to increased need as it was a response to increased opportunity. Although the need had existed for centuries, wage labor was now more readily available and improvements in transportation made regular travel to Mexico City possible. Early migration from El Alberto was typical of indigenous migration patterns, in which people move seasonally in rural-to-urban directions before extending to longer periods spent farther away in the United States. The jobs El Alberto's workers fulfilled—construction and domestic service—also reflect typical economic niches available to indigenous workers in Mexico. Today, residents of El Alberto have reproduced those same economic activities in the United States.[1]

Roberto, a Pentecostal man who was in his late fifties at the time of the interview, describes his gradual involvement in such widening spheres of migration. Today, Roberto runs a store in El Alberto and is an active member of Templo Sinaí. He was born among "poor people. My father didn't speak Spanish, nor my mother . . . they didn't know anything, they were totally secluded." Like Javier, Roberto used to accompany his parents as they made the three-hour trek to Ixmiquilpan to sell baskets. He left home at the age of fourteen to work in Mexico City. At first he worked in excavation, "with a pick and shovel." Then he worked in construction for two years. "But we earned very little. Very little, and we hardly earned enough for the family, for a week's worth of food."

Fortunato[2] also recalls having a difficult time making ends meet during an early venture away from home. Traveling to Mexico City from Guadalajara as a young man, he and his friends found a construction job in Mexico City, but they had spent all of their money on a bus ticket and had nothing left for food. They worked for three, four, five days straight without eating. When he and his companions became too weak to continue, their supervisor noticed that they were hungry and gave them some tortillas and a pancake. "So we made tacos with the pancakes inside," he remembers. "We pretended we were just having fun, but really we were so hungry we made pancake tacos."

While men often returned home on weekends, women remained away from El Alberto for months or years. Since domestic labor provided food and shelter, families were able to ease their financial burdens by sending daughters off to work. Some women were young children when they first left home. Yolanda began working as a maid in Mexico City when she was eight years old. She explains, "I didn't have a father. That is, I was really little when my dad died. . . . And, so we went to earn a peso, among us kids. Because my mom was widowed, there was no money." Things were very difficult at first. The first family she worked for did not give her enough to eat. "I was always afraid. They'd give me a cup of coffee and a roll for the whole day, and I'd be so hungry. . . . Until four in the afternoon, or five, they'd give me more food. And that was it. Until the following day." Yolanda spoke little Spanish at the time. The owner of the home scolded her continuously because she did not know how to clean. "In my town, everything was just dirt, no beds, nothing. . . . And there in Mexico City many houses are elegant, lots of furniture. Since I didn't know about those things, it cost me. It took me a while to learn. But yes, I learned."

The first household paid Yolanda about 90 *centavos* a month. After a few weeks she left to work with her sister, where she stayed for eight months. "At that time I earned about two hundred pesos a month. Back then, well that was plenty of money. . . . I remember when they'd send me to the store, they'd give me one peso, and I'd bring back a bag of bread this big," Yolanda demonstrated, holding her arms open wide.

Marta's story mirrors Yolanda's in many ways. It also sheds light on the gendered dimensions of early migration, as well as on the ways in which cross-border inequalities shaped migrants' experiences before they set foot in the United States. Thirty-four at the time of the interview, Marta first worked in Mexico City as a young girl. Unable to understand Spanish, she had no more cleaning experience than Yolanda, having been accustomed to dirt-floor dwellings. As Marta relates, the señora would say to her, "'Did you finish sweeping?' And I tell her, 'yes.' 'You didn't sweep it well. Sweep again,' and 'sweep again.'" Discouraged, Marta joined her older sister, who was working as a maid in a different household. She became a burden to her sister, though, for she was still very young. When the 1985 earthquake struck in Mexico City, Marta's mother bade her to return home. "And back here, I put myself to work. . . . I'd look for *quelites* [wild greens], *epazote* [a pungent herb native to Mexico], whatever I could find in the countryside to go and sell." Soon after, Marta met a woman in the market who offered her a job as a maid in her daughter's household in Tijuana. Marta's new employer worked across the border in San Diego. In addition to cleaning, Marta looked after the family's children, who were older than she was. Marta stayed at the house in Tijuana for a year and a half, "without once talking to my parents or going home, without hearing a thing from them," for there was still no telephone access in the *pueblo*.

Marta's employers forbade her to visit home. Finally, Marta got up the courage to tell her boss that she had decided to leave, with or without permission. Although Marta earned very little, the señora tricked her out of her pay by stating that she had already paid Marta's mother part of the sum during one of her recent trips to Ixmiquilpan. She warned that the bus ride would be dangerous, for "bad men go there; they rape a lot of girls." But Marta went home anyway. Unbeknownst to Marta, her family had sent her brother to look for her, borrowing five hundred pesos to pay for his trip. They had just missed one another—but Marta arrived on her own, safe and sound. She was only thirteen.

While the long separation from her family was difficult, some good came of the ordeal. After such a long time of "not even hearing Otomí again," Marta had learned to speak Spanish. After a brief stay in El Alberto, she returned to Tijuana, now with greater confidence. She found work with a different family, and "this time, they paid me 110 pesos a week. A week!" After another visit to El Alberto, two other girls from the community decided to join her in the border city. Due to a fluke of travel—the girls missed a bus—they ended up in Guadalajara, thus laying the groundwork for a pattern of migration that continues to this day, as young women from El Alberto travel to Guadalajara to work as maids. They go there, Marta explains, "because one doesn't finish one's education, doesn't know how to do other types of work, the only thing is housework." But the pay is good. "You don't pay rent, or electricity, or water . . . and the girls are now earning a thousand pesos," or roughly eighty dollars, a week.

Marta and Yolanda's stories provide a simple yet necessary reminder that labor migration thrives when migrants and their hosts share different conceptions about acceptable treatment and adequate pay. Marta's first boss benefited from her youth, her innocence, and her limited Spanish abilities. Yet Marta recalls that the family at least saw to her basic needs. "They dressed me and put shoes on my feet," she recalls. "Everything their daughter didn't want anymore, they gave to me." Clothing and shoes might seem like little compensation for live-in labor. But for Marta and Yolanda at that time, work was not necessarily a means to save money and get ahead. Rather, work was about earning the means to survive. Marta's story is indicative of a systemic exploitation of indigenous labor in Mexican society. It also illustrates how migrants from El Alberto experienced transnational inequalities before setting foot in the United States. Marta cleaned the house of a woman who crossed the border on a daily basis, and she attended to the "needs" of teenaged children whose upbringing in the borderlands was lined with comforts and expectations she had never dreamed of.

The working conditions that early migrants from El Alberto faced had lasting effects upon their personal relationships. The effects on men were not quite as pronounced, as male migrants usually returned home on weekends. But those who left home as young girls spent their early years immersed in the homes of *mestizo* families who viewed them not as children, but as sources of labor. Marta became a virtual mother to her some of charges. The little girl whom she cared for in Guadalajara asked her mother if she could go with Marta when it came time for Marta to leave the job. As often occurs in situations of domestic labor, Marta's status as a worker served to mask and discredit her value as a human being.[3] Women from El Alberto would experience similar tensions and tradeoffs as they engaged in domestic labor in the United States. But even though Yolanda's and Marta's early years of work were not easy, they do not speak about those years from the point of view of victims. They emerged from their trials no longer shy, frightened children but rather strong, independent women, who had gained the confidence to reject abusive work situations and seek better treatment and higher pay. Perhaps most importantly, they learned to speak Spanish. Today, women who worked in domestic service as young girls are some of the most fluent Spanish speakers of their age group in the community. In a culture that is still highly patriarchal, that is no small benefit. The language abilities gained through domestic employment also helped give some women the confidence necessary to venture across the border to the United States.

For young evangelicals who were raised in the faith, early migration was a testing ground that brought them out of the supportive structures of family and church. Fortunato, the man who recalls going hungry while working in Mexico City, is the son of El Alberto's first evangelical pastor and was raised accordingly. Nonetheless, he states that he did not consistently practice the religion during his youth. At one time, he even resorted to selling Catholic devotional cards while searching for work in Guadalajara, for his pride prevented him from going to a nearby evangelical church to ask for help. He eventually arrived among a group of *hermanos* who chided him for not seeking them out sooner. With their help he found work and saved enough money to get to Mexico City.

Like Fortunato, Marta was brought up as an evangelical. Her mother converted before she was born, and her father converted shortly thereafter. Marta states that she would not be the person she is today were it not for her father's conversion. Although Marta was too young at the time to remember, others say that her father's conversion produced such a dramatic change in his personality that she scarcely would have recognized him. When Marta was young, however, her faith was not strong. Her parents were loving and kind, yet they were often too preoccupied with daily survival to sit and reflect with their children about religion. "My mom was always busy with work," Marta explains. "And 'you, child, go get firewood, you go pasture [the sheep and goats], you go spin thread'—and that's how we spent our time. We didn't sit like this to talk, to discuss things. We were . . . always in a rush to do something." Marta had every intention of maintaining her religious practice when she first arrived in Tijuana. But it was difficult to do so without support. At first she would tell her employers that she was going to go to church, "but they never helped me find [one]." Instead, the teenaged children of the household took her to dances, where Marta would wait for them outside in coffee shops. "I stopped being careful," she explains. "If one stops participating, one loses heart, and soon one is discouraged. So it was a time that yes, I was sad, lonely, without remembering God."

The stories of both Marta and Fortunato, who went through religious dry spells when they found themselves far from home, reveal how important the social body is in providing a nurturing context for religious practice. Nevertheless, Marta did not comment upon her religious experiences until I asked her about them directly. And although Fortunato shared how he strayed from the faith during his youth, I found stories like his to be few. Unlike the stories of development outlined in chapter 1, early migration experiences are not, in general, cast into a shared religious narrative by evangelicals. This is perhaps because, unlike development, early migration was a relatively lonely endeavor. Perhaps an Exodus-inspired narrative would have emerged if El Alberto's residents had emigrated en masse or if, as a group, they had been forcibly displaced. But as things transpired, there was no collective migration story to tell. To this day, it is common for people to depart for El Norte suddenly, in the night, without telling their neighbors or in some cases even their spouses.

One thing we can learn from early stories of internal migration is that neither religious conversion nor economic development brought an end to people's suffering. Indeed, the fastest rate of evangelical growth in Mexico from the 1950s through the 1970s occurred among those who were the most marginalized and thus had the least to gain from Mexico's economic boom.[4] By the early 1980s, people in El Alberto were still poor, evangelicals included. Although Marta's father's conversion caused him to stop drinking, her parents were still so preoccupied with daily survival that they had little choice but to allow their young daughters to work in the houses of strangers. And although Fortunato came from a prominent family as the son of El Alberto's first pastor, he still had little choice as a youth but to seek employment in Mexico City. Thus, migration emerged as a parallel, interrelated response to the same desperation that drove religious change. It would not be long before people would travel even further, to seek their livelihood across the border in the North.

The Rise of U.S. Migration

By the time residents of El Alberto finally ventured into the United States, a "clandestine form of cross-border interdependence" had been developing between the two countries for decades.[5] The rise of so-called "illegal" Mexican immigration must be understood as the by-product of recurring efforts by the U.S. government both to attract and to restrict

Mexican labor in response to economic change. While the United States deported Mexicans en masse during the Great Depression, the tide turned following labor shortages during World War II. Through the Bracero program, initiated in 1942, the United States invited millions of Mexican contract laborers north. These documented laborers were accompanied by millions of undocumented immigrants who encountered little restriction at the border and found abundant employment in the Southwest. No sooner had U.S. agribusinesses become dependent on Mexican labor than the United States initiated Operation Wetback, which deported hundreds of thousands of undocumented immigrants back to Mexico. Later, as the Bracero program was officially ended and the 1965 Immigration Act placed new restrictions on the number of visas for people from the Western Hemisphere, these measures were countered by a corresponding surge in undocumented immigration from Mexico.[6]

To the best of my knowledge, the first people from El Alberto to travel to the United States in search of work did so in the 1980s, and it was not until the mid-1990s that U.S. migration would become commonplace. El Alberto was not alone in this pattern. During this time, several factors converged to send members of Mexico's rural, indigenous populations north. With the exception of Mixtecs, Zapotecs, and P'urépechas, few indigenous groups were systematically engaged in migration to the United States until the 1980s.[7] As growing economic liberalization caused the Mexican government to cut crucial subsidies to peasant farmers, more and more indigenous people had to go on the move. The situation for rural populations became even more precarious as the peso collapsed and the North American Free Trade Agreement (NAFTA) went into effect in 1994. By some accounts, the peso collapse was part of a strategic move by the government to pave the way for foreign investment.[8] Indigenous farmers found themselves unable to compete with the plummeting prices of coffee, corn, and other agricultural products. During the years following the passage of NAFTA, Mexican government officials neglected small-scale agriculture, leaving members of rural populations with little choice but to seek their livelihood in agribusiness, urban wage labor, and U.S. migration.[9] It was in the midst of this increasingly hostile climate that migrants from El Alberto first caught wind of opportunities across the border.

Evaristo recalls that a group of seven people began to hear of opportunities in Texas while they were working in Tamaulipas in the early 1980s. "'In Texas they say there's a lot of work,' people began to say to one another. 'And they pay a dollar, or two dollars an hour,' and 'oh, is that true?'" The group eventually made it to Brownsville, where they worked in an oil refinery. Several years later, Roberto and his companions had a similar experience. As we have seen, Roberto had worked in construction in Mexico City. Enduring long days and meager wages, he and his companions heard of better opportunities in the North. "So we struggled, we were thinking, thinking, pretty much daily what we were thinking and hearing was that those who went there made money, enough to build a house, and buy a car. But not us, well we just stayed in the same routine."

After much deliberation, Roberto and three others finally ventured to the border in 1986. There, on a riverbank crowded with people, they met a *coyote* who knew the schedule of the local Immigration and Naturalization Service (INS) agents and advised them of the best time to cross. On reaching the other side, the companions remained hidden by walking through a bed of reeds. They traveled on foot for ten days and eventually arrived in San Angelo, Texas, where they found agricultural work. After several short-term jobs, Roberto found work helping a white farmer manage cotton fields near San Antonio. Roberto's job involved irrigation. He speaks well of his former boss. "A very, very good person, that *gringo*. . . . He gave me my house, gasoline, he gave me my pickup truck, and I went to my work as if it were my own home." The boss and his wife thought highly of Roberto, as well. "[O]nce a month they'd go buy clothes for me, pants, everything, shirts—they'd buy them for me! Because they liked me very much." One time Roberto's boss got sick and spent two months in California for treatment, leaving him in charge of the house and animals. "And when he came back from the doctors, he cried," Roberto remembers. "He cried! . . . He said, 'I'm not going to find another Mexican like you. Because other Mexicans have come here, they've robbed us, and they've gone,' he says. 'But you are a good Mexican. Good Mexican.' I fed his chickens, his cats, his dogs."

Roberto was already evangelical by the time he found work with the benevolent farmer. Although he is an active participant in Sinaí and readily talks about his faith, he made no mention of his religious experiences during that time. Rather, the bulk of his story centers on the bond of trust he forged with his employers. His use of racially charged words implies that his positive experience was an exception to the norm. Roberto's boss was not merely kindhearted; he was a kindhearted *gringo*. Roberto was not merely a trustworthy employee; he was a trustworthy "Mexican" upon whom the burden of proof for his own goodness rested. Roberto's case helps us to see, yet again, how deep structural inequalities condition certain people to embrace as opportunities situations that others would see as limited and oppressive. Although the bond he shared with his employers was racially charged and paternalistic, Roberto views the experience as a vast improvement over the low-paying excavation work he had done in Mexico City. Like the women from El Alberto who worked in domestic service as young girls, he does not identify as a victim but rather highlights what he learned from the experience. Roberto lasted two years in that place of employment. With the money he earned, he was able to build a house in El Alberto.

Just as Roberto's words of loyalty and friendship for his boss obscure his status as a low-wage worker, people's words about early border crossings obscure the fact that they were entering a country that welcomed their labor while denying their full status as human beings. Those who crossed during the 1980s and early 1990s state that the journey was relatively easy. Evaristo went to the United States for the first time the 1980s at the age of twenty-nine. Traveling through Nogales, he was guided by a young boy who charged nothing. They simply walked by when the INS agents were not looking. Evaristo's new boss met him at a McDonald's as soon as he made it across the border. Evaristo recalls eating two large orders of french-fries. He laughs as he remembers how he fumbled to work the ice dispenser on the soda machine. They arrived in Chandler, Arizona, at ten o'clock that night. "It was so easy," Evaristo recalls. "And now—no, man, the reality is totally different. Now, you really do suffer!" Marta's first trip to the United States was fairly simple as well. She and her husband passed through Nogales in the early 1990s. The journey took them scarcely ten minutes. They arrived at a Burger King, where a taxi was waiting for them.

Evaristo and Marta's experiences are typical of undocumented Mexican travel to the United States during that time. The immigration restrictions of the post-1965 era were not accompanied by increased border enforcement. Crossing the border remained relatively easy and inexpensive, with border apprehension efforts serving more as a symbolic gesture of control than as a genuinely effective deterrence policy.[10] As Douglas Massey, Jorge Durand, and Nolan Malone argue, the period of Mexican immigration to the United States from 1965 to 1985 was comparable to major waves of European immigration in the late nineteenth and early twentieth centuries.[11] That is, Mexico sent large numbers of immigrants to the United States as it underwent intensive industrialization. Left alone, migration levels would eventually peak and then start to decline, much as European-U.S. migration had done in the early twentieth century. Beginning with the 1986 Immigration Reform and Control Act, however, the U.S. government put a "wrench" into the "well-ordered machinery" of Mexico-U.S. migration by implementing a series of restrictive border policies that blatantly contradicted the increasing economic integration of the continent.[12] Until the mid-1990s, however, cross-border travel for residents of El Alberto remained fairly fluid. Many found ready employment in the housing boom of the Southwest. Some of the town's men worked for a year or two at a time while their wives and children remained in Mexico. Others started families in the United States. Many of those who arrived in the United States by the 1980s were able to secure papers for themselves and their families under the general amnesty extended by the Reagan administration.

Today, El Alberto's population is about equally divided between Mexico and the United States. Although the town's members have traveled as far north as Washington State and as far east as Florida, it is Las Vegas that hosts the town's largest concentration of immigrants, followed by Phoenix and Salt Lake City. This trend reflects larger geographic shifts in Mexican migration. Whereas California, Texas, and Illinois were once the top destinations for Mexican immigrants, by 2010 these traditional "gateways" had been replaced by cities such as Atlanta, Phoenix, Las Vegas, and Raleigh.[13] Such changes are partly the result of state-level shifts in immigration enforcement. The new geography of Mexican migration is also linked to demographic shifts among the U.S.-born. As middle-class and retiree African Americans and whites flock to "New Sunbelt" states such as Nevada, Arizona, Georgia, and North Carolina, these states' major cities have witnessed a rise in service-sector jobs that have attracted, in turn, large numbers of immigrant workers. In Las Vegas, two unlikely migration streams have converged: American workers from the declining industrial centers of the North and immigrant workers who hail from the very countries to which American manufacturing jobs have fled.[14]

Eyes to the North

While religious themes are scarce in early stories of internal migration, they are even scarcer in early stories of migration to the United States. This is perhaps because, at least in the early years, U.S. income offered a solution to hardship that, in its efficacy and power, rivaled religious conversion. Mateo, who now lives in Salt Lake City, first traveled to the United States in the 1980s. He explains that the country "hasn't made us kings, but . . . we've built houses, we've bought cars, we've dressed well, we have done things we hadn't done twenty or thirty years ago. And all from what we have earned in the United States, from dollars." What people love about the United States, Mateo explains, is the fact that its money "yields":

> For 100 dollars, you get about 1,400 or 1,450 pesos. . . . Yes, so that's what the United States has done for us. Yes. . . . we worked a lot; I worked even on Sunday nights, from Monday to Sunday. We didn't know what it was to take a break, but for me it was good, because we earned well. [At first] I earned about six dollars an hour. And six dollars an hour—you do the math—how much is *that* in two weeks!

While recognizing that he has worked hard in the United States, Mateo also highlights the marvelous ability of U.S. dollars to multiply and expand. Working there did not merely enable people survive from day to day. Rather, it brought them the ability to acquire material things they had once never dreamed of owning. Today, the salvific promise of dollars is frustratingly out of reach for many of El Alberto's residents, as newer generations of migrants face apprehension, detention, and deportation at the U.S.-Mexico border. Yet many continue to attempt the journey.

In a rapid-fire breakdown of earnings and expenses, a young man named Heriberto explained the tremendous temptation of U.S.

earnings. Heriberto has never been to the United States, but says that he would like to obtain a master's degree in order to work there as a teacher. The basic daily wage in Mexico, he explained, is about 150 pesos. About three years ago, Heriberto worked as a quality inspector in a clothing factory. His job was to ensure that the products' seams were in good order. He began work at eight in the morning and left at six in the evening, Monday through Friday. Heriberto made 900 pesos, or $71 a week, which works out to about $14 for a ten-hour day. He recalls:

> I spent 300 pesos a week on gas, so that leaves me with 600 pesos. And sometimes I would give my mom money, 100 or 200 pesos, so that leaves me with 400 pesos. And to go have fun on the weekend, at the dances, another 200 pesos. So that leaves me with 200 pesos for the week. And if I want to buy a pair of jeans, well, I have to work a whole week just to save enough to buy a pair of jeans. Or a shirt. So you see? You can't save anything. And to build a house, or buy a car? Forget about it.

Heriberto explains that many people go to the United States expecting to earn in a few hours what they would earn in a whole day in Mexico. The trouble is that they underestimate how long it will take them to save money, given the higher cost of living in the United States. Often people plan to return after one year, once they have earned enough to build a house in Mexico. The year comes and goes, and they find that they have not met their goal. As they continue working, their needs and desires continue to grow. Even after they return to Mexico, they are soon itching to make the journey back.

The attraction of dollars in El Norte is foreshadowed by a folkloric belief about mountains in the Valle del Mezquital. In hñähñu cosmology, mountains are held to be the source of rain and other benevolent forces. They contain circulating breezes and bodies of water that connect to the ocean.[15] They also occasionally open up to let forth animals and *nahuales,* or human-animal doubles, which travel to human settlements to lure young people back inside. Time passes differently inside the mountains than it does in the outside world. While a young person may feel that she has spent several hours within the mountain, a year may have passed within the life of the town.[16] Like the mountain of the legend, the United States is a marvelous place that offers opportunity but also danger. Like the elusive entrance to the mountains, passage to the North is available only to certain people, at certain times. When young people emerge from the United States, as from the fabled mountain, they find that their sense of time is out of sync with those they left behind. A visiting pastor to a Pentecostal church in Phoenix captured the magical appeal of the North in a sermon in the spring of 2010. While preaching to a congregation that included at least a dozen immigrants from El Alberto, he made a play on Psalm 121. "Many people in Mexico say, 'I lift up my eyes to *el Norte,* from whence cometh my help,'" he cried. "From the North comes my support! From the North comes my check! But then, when we've made it to the North, to where do we turn our eyes?"

Economic need initially drove El Alberto's residents beyond their town and, eventually, to the United States in search of work. Their early journeys within Mexico were not easy. They encountered discrimination, loneliness, and hunger. Gradually, their opportunities increased and their horizons expanded. U.S. migration arose out of the same quest for survival that drove early internal migration. At first, the benefits of working in the United States were so great that the pull of dollars rivaled the pull of faith. The promise of the American Dream appeared to be close within reach—at least for the time being. Yet it would not be long before transnational life produced challenges of its own. U.S. migration brought not only money and consumer goods, but also new worries, needs, and desires. It brought the pang of family separation and the ever-present threat of apprehension and deportation. As the pursuit of dollars produced new forms of physical and psychological strain, evangelicals in El Alberto would turn more strongly to their faith. The next chapter explores how Pentecostals draw upon religion today to negotiate the day-to-day challenges of transnational life.

PART II

4

Send Us Power

The house where I would wash my clothes while I was in El Alberto belongs to the brother of my host. To reach it, one goes through an iron gate and over a hexagon-brick path. The home is painted white, unlike the bare concrete of so many other homes left behind by emigrant families. The house is surrounded by overgrown fruit trees and weeds, slowly reclaiming what was once theirs. A mop-head sits inverted on a piece of rebar. Elephant-ear seedlings grow in rusted coffee cans. A papaya tree crowds the house's dark-tinted windows, its spindly trunk topped with lobed leaves and a single green fruit. A water bottle with a Western Union logo lies near a broken high-chair under a banana tree whose leaves are torn by the wind.

    This house is not an unusual sight in El Alberto. The town's landscape is dotted with empty concrete houses in various stages of completion. Some are mere frameworks with grand columns and arched windows that open onto empty land and sky. Some are locked tight like treasure chests, holding plastic-covered sofas and polished wooden tables. Others evoke a Pompeian vision of life swiftly interrupted. Such is the ecology of dwelling places in a migrant town. Houses lay vacant when families pack and leave with *coyotes* in the night. The only signs of life around them are the weather and the weeds and the occasional flock of turkeys wandering through in search of food. Occasionally a neighbor or relative stops by to ensure that nothing has been stolen. Yet eventually fate shifts and homes come back into life. Families return from the United States. Perhaps they have been deported or perhaps they come home to tend to a sick relative. A husband arrives and then sends for his wife and children. The families open the doors and take the covers off the couches and bang the kitchens back into shape. The children learn to speak hñähñu with their grandparents and cousins. Life, the alternate Mexican life that they have kept on hold for years, settles back to normal.

Other homes host rotating traffic, as relatives cycle through between stays in the United States. At one time a man, his sister-in-law, and his father might share a roof; now, a woman with her daughter-in-law and grandson, or an elderly couple with grandchildren sent home by their daughter in the United States. Students in El Alberto leave their classrooms mid-year when their parents bring them north. Others arrive from the States and gradually fall back into stride with cousins who have never left home. A third of the elementary school classrooms lie empty; they were built in years before migration. The high school classrooms are the emptiest of all.

The absence that is so visible in the architecture of this migrant town is also palpable in church services. During each worship period, Brother Elpidio,[1] pastor of Bethel Pentecostal Church, sets aside a moment of prayer for relatives and loved ones in the United States. As many as half of the nearly one hundred congregation members gather near the altar. Some stand, others kneel. One person leads the prayer on a microphone. Her voice is soon enveloped by a chorus of voices that rise to a crescendo of shouts and tears. Some call out in Spanish, some in hñähñu. The prayer lasts a full five minutes. During *casa cultos*, when services are held outside at congregation members' homes, the effect is particularly moving. In a space where no roof separates the people from the stars, one can feel the prayers spiral upward through the night air toward relatives across the border.

During my time in El Alberto, I experienced how frustrating it can be to try to communicate with those in the United States. International phone calls are expensive, and connections are halting and erratic. As I joined townsfolk at the altar during the migration prayer, I would strain to catch individual words within the sea of voices. "Give him work, Lord!" "Give her wisdom. Protect her." "Heal him!" "You're the one who opens doors, who makes all things possible." "Find him a good job!" As individual prayers intertwined, anguish would leave the confines of the individual chest to be shared by all. I have seen a grown man crying about a brother who was suffering from alcoholism in the United States, and then praying aloud for a nephew who was in a detention facility in Arizona. By praying together, migrants' relatives intensify bonds of compassion and solidarity. Yet I would be neglecting the richness of the situation to claim that what is going on in these prayers is simply the externalization of private concerns. Those who gather at the altar during each service seek more than mutual support. They seek to procure health and wellbeing for their relatives in the North, and they do so by making their bodies sites of active exchange with the divine.

As we have seen, people in El Alberto turned to Pentecostalism just as national development projects began to make headway into the Valle del Mezquital. Conversion occurred amidst the social and ecological shifts that emerged as wage labor became increasingly available and Mexico made a concentrated effort to develop its rural areas. Despite the enormity of the religious transformation involved, the logic of exchange that underlay indigenous *costumbre* and the Catholic *fiesta* system was not lost. Rather, it was redirected. Pentecostals sought in worship and prayer the tools and empowerment necessary to engage with bureaucratic government offices and employers in distant cities. Later, as international labor migration became commonplace, they would draw upon Pentecostal practices to negotiate their relationships with relatives across the border.

This chapter focuses on the experiences of Pentecostals who remain behind in El Alberto while their loved ones are in the United States. We have seen that early Pentecostal converts drew a distinct connection between religious faith and material well-being. Today, however, the quest for a better life has become an increasingly complicated endeavor. I argue that Pentecostalism in El Alberto has become intimately connected to the daily, relational challenges of migration, even for those who have never set foot in the United States. The religion's embodied practices resonate with indigenous notions of reciprocity and exchange. At the same time, Pentecostal prosperity theology appeals to those whose personal and economic lives are intertwined with loved ones in the North. Faced with restrictive border policies, erratic deportations, and an unpredictable U.S. economy, worshippers in El Alberto embrace a spiritual economy in which dollars interlace with prayers. As migrants send remittances home, those who remain in Mexico implore God to protect their relatives and help them find work. They draw upon fasting, faith healing, and prayer to absorb the tensions and uncertainties of migration in their bodies.

A Cell Phone on Her Pillow

Emilia sleeps with a cell phone on her pillow. The space beside her on the bed is empty because her husband is working somewhere in Washington, and she has not heard from him since he left Las Vegas. Emilia is in her early fifties, and she has lived a life divided by migration for over thirty years. While she remains in El Alberto, her husband has U.S. residency and can travel across the border and within the United States with relative ease. Even so, uncertainties are always present. Jobs are scarce. Her husband has worked in the construction industry for many years, but recently he has suffered long dry spells between jobs. He might call at any hour of the night. When he does, greetings are rushed, a pen and paper must be quickly found, and an address and phone number jotted down before the minutes run out.

Emilia's days are filled with many tasks. In the daytime, she manages a small store, where she sells bottles of soda, bags of chips, Tylenol, and candies for a peso each. The store's shelves hold hand-embroidered bags, tourist souvenirs, cans of Ajax, and bottles of bleach. Emilia also owns a *molino* (mill) where neighbors come by to grind buckets of maize into the dough for their daily tortillas. On weekends, Emilia makes food to sell to tourists beside the swimming pools in the park. At night, she joins a team of women who serve coffee, bread, and *atole* (a hot drink made of ground corn) to tourists who have just finished the Caminata Nocturna. Sometimes they do not close the kitchen until two or three in the morning.

In times of harvest, Emilia can be found in the fields with members of her household and with neighbors, cutting alfalfa with a scythe and carrying it on their backs to a pick-up truck parked along the road. They grow the alfalfa for the goats and sheep that they butcher for festivals, as well as for household consumption. They also cultivate enough maize, beans, and vegetables to feed the family year round. Herbs, good for teas and home remedies and for flavoring meat and beans, grow in the shade along the sides of the fields. Pomegranate trees border the road, and Emilia helps her family pick the red fruits each year to sell in the market in Ixmiquilpan. She and her neighbors have been selling the fruit that way for years, although competition from commercial growers has driven prices down in recent years.

Emilia tends a parcel of land that she inherited from her parents. She has a pig and some goats. A surly little dog named Amigo keeps guard. From time to time, she travels up into the hills to collect firewood. In the *sierra,* the uncultivated hill land on the outskirts of town, sustenance is there for those who know where to look. To find firewood, one must contend with cactus spines, rocks, and tough walking. The wood isn't heavy, but it is awkward to carry. Although Emilia has a natural gas stove in her house, as most families do, the price of gas has skyrocketed in recent years, and so her husband has built an outdoor kitchen with a wood-burning stove, "like in the old days."

When she is not at her store, in the fields, or selling food, Emilia can be found in her home, washing clothes or preparing meals for her family. She occasionally takes in visitors like myself for a small fee. There is always a son or a nephew to feed, or a grandchild to chase after. Between tasks, she knits sponges from agave fiber to contribute to the women's cooperative founded by members of her town. She also sells Forever Living products, a line of cosmetic and health items manufactured by company based in Scottsdale, Arizona, which champions aloe as a cure for nearly all ills.

Emilia must fill her days with many such tasks, for the income from her husband's job is not always enough. Ever since the recent housing bust in the Southwest, he has had trouble finding work. This window onto Emilia's life shows but a small portion of the larger migration reality within El Alberto. Yet we can draw from it some important observations. Emilia's daily experience is one of being in an intimate, interdependent relationship with individuals who are absent. Moreover, it is an experience of being in relation with people whose labor, in the eyes of the United States government and populace, is expendable.

Although Emilia's husband is fortunate enough to have U.S. residency, his recent travels from Las Vegas to Washington State suggest that he is embedded in an economic system characterized by what David Harvey[2] refers to as flexible accumulation. In order to compete within a rapidly changing global market, Harvey argues, corporate leaders embrace flexible strategies such as outsourcing and subcontracting that condition workers to accept short-term, geographically shifting work as the norm.[3] Immigrants in the construction industry must adapt to unpredictable hours, often taking back-to-back shifts or working at night. One man from the neighboring community of El Dexthi installs flooring in gyms, banks, hospitals, and nursing homes in Phoenix. He often does not know what his schedule will be from one day to the next. Day shifts alternate erratically with night shifts, interrupting the natural rhythm of wakefulness and sleep. His personal life and religious activities must defer to the schedules of those whose needs and wishes take precedence.

The lives of U.S. migrants from El Alberto are fraught with unpredictability. Given current anti-immigrant initiatives in the United States, their lives are also marked by a sense of precariousness. While migrants absorb the shock of a fluctuating U.S. economy and draconian deportation regimes, their relatives in Mexico absorb that shock a second time over. To be the relative of a migrant is to be divided by a border yet to have one's life, one's sustenance, and even the wellbeing of one's children enmeshed with the life of a person on the other side. It is to be partially dependent for one's survival upon a person who is, in turn, vulnerable to the variations of the U.S. market. Emilia lives in just such a divided and changing household. During my first visit, her nephew came to live with her when he was deported after serving time in a U.S. detention facility. A few years later, her son was deported. He now lives with her, along with his wife and young son.

Emilia is not the only one who must be resourceful in order to make ends meet, in El Alberto or in Mexico as a whole. Since the 1980s, scholars have spoken of various "household survival strategies" or "resources of poverty" adopted by members of Latin America's poor.[4] Faced with limited employment opportunities, people live in extended family households that allow them to pool their resources more efficiently. Since households mediate between the individual and larger, macroeconomic processes, their effective management can make the difference between wellbeing and misery. Women play a key role within the household, for they convert wages into sustenance and build social networks that are crucial for survival. Due to the growth of neoliberalism in Mexico, however, today even a carefully managed, extended family household is not always enough to buffer people against poverty.[5] After the devaluation of the peso following Mexico's debt crisis of 1982, formal employment in the country declined, and informal sector employment rose exponentially. When Mexico signed the General Agreement on Tariffs and Trade in 1986, foreign goods flooded the market, and more jobs were lost. Households have become more crowded, and growing numbers of women have moved beyond the home to seek employment in the informal sector.[6]

Poverty in El Alberto is somewhat different from the urban poverty referred to in the literature on household survival strategies. As a *comunidad*, the town's shared land and extensive kinship bonds offer an extra buffer against economic instability. Nevertheless, recent neoliberal restructuring has constrained the options available to migrants and their families. Viable employment has declined in Mexico as a whole. Some young people from El Alberto try their luck in cities like Pachuca, Mexico City, and Guadalajara, yet as they do so, they compete with urban-born youth who themselves feel increasing pressure to migrate to the United States.

So dire have the social effects of neoliberalism and globalization been in recent decades that some scholars and global organizations suggest that it is no longer enough simply to speak of poverty. Rather, we must try to understand the vulnerability that people face as a result of "the increased riskiness of life in today's world" and "the erosion of coping mechanisms to survive and recover from such risks."[7] When large numbers of people lack access to stable employment, they turn to new coping strategies, such as unauthorized migration, crime, and the drug trade. The concept of vulnerability is especially relevant to Mexico, where drug-related violence has been rampant in recent years, and the social climate is increasingly fraught with fear. Increased risk contributes to the appeal of salvation-oriented religions like Pentecostalism, as well as the appeal of gang membership. The fact that El Alberto's youth have become involved in gangs at the same time that their parents turn to evangelical Christianity speaks to the fact that both activities offer resources for coping with the sense of dislocation brought about when employment options are few, and migration disrupts conventional reference points of self and community.[8]

As the wife of a migrant facing sporadic working conditions in the United States, the mother of a son facing limited employment in Mexico, and the grandmother of children whose parents could be deported at any moment, Emilia finds that her material efforts are simply not enough. Throughout her daily activities, Emilia invests significant time and energy in spiritual practices. These, I argue, are just as survival oriented as her other pursuits.

"Send Them Work"

Emilia attends church services two or three nights a week. Each service lasts anywhere from two to three-and-a-half hours. On some nights, she prepares tacos or sandwiches to be sold after the service to raise money for the church treasury. When I last visited, Emilia was also part of a committee of women helping to plan the pastor's birthday celebration.

A typical service begins within over an hour of song. First are the songs of *adoración,* slow, heartfelt numbers that center the worshipper and facilitate transition into a devotional state. They are followed by songs of *alabanza,* or praise, accompanied by drums, keyboard, guitar, and bass. No hymnals are needed, for most of those gathered know the verses by heart. The title of this chapter is adapted from one such song. "Send us your power, Lord!" worshippers belt out, in a cascade of repeating verses. "We want more power, we want more power! Send us your great power, to every heart!" The lyrics act not as poetic descriptions but as visceral incantations that invite the Holy Spirit into the congregation's midst. Prayers are composed on the spot.

As Jean-Pierre Bastian argues, although Protestantism is often understood as making a sharp break with the ritual practices of Roman Catholicism, expressions of Pentecostalism in rural Mexico do not necessarily involve a shift toward rationalized, text-based worship. Rather, they involve a reinterpretation of traditional oral and performative culture.[9] Although each person follows along in the Bible as the scripture is read aloud, the very redundancy of the gesture suggests that the Bible's presence and physical accessibility are as important as the word it contains. Scripture readings start and end with prayers, during which all gathered ask God to open their minds and hearts to make them better able to receive the word. In an activity known as a *lluvia de versos*, or "rain of verses," those gathered call out treasured passages and challenge one another to locate them in the text. Worshippers strive to memorize verses because, within Pentecostalism, the word itself has incantatory power. It can cast out demons and heal. The repetition of biblical passages in worship and devotional songs helps commit them to memory so that worshippers can access them the instant that adversity arises. When a man from an affiliated congregation in the region faced kidney failure after a motorcycle accident, he says that he put his hand to his wound and said, "*todo lo puedo en Cristo que me fortalece*": "I can do all things in Christ who strengthens me." The words are from Philippians 4:13 in the Bible. They also form part of a popular evangelical hymn. The words had slowly woven into his being during the months before the accident, and they emerged into his consciousness in his moment of need. When I met him, the man was still unable to walk, but his kidneys were functioning well.

The oral nature of Pentecostal worship is apparent in sermons. Pastors rely very little on notes. Their sermons, as Bastian puts it, fulfill a role once covered by the myth-making of the past.[10] Pastor Elpidio is a master storyteller, and his sermons draw liberally on Old Testament themes. His references to the pastoral activities of the ancient Israelites evoke the daily reality of those gathered, many of whom are familiar with the rhythm of raising and butchering animals for their sustenance. Stories of the Hebrews' covenant resonate with worshippers' identity as members of a *comunidad* that is collectively judged and blessed. Stories of struggle against the religion of the Canaanites speak to struggles against the "idolatry" of Catholics, and stories of Babylonian captivity resonate with the challenges of surviving as a minority community in the face of exploitative Mexican authorities and an ambivalent superpower to the North.[11]

Worshippers are encouraged to respond to sermons with multiple *amen*s and *aleluya*s. They are also encouraged to attend as many services as possible. Absences do not go unnoticed. One sermon taught that the people "kill their church" by missing services, arriving late, neglecting to tithe, or by worshipping for the wrong reasons. These words express the underlying conviction that worship is not a solitary endeavor.

Early Protestant reformers insisted that even as people gather in groups to worship, it is each individual soul that ultimately connects with the divine. In this respect, Protestant reformers broke with the Catholic tradition in which salvation is achieved only through the intercessory efforts of a priest and various saints. Worshippers at Bethel are firmly Protestant in their emphasis upon the direct and unmediated relationship between individual human beings and God. Yet they also recognize that there is strength in numbers. For them, the collective nature of worship matters because the goal of worship is not simply to achieve inner tranquility. Rather, worship is a practical effort intended to produce tangible results in the material world. Regular attendance is not simply a matter of respect. It is a matter of necessity, for the larger and more unified the congregation, the more efficacious its prayers.

As a sense of the Holy Spirit begins to manifest in the burn of clapping palms and the hypnotic rhythm of song, the pastor invites those present who have loved ones in the United States to come to the altar to pray. Worshippers call upon God to bring health to their relatives in the North. They ask God to grant their loved ones protection and to give them wisdom and strength to survive and flourish in difficult conditions. Most of all, they ask God to help their loved ones find work. More than just expressions of concern, these prayers are practical efforts urging God to alter the physical circumstances of migrants' lives. Worshippers frequently buttress their prayers by fasting.

Spiritual Nourishment

Fasting is a regular practice within both Bethel and Sinaí. Although people fast individually from time to time, group fasts are also quite common. The Spanish term for a fast, *ayuno,* connotes far more than the act of refraining from food. Individuals begin fasting the night before in their own homes. The next day, they gather for hours of prayer, preaching, and song, before breaking their fast through a shared meal in the mid-afternoon. During my stay in El Alberto in the summer of 2009, Bethel's congregation held *ayunos* twice a month in private homes.

Well into the first group fast in El Alberto in which I was a participant-observer, I began to feel extremely hungry, and a headache pressed upon my temple. But the presence of those beside me forced me to remember that I was not the only one experiencing discomfort. Many of those gathered were elderly. There were also pregnant and nursing women, as well as people in poor health. The smell of tortillas wafted over us as people walked by carrying plates of food. But the pastor pushed us onward in prayer, song, and scripture readings. When at last the hour arrived to break the fast, we sat at plastic tables and quietly partook of barbecued goat, tortillas, and bowls of rich broth flavored by onion and wedges of lime. My headache persisted for the rest of the day. I provide these details in order to convey something of the physicality, even the banality, of the act of fasting. Fasting for short periods of time is not glorious, and the physical changes it spurs are not enough to produce mystically altered states. Fasting is simply an inconvenience that one endures in the company of others. And yet this shared inconvenience works to sharpen the senses and foster a sense of common purpose.

Members of Iglesia Bethel describe fasting as both an ascetic act used to hone one's faith and a practical effort intended to produce a transformation. It is a way to humble oneself before God in order to improve the chances that God will listen to one's prayers. Fasting is more powerful than prayer alone, a worshipper explained, for it demonstrates an extra degree of earnestness and commitment. It shows that one is willing to accompany prayer with action. Yet fasting is not simply about denying the flesh in order to better reach God through the mind. Pentecostals view the body not as an obstacle to be overcome but as a "good and reliable conduit to the ultimate."[12] Rather than repressing the flesh, fasting strengthens the body's ability to connect with God. In Phoenix, where work schedules prevent worshippers from holding group fasts during the day, Pentecostals fast on their own. They supplement these daytime efforts by gathering for nighttime vigils, or *vigilias*. While fasting is not a part of these vigils, the dynamic is similar. A woman who works a twelve-hour shift at a Phoenix hospital told me that the palpable sense of the Holy Spirit generated during *vigilias* fills her with such energy and strength that her coworkers have begun to seek her out for spiritual guidance.

As people fast, they voluntarily reproduce the all-too-familiar reality of hunger and exchange it for spiritual nourishment. The words of several worship songs underscore the logic of exchange. In one worshippers call God to "send us power"; in another, they urge God to send "fire from heaven"; and in yet another, they ask God to "send rain." While the members of previous generations called for actual rain during their religious rites, Pentecostals call for the metaphoric "rain" and "fire" of a Holy Spirit that has the power to nourish, animate, and transform. Just as one exchanges physical labor for money during work, one can use fasting and prayer to gain better access to the flow of the Holy Spirit and then direct that flow toward loved ones in other places. Fasting thus becomes part of a spiritual exchange in which the Holy Spirit serves as currency. Indeed, in the eyes of worshippers, the Holy Spirit is a form of currency that is more versatile than money. Like money, the Holy Spirit can go anywhere. It circulates the globe. Yet it can also answer to the needs of those who are deeply invested in local contexts. Those who need irrigation can call upon the Holy Spirit for help. Those battling envious neighbors can call upon the influence of the Holy Spirit to smooth things over. While money can pay for medical care, accessing the Holy Spirit can circumvent that step and take one right to the divine source of health. While money is finite, the Holy Spirit is available to all.

At the same time that fasting builds upon the indigenous tradition of reciprocal exchange with the divine, it adapts that tradition to the new conditions introduced by labor migration. In one group fast I attended, those gathered sought to call divine attention to the dangers facing the youth of the town. Other fasts center on migration more directly. I have observed people in El Alberto fast for relatives in the United States, and I have met women in Phoenix who fasted in the hope that God would help bring their deported husbands back home. During a visit to El Alberto in August of 2011, I witnessed Pastor Elpidio asking the congregation to fast on the day of his family's long-awaited immigration appointment in Ciudad Juárez. He later called to report that the appointment had been successful, and that his wife and children would be able to travel with him to Phoenix the following week. Buttressed by the power of fasting, prayers interlace with dollars in a bi-directional exchange across the border. As Pastor Elpidio explains, although migrants are in the United States, "we who remain here set aside a time to ask God for their health, for good work, for a good salary. That God will bless them there."

Spiritual and Material Blessings

While today's worship practices draw on indigenous notions of embodiment and exchange, we must be careful not to overlook the effects of global beliefs and practices on local expressions of Christianity.[13] Pastor Elpidio's words indicate another influence within Pentecostal fasting and prayer: prosperity theology. Popular within many evangelical and charismatic circles, prosperity theology, or the "gospel of health and wealth," holds that God rewards the faithful not only with spiritual blessings, but also with health and material wellbeing. The teaching has deep roots in North American Protestantism. As early as the colonial era, Puritan settlers looked to material wellbeing as an indication of divine favor. When the practice of tithing grew during the nineteenth century, some Protestants began to assume that the more money they gave to the church, the better they themselves would thrive financially.[14] Prosperity theology later spread through the efforts of twentieth-century radio preachers and televangelists. Today, the "gospel of health and wealth" is especially prominent in third-wave or "neo-Pentecostal" churches, which tend to place less emphasis on glossolalia than they do on practices of spirit exorcism and divine healing.

Members of Bethel accept prosperity teachings with caution. I once heard the pastor in Phoenix warn his congregation about the dangers of a local Christian radio program that was attempting to lure people into donating large sums of money for supposed spiritual gain. Yet members of Bethel insist that faith has the power to heal, that prayer can help barren women to conceive, and that spiritual activities can result in improved financial circumstances. In the words of one worshipper, "when you put God first, God blesses you, spiritually, and also materially." There is even an enchanted quality in their words about the power of prayer. I have heard members of Bethel cite wonder stories of traveling evangelists who instantly transform people's decayed teeth into beautiful, unearthly teeth of shimmering colors. As Virginia Garrard-Burnett argues, contemporary forms of prosperity theology have something of a "miraculous quality," for they foster the expectation that God will instantly send forth material blessings.[15] Jean and John Comaroff draw a connection between magical treatments of wealth within contemporary charismatic faiths and the apparently salvific nature of global capitalism itself.[16] The current world economy presents itself as having the power to save people from poverty, the Comaroffs argue, yet it produces grave inequalities. At the same time, the proliferation of the mass media and the culture industry serves to sharpen people's desires. As the possibility of wealth hovers just beyond reach, magical, get-rich-quick schemes abound in churches and the informal market alike. Part of the appeal of Pentecostalism and other spirit-centered religions is that they help people to wrestle with this reality. In the words of Manuel Vásquez, these "pneumacentric" religions help people to "deal with desire and materialism in a world of limited means and lack."[17]

Prosperity theology speaks to El Alberto's history of overcoming extreme poverty. The doctrine also speaks to the contradictions of the current global economic system, in which luxury and poverty lie in close proximity and some goods and people flow freely while others are subject to restriction.[18] For many of El Alberto's residents, the abundance of the U.S. economy is close yet unobtainable. Prosperity teachings offer spiritual tools that help the faithful avoid being paralyzed by frustration as they rely financially upon migrants who are subject to the whims of the U.S. economy. When their resources are exhausted, when no more food can be gleaned from the soil and no more money can be saved, worshippers have recourse to an alternate source of sustenance. They can bypass the pursuit of dollars and go directly to the divine source of all power. They can call upon the healing, nourishing power of the Holy Spirit.

Christians and non-Christians alike often criticize prosperity theology for its excessive attention to worldly concerns. For members of a tradition whose founder claimed "blessed are the poor" and called upon the rich to shun earthly goods, the notion that faith brings material comfort may seem simplistic, even heretical. Yet we must recall that for evangelicals in El Alberto the notion that prayer can bring about material change is rooted in something deeper than the pursuit of wealth. It is rooted in the cultural assumption that material and spiritual reality are inseparable. The religion that Pentecostals draw upon as they ask God to help their relatives find jobs is the same religion that once made the difference between raising children who lived and raising children who died of malnourishment or were killed by witches. We can see why the faith in God's power to shower material blessings is so firm. Nevertheless, the fervent tenor of today's cross-border fasts and prayers suggests that Pentecostal strategies for mitigating the challenges of migration are being stretched to a breaking point. It is partly the strains and uncertainties described here that have driven some evangelicals to join their neighbors in seeking migration alternatives outside of the church, through ecotourism. In order to more fully understand the extent of migration's collective impact, however, a few dimensions of Pentecostal practice remain to be explored. One of those dimensions is spiritual warfare. With the rise of globalization, the Holy Spirit is not the only spiritual agent that enters into bodies, crosses borders, and circulates the globe. The same can be said of the "enemy," Satan.

5

To Crush the Devil's Head

Evil is alive and well today, the pastor of Templo Bethel assured me one summer as we stopped for gas at a PEMEX station on the way to a worship conference. As he drove the minivan, cell phone in hand, he and the other passengers had been telling me about the past. They spoke of how frequently children used to die of malnutrition and witchcraft. The pastor's monolingual grandmother listened silently in the back of the van as the others told me that she had once worked as a healer who sucked children's eyes to rid them of curses. Although witchcraft may have declined, my fellow passengers said, it has not disappeared. According to the pastor, a young man in the nearby city of Ixmiquilpan turns into a wolf each full moon. He had been studying magic and had made a pact with the devil to gain power, but since he did not fulfill his end of the bargain, he was transformed into a wolf as punishment. The family keeps him enclosed, and many people go to see him.

The wolf-boy is not an isolated case. People also tell of a woman who changed into a turkey. As the turkey went walking along the side of a road, a man found her and put her in the back of his truck. When he arrived at his destination and opened the back of the vehicle, he found no turkey at all but rather an old woman. "But she was kind of still half-turkey, with turkey-like skin," the pastor explained. The others in the van gave murmurs of agreement.

My traveling companions told me this sort of thing is nothing new. People have long turned themselves into animals. Not everyone has the power to do so—only those who make a pact with the devil. But such practices occur on a global scale. While the particular form of evil varies from place to place, people throughout the world make pacts with the devil to obtain power. Pastor Elpidio stated that he has a friend who is a missionary in Africa, in Equatorial Guinea. The friend had told him that people turn into animals there, as well. The people there keep cows, the pastor continued, but they do not eat them. Neither do they drink the cows' milk. Instead, they worship the cows as gods.

Although my traveling companions were devout Protestants, their stories brim with indigenous Mesoamerican elements. The notion of human-animal transformation derives from the Mesoamerican concept of the *nahual,* and the notion that supernatural power can be obtained through pacts with the devil resonates with hñähñu popular Catholicism. Yet my companions also express a global awareness, a sense that spiritual danger lurks in distant reaches of the world.

We have seen that Pentecostals cast El Alberto's impoverished past into moral terms, attributing illness and infant mortality to acts of witchcraft and sorcery. They state that spiritual attacks declined as people turned to evangelical Christianity in growing numbers. Ethnographer Sergio Sánchez Vásquez has even found that some residents of a nearby town in the Valle del Mezquital attribute the decline of witchcraft to the introduction of electric lighting.[1] Not only are there fewer shadows for witches to lurk in, but "every one of the [utility] poles is a cross, and also when they try to fly they get tangled in the wires."[2] Yet Pentecostals recognize that modernization and migration have not come without a cost. The town's members continue to live and work in an imperfect, fallen world where they are never wholly safe from Satan's grasp. The very electric wires that trap witches in their paths also bring the potentially corrupting influence of global culture into the bosom of family life. Evil enters homes through the tattooed bodies of return migrants and poisons children's minds through television and radio waves.

This chapter looks beyond migration to examine the effects of other forms of mobility upon people's spiritual lives. Evangelicals state that God delivered them from the rampant sorcery of the past, yet today the pursuit of consumer goods has exposed their bodies to new sources of danger—as has the ubiquitous presence of media technology. I argue that worshippers draw on global Christian notions of spiritual warfare to chart a safe path through the chaotic "landscapes of possibility" that they now face on a regular basis.[3] Much like prosperity theology, the logic of spiritual warfare resonates with traditional hñähñu understandings of personhood and agency. It is grounded in the assumption that a person's moral and physical states are seamlessly combined. While the sacred landscape of hñähñu tradition teemed with myriad other-than-human beings, today it is also infused with images and symbols from the media and from global entertainment culture. Drawing upon the tools of spiritual battle, Pentecostals seek to control the many unseen threats introduced by the global movement of people, products, and images. Their efforts reveal deep concerns about rapid intergenerational change, as well as a deep commitment to protecting their youth from harm.

Danger, Protection, and Empowerment

We have seen that early evangelical conversions in El Alberto often centered on issues of illness and healing, as desperate patients and their families turned to Pentecostal prayer as a last resort. Often the illness in question was attributed to supernatural causes. Two additional conversion stories can help us to better understand the role that sorcery beliefs played.

Marta, the woman whose story of working as a maid in Tijuana was given in chapter 3, says that witchcraft-induced illness prompted her father's conversion. Marta's father was once a tough man. He treated his wife badly and fought with neighbors. But one day he fell ill. He "got a bad illness, bad, it wouldn't get better." The illness, Marta explained, was caused by sorcery. "It wasn't something a doctor could treat. Someone had done him evil." Thin and virtually lifeless, Marta's father could scarcely muster the energy to move from the sun to the shade while resting outside. He was wasting away. He sought help among the evangelicals in Ixmiquilpan, to whom his wife had already gone.

"And then they told him, 'You know what? You've got to get on your path. You've got to recognize that you've failed, and that God will heal you.'" The evangelicals insisted that God could heal Marta's father, if only he had sufficient faith. "'Don't be playing around with God,' they told him. 'God is not a game. Just as He can heal you, He can also not listen to your prayer.'" After giving himself entirely to God by renouncing his former ways and dedicating himself to regular prayer, Marta's father was healed.

Witchcraft also played a role in the conversion of Roberto, the man whose story of working for a farmer in Texas was also recounted in chapter 3. Roberto did not wait until he fell ill. Like Marta's father, he had a bellicose temper in his youth. Roberto had been training to become a *lucha libre* fighter, or Mexican freestyle wrestler. He was short, he said, but he was tough. At one point he was attacked by fifteen gang members in Mexico City. He fought them off singlehandedly. In those early years, Roberto said, he had no respect for community.

"Oh, I was rebellious," he remembers. "So here in the town, I had my enemies. Here they were going to—they were going to bewitch me. They were going to curse me. I had heard that those who become evangelicals, even if 100 enemies bewitch them, it won't hurt them. So that motivated me," Roberto explains. "I became evangelical. . . . I was afraid that the people were going to kill me. . . . I'd be better off converting." Now, Roberto insists, God is his protector. "God defends me. That was already His purpose . . . that I was going to serve Him. . . . To this day He defends me! Whatever person, or whatever enemy, even if they don't appear, I offer them friendship. I love them."

In both Marta and Roberto's stories, we gain a sense that God is not the only actor on the scene. The stories depict a world that is infused with hostile and threatening forces. Rather than reject or dismiss beliefs about witchcraft and sorcery, Roberto and Marta's father sought within evangelicalism a new, powerful way to counteract spiritual threat. They sought not only salvation in the next world, but also this-worldly protection. A similar dynamic of danger, protection, and empowerment emerged in my conversation with the pastor and his family on the way to the worship conference. I had asked whether witchcraft could affect people who do not believe in it. At first the pastor answered no. "If you believe in God, then you've got the blood of

Christ surrounding you, protecting you," he explained, "and nothing can do you harm."

I rephrased the question. If a person does not believe in witchcraft, but does not believe in God either, can witchcraft affect them? "Of course," the pastor responded. "Because evil exists. Satan exists, and he's very, very powerful. But God exists too, and He is more powerful. We, alone, are only this powerful," he said, measuring a few inches with his fingers. "But if we call upon the power of God," he insisted, "which is so enormous, so much larger than us, we are protected." The pastor insisted that good and evil exist in dynamic tension. He insisted on the unshakeable reality of God and Satan alike. Far from mere superstition, he made clear, witchcraft and sorcery are real.

Witchcraft, Sorcery, and the Hñähñu Cosmos

Although Pentecostal discourse emphasizes a radical break with the past, the religion is in many ways continuous with hñähñu cosmological understandings. Within the hñähñu cosmos, sorcerers and shamans alike enlist the aid of animal doubles both to curse and to heal. As in other parts of the Americas, the interlocking struggle of killing and curing is understood as a necessary dynamic that makes social life possible.[4] The actions of these spiritual practitioners are essential, for humans share the world with myriad non-human beings capable of sending both wellbeing and harm.

As discussed in chapter 1, hñähñu religion is grounded on principles of balance and reciprocity, as people seek to maintain harmony with the wide range of beings that occupy the many levels of the cosmos. Among those beings is the primordial couple, Zidada and Zinana,[5] associated with the celestial bodies as well as the Christian God and Virgin Mary. The heavens are also home to Catholic saints and various indigenous intercessory figures known as the "ancient ones."[6] In the earthly realm below dwell animals, plants, and humans. Yet the earth is also home to water spirits, sometimes referred to as *sirenas* or sirens,[7] to mountains that serve as intercessory beings, and to seed spirits whom shamans call upon during agricultural fertility rites.[8] Traces of ancient beings are found in the soil, as well. Farmers occasionally uncover *wemas*, which are the bones of ancestor giants who have the power to cure and to send illness,[9] and *cangandhos*, which are carved stone statues that were presumably created by the Otomí years ago and are believed to be very ancient gods.[10] As these beings can be both benevolent and harmful, people must placate them with offerings of food and *pulque*, a drink made of fermented agave nectar. Like the heavens, the underworld is also home to various beings capable of acting upon human life for good or for ill. *Los muertos*, the dead, must be properly honored with offerings, for they have the power both to send sickness and to heal.[11] *Malos aires*, or "evil winds," can bring harm to those who encounter them.[12] Moreover, in the Valle del Mezquital, evil winds are joined by *tierras malas*, or "dust devils," which can provoke *susto*, or fright.[13]

From this brief overview, we can see that the traditional hñähñu cosmos brims with diverse beings, and that the social and natural worlds are deeply intertwined. To live harmoniously within so vibrantly populated a world is not an easy endeavor. Although evangelicals no longer believe in all of the beings described above—the pastor once joked while driving past the town cemetery that *"los muertitos"* here do not bother the living—not all beings have entirely disappeared from view. For example, Pastor Elpidio told me that sirens occasionally appear near the river, though the saved cannot see them. On another occasion, as I struggled to speak hñähñu one night with an elderly evangelical woman, she pointed to the moon and referred to it as Zinana, or "Holy Mother." And another time, while I was helping a member of the Iglesia Bethel in the fields one day, she stopped to embrace a rue plant, explaining that the herb can help protect one from *malos aires*. Sánchez Vásquez writes that some evangelicals fear the power of *cangandhos*, those ancient stone figures that farmers occasionally unearth in their fields, and historian Gabriela Garret Ríos has found that in cases of crop failure or other severe misfortune even firmly evangelical communities in the Valle del Mezquital have returned to long-abandoned rites of reciprocity in an effort to restore harmony with the natural world.[14] Rather than anecdotal survivals, the examples above are evidence that an underlying relational ethic continues to shape the worldview of evangelicals in the Valle del Mezquital.

For evangelicals, as for practitioners of hñähñu shamanic religion, the world is steeped in agency. But there is more to the story. Within the traditional religion of the region, human beings do not simply relate to the natural world through rites of reciprocity. Rather, they understand themselves to be directly linked to the natural world through their life forces. Among the Sierra Otomí, who dwell in the eastern highlands of Hidalgo and the neighboring states of Puebla and Veracruz, plants, animals, and humans alike share a life force known as *zaki*. Each human being also has a breath soul, or "shadow," that he or she shares with a specific animal.[15] Ritual specialists known as *bãdi*, or "one who knows," call upon the power of their animal doubles to heal or to harm.[16] *Bãdi* often work by cutting paper into figures representing the life forces of various beings, and then manipulating the paper cuttings in order to send healing or harm to the person in question. *Bãdi* are not bound by space in their work.[17] Nor are they deterred by international borders, for some may even conduct rites to influence the *zaki* of migrants in the United States.

While ritual paper cutting is more prevalent among the Sierra Otomí than in the Valle del Mezquital, the logic of causality used in healing is similar in both regions. Ritual practitioners work to produce concrete changes in patients' physical and psychological states by manipulating objects in which they are emotionally invested.[18] In "sucking," for example, a healer chews tobacco and sucks the body's surface to remove harmful objects believed to be implanted by sorcerers, and in *limpias*, or "cleansings," bundles of herbs are swept across the patient's body to clear away malevolent influences.[19]

The witches and the turkey-woman my informants describe derive from another type of being commonly believed to exist throughout Mesoamerica—namely, bloodsucking witches.[20] Usually female, witches have the power to transform into turkeys, dogs, fleas, ants, and other animals. Once transformed, they sneak into sleeping children's chambers to attack them. While Pentecostals have told me that witches gain power by making pacts with Satan, hñähñu tradition holds that they are born with their condition and are thus incapable of controlling their furious desire for blood.[21] The distinction between witches and sorcerers may not always be easily drawn, however. Neil Whitehead and Robin Wright propose the term "dark shamanism" to encompass the predatory dimension of various ritual specialists.[22] While their observations concern Amazonian societies, they can also help shed light on sorcery beliefs in hñähñu *costumbre*. The authors argue that shamanic healing cannot be understood apart from killing. Light and dark shamans engage in a perpetual struggle that keeps the cosmos in motion. Rather than condemning dark shamans' actions as sinful, people recognize them as an "inevitable, continuing, and even a necessary part" of existence.[23] Dark shamans help make the social world possible, for they provide a manageable focus for the otherwise overwhelmingly harmful potential of the cosmos.

Hñähñu tradition is replete with predatory beings, whether they are sorcerers who send *nahuales* to attack victims' life forces, witches who suck children's blood, or *malos aires* that catch unwitting travelers in their paths. Ritual practitioners work to protect and strengthen people within this dangerous cosmos. For today's Pentecostals, the cosmos has not lost its predatory nature. Just as light shamanism cannot function without dark shamanism, the healing power of the Holy Spirit cannot be understood without the presence of Satan and his agents. Pentecostal sorcery beliefs extend the "active, participatory relationship with the cosmos" that characterizes shamanic systems.[24]

As we have seen, a theme of danger, protection, and empowerment lies at the heart of early Pentecostal conversion stories. We must go further, however, to understand the uniquely global nature of the sorcery beliefs that my informants express. Pastor Elpidio makes mention not only of wolf-boys and turkey-witches close to home, but also of flying sorcerers in Africa. He insists that people make pacts with the devil just as frequently in the United States as they do in Mexico. Evil is expressed in El Norte not only through such vices as drinking and drug addiction, but also through practices like the use of Ouija boards for divination. As international migrants and as consumers of global entertainment media, Pentecostals from El Alberto occupy a cosmos that is ever shifting to encompass new images, people, and material goods. While the logic underlying Pentecostal sorcery beliefs draws heavily from hñähñu shamanic principles, we are still faced with the task of understanding which symbols, which objects, and which people Pentecostals perceive as evil today, and why. We must also understand how El Alberto's Pentecostals draw upon the larger evangelical lexicon of spiritual warfare to make sense of their place in global space and time. To explore these questions, I turn to a PowerPoint presentation that Pastor Elpidio gave with a sermon during an evening service at Bethel in July of 2009.

"My People Are Destroyed from Lack of Knowledge"

The pastor had recently returned from a two-week visit to Bethel's sister congregations in Phoenix and Las Vegas. Just off the plane, with stories and greetings from fellow *hermanos* fresh upon his lips, he roused the congregation with the usual opening songs. Rather than giving a sermon, however, the pastor told us that he had something new in store that evening. He was going to teach us to recognize a range of evil symbols that surround us, symbols that can corrupt our lives if we are not careful.

The pastor opened by reading from the Bible: "My people are destroyed from lack of knowledge."[25] He then proceeded to unveil, slide by slide, a series of images from ancient religions and contemporary culture. He told me later that he had purchased the presentation at a Spanish Christian bookstore. The symbol on each slide was accompanied by a brief written interpretation. The pastor read the interpretations and elaborated upon them. There were at least a dozen symbols, perhaps twenty. Many hailed from the ancient world. There were symbols of Celtic, Mediterranean, and ancient Indian origin. These were pagan symbols, the pastor told us, through which sorcerers have long called upon the powers of Satan to bring evil into the world. None of the symbols depicted were of pre-Columbian origin.

"The pentagram," the pastor explained, showing us a five-pointed star surrounded by a circle, "represents the four elements, surrounded and controlled by the Evil Spirit"—which is also embodied by the star's fifth point. The elements of earth, air, water and fire are important within hñähñu cosmology and are symbolically represented at the closing of the Caminata Nocturna. By manipulating representations of those elements, the pastor suggested, sorcerers act upon the elements themselves. The next symbol was the hexagram. The hexagram resembles the Star of David, the pastor noted. Unlike the Jewish symbol, however, it was surrounded by a circle and thus, like the pentagram, enveloped in evil. The logic involved in the pastor's explanation is not unlike that involved in the practice of ritual paper cutting among the Sierra Otomí. By acting upon the paper representations of a person's life force, the ritual practitioners known as *bädi* influence that force itself and thus affect the wellbeing of the person. Similarly, drawing a circle around a representation of the four elements is an essentially dangerous act capable of affecting the physical world.

The next symbol was the ankh. The pastor explained that the ankh is an ancient fertility symbol. Today barren women wear the ankh as a pendant in the hope that it will help them conceive. The pastor maintained that there is nothing wrong with seeking fertility, but one must not call upon dark powers to do so. Instead, infertile women must place all of their trust in God. To reinforce this point, he shared the story of a woman from a neighboring congregation who had tried everything possible to conceive. Even the doctors could not help her. She finally became pregnant after putting her faith in God.

The slideshow continued with symbols of more recent origin, including the swastika, the angular "SS" of the Nazi Schutzstaffel, and the peace sign, which the PowerPoint slide described as a broken cross. The accompanying text explained that the initials SS stand for *Servicio Satanás*, or "Satan service." The jagged double "S" also appears in the name of the rock band KISS, the slide's text explained. The pastor shifted to a discussion of popular music. That summer the death of Michael Jackson was fresh in the public imagination. News of the event flooded the television channels, and bootlegged CDs of his music were available by the dozen in the market in Ixmiquilpan. The late king of pop, the words on PowerPoint slide explained, had become famous not by natural means but because he had made a pact with the devil. "We have no problem with rock and roll," read the text. "God created music. We are not opposed to rock and roll but rather opposed to people like Michael Jackson who sell their souls to the Devil in order to become rich and famous."[26] The star's premature death, the pastor continued, is a sign that the devil claimed him in the end. Pastor Elpidio elaborated upon Michael Jackson's satanic dealings by drawing upon observations from his travels in Mexico City and the United States. Today, he explained, some young people—*los chicos emo*, the "emo kids"—also make pacts with the enemy. He referred here to a style of self-expression popular among young people at the time. You can tell who they are, he noted: emo kids paint their nails black, cut their hair in strange styles, and sport tattoos on their flesh.

We have before us a rich array of symbols, some from ancient culture, some from the entertainment industry, and some from youth culture.

Michael Taussig's observations may help us begin to unravel the significance of my informants' references to the devil.[27] Taussig argues that devil beliefs among laborers in Colombia and Bolivia are deeply tied to economic change. By making a pact with the devil, these laborers believe, individuals can obtain quick wealth. Such pacts produce intensive short-term gain but are ultimately unsustainable. By objectifying individualistic greed and exploitation in the figure of Satan, Taussig argues, laborers on the fringes of a capitalist economy manage to retain a critical awareness of their situation.

Like the laborers that Taussig describes, residents of El Alberto are poised between the global capitalist economy and the traditional, collective economy of their hometown. Many have worked for years in the United States yet remain deeply invested in El Alberto's communal labor system. Although agriculture is no longer the main source of subsistence in the town, the ecotourism park offers a new framework through which traditional forms of work continue. We may well ask whether the witchcraft, sorcery, and devil beliefs discussed here serve to mediate the tension between the two economic systems. Yet Pentecostal sorcery beliefs do not condemn wealth and capitalist accumulation per se. Indeed, the religion's heightened focus on personal salvation generally serves to deflect attention away from economic differences between worshippers.[28] But what Pentecostal sorcery beliefs do express is a deep anxiety about the unknown dangers that accompany their involvement in the global economy, as well as a desire to become aware of and exert control over those dangers.

If we look closely at accusations of sorcery, we can see that they are directed not toward residents of El Alberto but rather toward outsiders: Michael Jackson, teenagers in Mexico City, an unknown woman traveling by the side of the road. Often the accused work in secrecy. In much the same way that priests bless objects and places with holy water, the pastor explained, Satanists apply harmful substances to pentagram necklaces, ankh amulets, and other pieces of jewelry before selling them to the unwitting public. Christians can counteract Satanists' efforts by applying holy oil to objects and spaces, for the oil represents the Holy Spirit. These efforts mesh with Birgit Meyer's observations among Pentecostals in Ghana.[29] Because commodities are produced by distant, unknown actors, Ghanaian Pentecostals view them as highly dangerous and thus even "able to impose their will on their owners."[30] However, prayer transforms consumer goods into innocuous utilitarian items. In a new spin on Marx's notion of commodity fetishism, Ghanaian Pentecostals are not blinded by the illusions of capitalism. By attributing agency to products, they recognize that, in buying them, they are stepping into a set of relationships with unknown beings. Behind each product lie globally dispersed designers, investors, and advertisers who do not necessarily have the buyer's best interest at heart. Prayer is an attempt to strip the product of its dangerous potential, much as rites are used to integrate initiates or transition individuals within society.

For El Alberto's Pentecostals, threats arrive not only in the form of products purchased abroad, but also in the form of outsiders who pass through the town. One evening an older evangelical couple from El Alberto who live in Phoenix began telling me about life when they were children. When they repeated the familiar narrative trope that life in the past was fraught with poverty and conflict, I asked if they had any positive memories of those times. After some thought, the husband, who is now a U.S. citizen and visits El Alberto once a year, answered that in the past there was "no theft." No one went anywhere, for no one had a car, a horse, or even a bicycle. And nobody from the outside came in. Everyone dressed the same, because they could not afford nice clothes. Despite the drinking and fighting, "the town was a safe place." Life was simple and one knew what one had to contend with. Today, greater wealth has come at the price of uncertainty. Again, this man does not condemn the evils of wealth and consumerism for their own sake. Rather, he expresses concern about the *inseguridad*— the lack of safety—that has inevitably followed as the town opens itself to migration and does business with the larger public. The town has grown so much that people do not always know their neighbors. Tourism has brought profits, but it has also brought danger. When I visited El Alberto in 2011, there was talk of a mysterious outsider who wore a wig and women's clothing and hid in the cornfields at night as he waited to rob the houses. One could tell he was not from El Alberto, people explained, because he was tall like a *gringo*.

Through the PowerPoint presentation, Pastor Elpidio sought to provide viewers with the knowledge necessary to arm themselves against external danger. The presentation suggested that danger travels through products and youth culture, and also through the global entertainment media. Evil is embodied in the music of Michael Jackson and in the music of the band KISS. Danger is present, too, in Spiderman films and film-related products. Like foreign-made objects bought in the Ghanaian market, rock music and blockbuster films are not neutral. They act upon the consumer as much as the consumer acts upon them. Movies look back at the viewer. Music shapes the mind of the listener. Rather than sit passively awash in this sea of dangerous influences, Pentecostals arm themselves with prayer to protect themselves and their loved ones. However, we are still left to understand the eclectic mix of symbols within the presentation, for the slides included not only images from the entertainment industry and global youth culture, but also religious symbols from the ancient world. Michael Jackson and the ankh, "emo" kids and the broken cross, the Nazi SS and the pentagram whirl together in a phantasmagorical cross-section of an imagined world landscape.[31]

Navigating Satan's Web

As Arjun Appadurai argues, the images, symbols, and products shaping people's imaginations today are not contained within the boundaries of nation-states but rather flow throughout the world in complex and often disjointed ways. Migrants cross borders; transnational corporations manage money at lightning speed; and news broadcasts reach opposite sides of the globe instantaneously. As "money, commodities and persons are involved in ceaselessly chasing each other around the world,"[32] the task of achieving coherence falls to the individual imagination. The imagination is, as Appadurai puts it, "a form of negotiation" through which actors assimilate, contest, and sometimes subvert the "globally defined fields of possibility" they face on a daily basis.[33]

As Pastor Elpidio interpreted each symbol from the PowerPoint presentation, he drew upon local examples and invited responses from those present. Yet because he had bought the presentation at a Christian bookstore, the symbols it contained had been assembled by others. Hence, the service that day was a veritable laboratory for "glocalization," or the mutually transformative exchange between local and global ideas and practices.[34] While the pastor drew upon ethnically specific understandings of witchcraft and sorcery in his sermon, he also drew upon themes embraced by other evangelical and charismatic Christians worldwide. In particular, he drew upon the language of spiritual warfare.

Popular within Pentecostalism and other charismatic forms of Christianity, spiritual warfare is at once a theological orientation and a prayer technique. It is a natural extension of Pentecostals' strong emphasis on the active intervention of the Holy Spirit in the world through divine healing and prosperity theology. For Pentecostals, just as the Holy Spirit is capable of acting upon the world in a very direct way, so too is Satan. Since problems frequently have spiritual causes, they must be confronted through spiritual battle.[35] The logic of spiritual warfare is perhaps most clearly expressed in the Bible verse that defines Christian struggle as directed "not against flesh and blood, but against the rulers, against the authorities, against the powers of this dark world and against the spiritual forces of evil in the heavenly realms."[36] For proponents of spiritual warfare, a life of faith demands not only regular efforts to deepen one's relationship with God, but also unrelenting battle against Satan and his agents.

The geographical origins of spiritual warfare are difficult to trace, partly because the teaching is so effective at absorbing and reframing local cosmologies. North American notions of spiritual warfare have not emerged in isolation, but rather have taken shape through constant, multidirectional dialogue with newly converted evangelical Christians across the world. The Brazil-based Universal Church of the Kingdom of God, for example, thrives on exorcising the spirits of the African-derived religions that many of its converts are familiar with.[37] The situation is further complicated by the reverse-mission dynamic in which evangelical Christians from former European colonies seek to spread the gospel in the very countries that once sent missionaries to their own shores.[38] Yet U.S.-based evangelists have also had a heavy hand in shaping the language and imagery of spiritual warfare. Prominent U.S. evangelist C. Peter Wagner, for example, has helped popularize the process of "spiritual mapping" to reveal evil spirits' locations.[39] Not only individuals, but also entire households, towns, cities, and nations are believed capable of falling into Satan's snares. Wagner identifies multiple levels of spiritual warfare, including a "strategic" level in which worshippers map out vast reaches of the globe that have come under satanic influence.[40] Practitioners of "strategic level" spiritual warfare draw heavily upon the language of actual international conflict waged by the U.S. military, referring to prayer efforts, for example, as "Operations."[41]

Multiple levels of spiritual mapping were at work in the sermon at Bethel that night. As the pastor elaborated upon the symbols in the PowerPoint presentation, he sought not only to draw attention to the wiles of sorcerers, but also to map the spiritual contours of the globe. Recall that an Otomí shamanic healer is, literally, "one who knows." That night the pastor strove to render the hidden spiritual dimensions of the world visible to the members of the congregation so that they would not be "destroyed from lack of knowledge." Like the cosmos of traditional hñähñu religion, this newly charted spiritual landscape was replete with danger. In this case, however, agency lay not only with the many other-than-human beings that inhabit the natural world, but also within global entertainment media and in the globally dispersed symbols from ancient "pagan" religions.

In addition to mapping the contours of the global space, the pastor charted out a sacred timeline. After discussing the entertainment media, he discussed evidence that we are entering the end times. One such piece of evidence was the Masonic all-seeing eye. The eye seated atop the pyramid, he explained, represents unbounded human power, human attempts to surpass God's omniscience. "If you've ever held an American dollar bill," said the pastor—and most of those in attendance had indeed done so—"you can find the all-seeing-eye upon it." During Pope John Paul II's visit to the United States, the pastor explained, the government made a pact with Rome to place the symbol on its dollar. Now, as a result, the U.S. economy was heading downhill. As the pastor spoke, the economic crisis in the U.S. was at the forefront of public conversation. In the past, the pastor continued, the U.S. dollar held the phrase, "God Bless America." And God indeed blessed the country. Ever since Americans put the all-seeing-eye on the bill, however, the economy has declined, while the euro has gained strength. And it is said that there will be but a single currency upon the earth during the end times.

At this point, one of the members of the congregation raised a question about the "www" typed in Internet website addresses and whether it has significance in Hebrew. Hasn't it been shown that the Hebrew letter "w" is equivalent to the number 6, due to its order in the alphabet, he asked? The pastor answered that this was indeed the case. "And what do the letters 'www' stand for, in English?" he continued. "'World' means *mundo*," he translated. "'Wide' means *ancho*. 'Web' means *tela*, like a spider's web." The Internet is like a global spider web, the pastor explained, through which the devil works to ensnare the world. After the service, I told the pastor that I would think twice the next time I used the Internet. He told me not to worry. "Everything is planned," he said. Although the signs of evil are present in the world, they have been foretold by the book of Revelation, and Revelation also foretells that good will ultimately prevail.

The PowerPoint presentation had several inaccuracies. The all-seeing eye, for example, has also been used as a Christian symbol, and its placement on the dollar occurred years earlier than the pastor indicated. The sermon also contained elements that may strike some people as humorous, such as the notion that "emo kids" are emissaries of the devil. Yet for those gathered, the task of explaining and ordering a chaotic and threatening reality was no laughing matter.

Part of Pentecostalism's worldwide appeal, as Manuel Vásquez argues, is due to the religion's ability to help people contend with a world inhabited by global forces they perceive as too extensive and mysterious to fully comprehend or control. Bethel's congregation members are not alone in their worries about unknown outsiders selling cursed objects to innocent youth, or in their concerns about the overseas workings of witches. Many immigrants who find themselves in close proximity with people from other parts of the world experience "a kind of urban paranoia about 'evil doers' who are out to cheat, deceive, rob and kill."[42] By combining "pneumatic materialism"—that is, an emphasis on the active engagement of spiritual forces with physical reality—with a dramatic, apocalyptic framework, Pentecostalism helps translate the diverse spiritual pressures of globalization into a form that can be more rapidly digested and shared with others.[43] In the case of El Alberto, spiritual warfare both simplifies the logic of spiritual struggle embodied in hñähñu traditional religion and projects it onto a global scale. When Pastor Elpidio spoke of Satan's "world wide web" casting a metaphoric spider-snare across the globe, and when he explained that this was but one of many signs of the imminent return of Christ, he guided his congregation in charting out a navigable path through a confusing and multilayered cosmos.

Protecting Youth

Pentecostal prayer does not simply help people to send the positive benefits of health and financial wellbeing to loved ones across the border. Prayer also provides an ongoing spiritual vaccination against the many dangers people may encounter at home and abroad, and divine healing offers a solution when things go wrong. In a sermon earlier that summer, Pastor Elpidio spoke of a young man from the neighboring town of Portesuelo who had returned home after working in the United States for seven years. During those seven years, he had managed to save seven thousand dollars. Yet by the time he returned to Mexico, the man had fallen ill with diabetes, leukemia, and gastritis.[44] He consulted *brujo* after *brujo*, each of whom charged steep fees and prescribed costly ritual procedures, to no avail. "He was just bones, that's all that was left of him!" Finally, a neighbor convinced him to attend a Pentecostal service. After the worshippers prayed over him, the man began to sweat profusely as the Holy Spirit chased out the illness.

The bodies of youth serve as a frequent focus for divine healing. During one evening service in June of 2009, about twenty people gathered at the altar. The pastor moved among them, touching each person on the head and praying over him or her in an effort to facilitate the Holy Spirit's entrance into their bodies. At one point, his prayers intensified. The worshipper in question was a young man whom I had never seen before in church. He had a shaved head, heavily tattooed arms, and wore a black T-shirt. All eyes in the congregation turned toward him. "He's here!" the pastor shouted, referring to the presence of God through the Holy Spirit. "Here! Yes! Yes! Yes! Yes! Let Him work! He's here with you! Now!" Several ushers gathered close, holding up their hands to catch the young man if he should collapse. The others held their palms open and aloft as though to channel the Holy Spirit toward him.

For a moment, the body of this young man had become a stage through which the ever-present struggle between God and Satan became palpable. The bodies of youth were a prominent focus in the PowerPoint sermon on evil symbols, as well. After speaking of "emo kids," the pastor warned about the "*cholo,*" or gang-style greeting in which people punch their fists together and slap palms. Giggles of recognition rippled throughout the congregation. The greeting is no laughing matter, the pastor continued; it is dangerous. Rather than shake hands in that way, he said, the people would do well to resurrect the greeting that their grandparents used. In that greeting, he said, there was true respect. I knew the greeting he referred to, for a few elderly people in the town have drawn my hand close to them, lightly kissed it, and indicated that I do the same.

It is the young people among whom the traditional greeting has been lost, the pastor implied, and it is the young people who are most in need of protection. Not only are their minds poisoned by the wrong sorts of television and music, but their bodies serve as sites for evil's transmission. Little children, in particular, must be shielded from spiritual harm. One of the images within the presentation's long succession of symbols was a picture of Spiderman. Some people laughed. Yes, even Spiderman is dangerous, said the pastor.

"What must we remember?" he asked. "No Spiderman———"

"Because that's bad!" yelled a little boy. Some laughed. It is important, the pastor continued, to protect children from seemingly innocent cartoons and movies that contain references to the dark side. We must also prohibit children from participating in Halloween. Halloween occurs at about the time of the Day of the Dead in Mexico, he explained, implying that the popular Catholic celebration is no safer than the American holiday.

The notion that children have a special vulnerability to spiritual attack has roots in Mesoamerican tradition. As we have seen, traditional hñähñu religion holds that infants and children can fall prey to bloodsucking witches or to *mal de ojo,* the evil eye. Yet the pastor's focus on youth during this presentation quite likely had to do with young people's position at the crux of massive social and economic change. Throughout my interviews, when I have asked Pentecostals about the negative influences of migration, most are quick to refer to *los jóvenes,* the youth. It is they who bear the contradictions of migration and social change in their flesh. While the first migrants traveled to the United States and worked their fingers to the bone, their children are the teenagers and young adults of today who often grew up with televisions in place of parents, and with the convenience of shoes and packaged food in place of moral foundations. While early migration was partly driven by the desire to keep children alive, today migration itself is exposing young people to new sources of danger. As travelers in global culture and consumers of global media, young people bring new objects, actions, and desires into the home. Their bodies are thus sites of potential danger that must be protected, mediated, and controlled.

The PowerPoint-guided sermon that night charted out the global spiritual landscape that townspeople inhabit today. Not only did the pastor map the contours of that landscape, but he also indicated how the members of the congregation might best navigate it. Immediately following the PowerPoint presentation, he presented a slideshow of photos from his recent trips to Phoenix and Las Vegas. The photos depicted neighbors and relatives from El Alberto, fellow brothers and sisters in the faith, in their homes and in worship. There were pictures of them preparing food and eating together. There were pictures, in particular, of children. The pastor introduced each person by name.

"There's the *hermana* Estela in Las Vegas, with her new baby Lucita—Estela's been in the U.S. five years and look, now she has a child. . . . Here's brother Carlos and his wife Natalia; they waited for us until three in the morning when we were driving in from Phoenix. . . . Here, this little one is their son Jonathan, born two months ago." Each photo produced murmurs of joy and recognition. It is significant that the pastor showed this presentation immediately after the presentation of evil symbols. If predatory sorcerers work to poison children's minds and curse the bodies of the youth, if the media projects dangerous images through the airways, if Satan spreads his web of evil across the world via the Internet, the pastor suggested that Christians can cast their own webs of protection in response. The final slideshow drew upon the tools of international travel and digital technology to send a protective circle of prayer and community around those *hermanos* and especially their young children in the United States.

As shown by the photo presentation, Bethel's members protect themselves from the dangers of mobility by embracing and redirecting the very deterritorializing forces that threaten them. Their focus on children and teens reveals a fierce commitment to protecting young people from harm. As we will soon find, this very same concern lies at the heart of the Caminata Nocturna. Pentecostals use worship and prayer to protect the bodies and souls of the youth from the spiritual dangers of mobility. Yet they also help stage the Caminata in order remove the need to migrate in the first place. Although the methods involved are different, the core motivation is the same. The beliefs and practices described in this chapter, however, do not account for the full range of challenges people encounter as they strive to make a living in a transnational context. El Alberto's residents face not only the strains of transnational family life and the diffuse risks of global mobility, but also the immediate, concrete danger of the undocumented journey. Since the mid-1990s, crossing the U.S.-Mexico border has become a potentially fatal endeavor.

6

Shielded by the Blood of Christ

Alejandro was in his early thirties when he survived the border accident that cost three others their lives. His wife was pregnant with their third child. Alejandro had been returning to his home of ten years in Las Vegas after a visit to El Alberto. The van that he and his companions were riding in was hit several miles north of the Arizona border, in what was apparently a chase by Border Patrol agents. Alejandro was in a coma for five days. When he awoke, he found himself paralyzed from the waist down. He was surprised that he had survived, for although the van was hit close to where he was sitting in the front, those in the back were killed. Among those who died were another man from El Alberto and two men from a neighboring town.

While he was in the coma, Alejandro recounted, he entered a different place. It was a wonderful place. Everything was clean, and nothing was lacking. It was peaceful. Many people had gathered for a banquet. Their clothes weren't like the clothes people wear here. They dressed in—"You know what God wears?" he asked me. "Like, dressed in white?" I answered. "Yes, something like that."

At some point, God came behind Alejandro and gently touched him at the back of his head. God showed him two places. One was the clean and wonderful banquet. The other was a place where everything was dirty. God told Alejandro that He still had work for him to do in the world. He was going to send Alejandro back to life, to choose the good path and to serve him. "There are only two paths," Alejandro stressed, in a phrase repeatedly echoed among Pentecostals. When Alejandro awoke, he says he felt a warmth moving up from his feet, through his body, and out through his head and shoulders. "It was the Holy Spirit," explained his aunt, who was listening by his bedside. Alejandro told us that God had put him through a trial. Now, he insisted, he had a message to spread. He wanted to share the message of salvation in evangelical churches throughout Mexico and, if possible, the United States.

Days later, about a hundred people gathered outside of Alejandro's house to fast. Most were evangelical, but a few Catholic neighbors and relatives joined the crowd. Alejandro sat in a wheelchair. The presence of his broken body beside the visibly pregnant belly of his wife and the couple's two small, rambunctious sons posed a sharp reminder of the promise and vulnerability of new life. Over the course of four hours, those gathered sang with Alejandro, prayed with him, recited Bible verses, and embraced him one by one. The pastor preached and pounded out songs of praise on his omnipresent electric keyboard. At last, the fast was broken with a feast of chicken *mole* and corn tortillas prepared by Alejandro's non-Pentecostal relatives. For a moment, the lavish banquet scene of his near-death vision had become an earthly reality. Alejandro's family members and neighbors transformed his near-death experience and miraculous recovery into something that was shared by all.

This chapter explores how Pentecostals in El Alberto are responding to the immediate, embodied challenges of the undocumented journey. In particular, I examine the narratives and practices through which Pentecostals make sense of the heightened danger they face while attempting to cross an increasingly militarized U.S.-Mexico border. Today, the town of El Alberto is famous for its border crossing simulation. References to migrant death—embodied in the vivid symbol of burning torches—imbue the tourist simulation with a sense of gravity.

Yet residents of El Alberto are also grappling with the dangers of migration in their churches, away from the gaze of tourists. By looking behind the scenes of the Caminata, we can better understand the full impact of migration upon people's lives. We can also better understand the larger context out of which the Mexican Dream has emerged. I argue that, just as religious groups use rites of passage to inscribe shared meaning into important life transitions, Pentecostals in El Alberto use prayer and worship to prepare migrants for departure and make sense of unsuccessful border crossing attempts. They are also working out an ad hoc theology of migration that addresses the contradictions of citizenship and exclusion in a bordered world. The faith they embrace supports their continued mobility, even while seeking to protect them from the dangers encountered en route.

Borders of Life and Death

For the millions of souls who have arrived in the United States by land or sea, migration has often served as a "theologizing experience."[1] Migration challenges group identity and stretches people's notions of belonging. The act also poses a host of challenges to the individual psyche. Just as immigrant groups have drawn upon religion to express their national and ethnic identities, individuals have turned to religion as they struggle to reposition themselves within American society. Immigrants have looked to religions for the narratives that help them reimagine past, present, and future, as they make sense of the shifting lines between self and other. Religions also serve a "theologizing" function for those who stay behind.

Folklorist Grace Neville observes that Irish immigrants at the turn of the century transformed a traditional death rite into an "American wake" for soon-to-be departed migrants. The improvised rite foreshadows the dance with death that undocumented immigrants and their loved ones face today. Many of the millions of Irish who left for the United States in the nineteenth and early twentieth centuries were very young. Knowing that they may never again see the young émigrés in the flesh, prospective migrants' families, neighbors, and friends offered the same send-off usually reserved for the dead: an all-night vigil, complete with feasting and dancing. The next morning the prospective migrant would depart for the harbor. Some carried bits of earth from their home communities in their clothing.[2] Although people wrote letters home and return migration was not unheard of, communication was sporadic. Some perished in the weeks-long passage across the Atlantic. Those who managed to return home were not the same as they had once been.

Just as death rites help the living negotiate their relationships to departed souls,[3] the American wake helped ease the transition of international passage and send migrants forth to new lives. For those who stayed behind, the rite granted preemptive closure in the face of uncertainty. For those who left, the ritual death provided preparation for rebirth on North American shores. In some ways, the transitions facing migrants from El Alberto today are far less drastic than those facing Irish immigrants of the nineteenth century. Cell phones, e-mail, and social networking facilitate near-simultaneous contact between those who leave and those who remain. Evangelical worship binds people across borders into a common system of mutual material and spiritual support. The task of ritual, for Pentecostals in El Alberto, is not to mourn the virtual "death" of loved ones who may never be seen again, but rather to ensure those migrants' souls—and their economic activities—will remain intertwined with those at home in lasting and meaningful ways. At the same time, as Alejandro's case makes clear, the need to contend with death is no less pressing today than it was a century ago.

Though they do not face the inevitable danger of nineteenth-century marine travel, El Alberto's migrants face the man-made danger of crossing a heavily militarized border. They face not sickness and ocean gales but rather an immigration enforcement regime that has transformed the border into an increasingly deadly and hostile realm. While the first people who ventured to the United States from El Alberto encountered little difficulty at the U.S.-Mexico border, the situation soon changed. During the 1993–1994 "prevention through deterrence" strategy embodied in Operations Gatekeeper and Hold-the-Line, the Immigration and Naturalization Service (INS) focused its border enforcement efforts on large urban areas such as San Diego, California, and El Paso, Texas. While migrants had for decades passed with relative ease through these cities, they now met with miles of chain-link fencing and greater numbers of Border Patrol agents. Rather than significantly deter migrants, the new enforcement strategy simply rerouted them away from urban areas.[4] "Prevention through deterrence" was more politically successful than it was practically effective. As Peter Andreas argues, images of orderliness at the border replaced images of a "border under siege," as undocumented immigrants were temporarily removed from the public view.[5] The reality for migrants, however, was grim. Migrants now risked crossing through remote desert and mountain areas where the likelihood of dehydration and exposure increased dramatically. By the year 2000, the Arizona desert had become the most common crossing area, setting the state as a key battlefront of the national immigration debate. Migrants would now risk extreme temperatures, exhaustion, and dehydration. The percentage of fatalities caused by environmental factors tripled between 1985 and 2000, and the rate of fatality during attempted border passage rose by over 400 percent from 1996 to 2000.[6] Death rates have remained high. At least 249 people died at the southern border of Arizona alone in 2010.[7]

As sociologist Jacqueline Hagan has argued, migrants increasingly turn to religious beliefs, practices, and institutions to help them face the danger and uncertainty of passage across the U.S.-Mexico border and along the larger migration corridor through Southern Mexico and Central America.[8] Such has been the case for people from El Alberto. When undocumented migration from the town increased in the mid-1990s, the town's members passed through the only routes available to them: the deserts and remote mountains where they were likely to confront excessive heat, cold, and exhaustion. Pentecostal informants state that religion has not always figured so prominently in the migration journey. Today, however, they risk greater danger due to exposure to the natural elements. They also risk falling prey to dishonest *coyotes*, border gangs, and vigilante groups. As Fortunato, an active member of the Iglesia Bethel, explained:

> The first time I went, truth is I didn't make any preparations. . . . But the last few times I've gone yes, I've asked for a prayer in the church. To cross. We ask God to take us safely because we know the danger we're running. . . . I've also heard that the Minutemen were really strong on that side. They even threatened people with firearms. . . . But what can you do! One has to survive.

As the danger of crossing the border has grown, the journey brings people face to face not only with the boundary between nations, but also with the boundary between life and death. Although Alejandro's accident was an extreme case, Pastor Elpidio explained to me the previous summer that it is not uncommon for people to begin to seek God during migration. He noted:

> There are many people there in the U.S. who didn't go to church here. But when they've arrived there, they've felt that need. . . . Many people have testified . . . when they go walking in the desert, and so many things happen to them, that's when they start to ask God for help. . . . Because it's such a difficult moment, that there in the desert no one reaches out their hand, only God. So only a miracle can happen.

Given the sheer depth of the existential questions it stirs to the fore, the act of undocumented border crossing can be compared to a life crisis.[9] Like fundamental transitions in human life—such as birth, puberty, and death—border crossing is a powerful personal experience that acts upon the body, posing challenges of meaning to the larger society. The journey sparks reflection upon life and death, and about the relationship between human and divine power. For El Alberto's Pentecostals, border crossing has sparked ritual innovation and theological reflection. In their eyes, the border is a human creation, put in place by political leaders who have neglected the divine mandate of brotherly love. True authority rests with God, and God has no borders. Some Pentecostals state that their faith in Christ literally shields them from harm as they attempt the undocumented journey.

"Blind the Eyes of the *Migra*"

Pastor Elpidio states that he typically offers three pieces of advice to prospective migrants. The first piece "is that they never forget God. Wherever they go, God should be in first place. Because God is the one who gives life . . . and God is the one who takes life away." His second piece of advice is that they remember the relatives who remain behind. Third, he urges potential migrants not to forget their community, for "the town is our home. . . . That's what has helped us and keeps helping us to maintain unity." Although migrants travel to the United States with the hope of advancing economically, Pastor Elpidio insists, it is important that "they don't forget their people. That they don't forget God. And . . . that they don't leave the family." Isaías, the pastor of Sinaí, offers similar guidance. He explains that whether or not people migrate is their decision. As a pastor, however, his role is to remind them "not to forget God." He advises potential migrants "to work, but by the sweat of their brow—they should save their money, and do something with it." If the migrant leaves a spouse behind, Isaías urges them to remember that marriage is a pact made before God.

These pastors' emphasis on family is a reminder that it is not only migrants, but also their loved ones, who need advice and support. Pastor Isaías notes that although some young migrants come to him for advice, more often it is their parents who seek spiritual support, much as Jacqueline Hagan has found to be the case among Pentecostals in rural Guatemala.[10] Pastor Elpidio explains, "before any relative goes [to the United States], we as a church put the person in God's hands. Because we know and we've seen God's marvels, so that motivates us to pray for them."

Pentecostals state that God literally shields his charges from harm at the U.S.-Mexico border. During a service at Bethel Centro Familiar Cristiano, one of Bethel's affiliated congregations in Phoenix, a man lead a prayer for two migrants who were about to make the journey. He implored God to make the men invisible to the immigration agents. "Lord, blind the eyes of the *migra*, so that our companions can pass safely!" he cried out. "Make them invisible, Lord; we know you have the power to make them invisible!" On another occasion, several congregation members were planning a trip to Las Vegas. I asked one of the *hermanos* if he was afraid to travel. Ever since the implementation of Arizona's S.B. 1070, which authorizes state law enforcement officials to ask about the immigration status of those whom they arrest if they have a "reasonable suspicion" that the person is undocumented, there had been greater enforcement levels at highway checkpoints. He answered that he and his companions simply needed to have faith, and no harm would come to them. The group passed without complications, and they considered their success proof of the efficacy of their prayers. Likewise, Pastor Elpidio states that his congregation continues to pray for migrants until word is received of their safe arrival. "Then we pray but now in gratitude to God. Because he took them safely." Successful border crossing attempts, in turn, become evidence that God has guided people's lives.

Migrants call upon divine aid not only at the border, but also while seeking work in the United States. As Pastor Elpidio explains, "when [migrants] are there . . . they start to look for a place where they can ask God for work. And they've gotten answers." Although crossing the border and finding work often involve great hardship, the spiritual rewards are great:

> Perhaps we don't have words to explain what God has done in our favor. Because although the border has been so difficult to cross, . . . we've seen that many people have succeeded. Because it's something lovely to believe in God. Many people when they have money, they think that money can make them great, but that's not so. Here we value the power of God.

As people are pushed to a state of heightened dependence on God during migration, their experience has breathed new life into the congregation as a whole. Pastor Elpidio explains that after they return home, many former migrants testify about how God acted in their lives when they were in the United States. "That pushes us, too, to depend more on God. . . . If God took you there, it's because God wanted you to be there. So, to depend on God is the most beautiful thing. Wherever one may go."

The migration journey does not always have the effect of strengthening people's faith, however. For some, especially teenagers and young adults, traveling to the United States brings new freedoms and with them, new opportunities for temptation. As Fortunato explains, "Young people who leave here, who are evangelical, who don't drink, don't smoke, don't do drugs here, but when they're involved in life [in the United States], their friends start to invite them." Freed from the structure of church and community, young people start to drink, have illicit sexual relationships, and become involved in gang violence. For some, however, the vices that they fall into in the United States eventually push them to seek salvation with greater intensity.

While migrants cross a literal desert in their journeys to the United States, errant youth wander about in a figurative desert of sin and spiritual isolation. Biblical desert metaphors have a special resonance among those so deeply affected by the migration journey. As a pastor visiting Bethel's affiliated church in Phoenix asked the congregation, "How many of you have crossed through the desert while coming here? Perhaps you don't want to be reminded. . . . But what does it mean to be in a desert? To be in a desert means to be in an empty place, a hot place, there's nothing there." Just as dangerous and isolating as the physical desert is the spiritual desert that people step into when they distance themselves from God. Pastor Elpidio made a similar connection. In a sermon in the summer of 2009, he drew a direct parallel between the thirst migrants experience in the desert and the soul's thirst for the Holy Spirit:

> I talked to a man who endured 3 days of hunger, and thirst, thirst, thirst, while crossing the desert to the U.S. And they found, by a miracle of God, a spring, a little spring of water, where the animals all went down to drink, and they lay down like animals and drank there from that water. Any you know, Christians often cross through the desert, but a spiritual desert, and what happens to a body without water? It can't live! And what happens to a person without the Holy Spirit?

Just as the body dies without water, the pastor implied, the soul soon perishes without the nourishment of the Holy Spirit. Some migrants experience total dependence on God in the desert after they are pushed to their physical limits. Fasting works through similar logic. During that same service, the pastor asked how many people in attendance had ever endured hunger. He was answered by a scattering of "amens." He then asked each person how long and in what context he or she had done so. One man responded that he had fasted for two days and a night on a hilltop. Others had gone hungry during migration. Still others had experienced both types of hunger: the intentionally induced hunger of a fast, and the necessarily endured hunger of border crossing.

Pentecostal prayer sends migrants off, follows them along their journey, and accompanies them throughout the time they live and work in the United States. Pentecostals also use prayer and worship to reincorporate people back into the church on returning to Mexico. In July of 2009, a family that had been in the United States for nine years was welcomed back into Bethel. Also present was a woman from El Alberto who had been away for eleven years, and had returned to visit with her new husband. The pastor called each person by name. Children who had been born in the United States stood up and waved for all to see. "When they left there were only two in the family, and now there are five!" the pastor exclaimed. He called the newly returned individuals to the front. One by one, members of the entire congregation passed to the altar. Some shook hands with the families, and others embraced them. Each was reincorporated into the group through the simple act of touch. The same action is used for other significant life transitions, including baptisms and birthdays. I was given a similar sendoff when I departed for the United States after a three-month stay in El Alberto one summer.

The migration journey is indeed a "theologizing experience" for El Alberto's Pentecostals, affecting not only migrants themselves but also their neighbors, loved ones, and friends. While the journey itself pushes some toward a deepened dependence on God, others state that their faith gives them a sense of protection and assurance before they even embark. Such is the case for Marta, the woman whose stories of working as a maid in Mexico City and Tijuana were recounted in chapter 3. An active member of Bethel, Marta has crossed the border multiple times. On several occasions she traveled with young children. Once, she was six months pregnant. Like Fortunato, Marta states that the migration journey is indeed more difficult today than it was in the past. Yet she knows that when she travels, she goes with divine protection. Marta states:

> Every time I go to the United States, I turn myself over to God. I say, "I'm going to make it, because I'm not alone." There are borders for human beings, but for me, a daughter of God, there should be no borders. I go with that security, with that certainty that I'm going to cross. Thanks to God, those times we've gone, we've made it . . . and I believe that if I go again, that I'm going to succeed.

Like the worshipper in Phoenix who implored God to "blind the eyes" of the *migra* and render those who cross the border invisible, Marta suggests that God offers not only other-worldly salvation, but also this-worldly protection to His followers. Such protection extends to other believers, as well. "Many say that the border is very difficult, but I've seen many people from the community of El Alberto, they've been able to cross, time and time again. And why? I say because they're guided." In some cases, Marta continued, people do not succeed. The mistake, she explains, is that they put faith in the *coyote,* or paid crossing guide, rather than in God.

> There are people who go with *coyotes*; they say, "This *coyote* is very safe." And then they end up saying, "This *coyote* has never failed, but failed this time." Why? Because they're putting their *faith* in human beings ... I say [go] with the help of a *coyote,* because he knows the routes. But I also say that God protects us every moment along the way.

In the summer of 2007 Pastor Elpidio told me that everyone from El Alberto who had attempted to cross the border had arrived safely. "To this day, thanks to God ... there hasn't been a single accident," he stated. The following year, however, that was no longer the case. The first person from El Alberto met his death at the border in April of 2008, and Alejandro survived to tell the story. The accident was a sharp blow to the residents of the town. Although the community had been depicting border danger in the Caminata Nocturna for nearly four years, this was the first time that one of their own had fallen. I was unable to attend the interfaith funeral of the other man in the car, but I observed the process of narrative and worship through which Alejandro and other Pentecostals made sense of his near-death experience. By telling and retelling the story of his accident, Alejandro and his fellow congregation members transformed Alejandro's individual experience at the border into a single, forceful testimony of salvation. Rather than shattering the group's faith, Alejandro's accident provided an opportunity for them to bear witness to God's presence in the world, and to the necessity of salvation.

A Near-Death Encounter

The seeds of Alejandro's story had been sown well before the accident. His narrative was not an isolated story but rather a shared product, worked out in the company of others. Before, neighbors told me, Alejandro's religious convictions had been weak. He occasionally attended evangelical services, but was not committed to the faith. The migration journey served as a catalyst that brought disparate pieces of his life together into a vivid, palpable vision of the afterlife. As David Smilde observes, a person's likelihood of conversion is strongly affected by his or her proximity to others of the faith. Through daily contact with evangelical neighbors and relatives, individuals are exposed to landscapes of possibility that crystalize, in the moment of conversion, into a coherent whole. Pentecostals then use narrative to chart past, present, and anticipated future events into a coherent storyline, weaving the particular details of their own lives into a shared vision of salvation.[11] Alejandro returned to life with a strong conviction that the afterlife was real. He also returned with the conviction that one's actions in this life will be punished or rewarded in the next. He stressed that God takes an active role in human life, and he highlighted the importance of choosing the "good path" that leads to salvation. Yet the vision he presented was a collective product. As Alejandro told and retold his story in changing contexts, and as relatives and neighbors came together to fast, pray, and worship over his paralyzed body, the details of his accident and recovery simultaneously drew upon and reinforced a common narrative canon about salvation.

Alejandro first told me about his coma while lying in bed at home. His aunt, mother, and nieces sat nearby. The stark presence of this formerly robust man's paralytic body imbued the conversation with a sense of immediacy, offering living proof that the accident had occurred. His fingers laced slowly together as he spoke. The stump of his leg lay barely concealed under a thin blanket, and a bag of IV solution hung on the wall. Alejandro noted that the story he was about to tell was merely a rough version. He wanted to refine his narrative and incorporate relevant Bible verses before speaking in church. At times as he spoke, he invited me to respond. At other times his aunt, Paula, joined in the conversation, and her contributions subtly guided the narrative in new directions. It was through an interview with Paula—the same woman whose observations on migration were described in chapter 3—that I had first heard of the accident.

Paula is an active member of Iglesia Bethel and is well respected for her leadership in the community. She has never been to the United

States, but her husband has spent many years working there. Paula states that her faith has given her invaluable support throughout the years as she has struggled to raise her daughters alone and maintain her marriage across the border. Paula first mentioned Alejandro's near-death experience to me in order to reinforce a larger point about the afterlife. "While some people work just to live well here," she explained, "thinking that when they die, there's nothing left, they are mistaken." There is an afterlife, Paula insisted, where we will be rewarded or punished. She explained that her nephew had recently seen the afterlife first-hand, and she proceeded to relate to me the story of the accident.

Paula's version of the story brought evil into the mix. She portrayed the border as a battleground between God and Satan. Paula pointed out that although the accident was a horrible ordeal, it had brought Alejandro into contact with God. Who caused the accident, I asked, God or the devil? "Look," she answered. "Between them both. Between both, because the enemy can do his thing, right? But God saved him in the middle of it." Although Satan had provoked the crash, "apparently when the accident was happening and he was able to see the Lord ... the Lord was there, He helped him. . . . God said, 'This one is going to serve me, so I'm going to save him.'"

Paula's narrative addresses the difficult issue of theodicy. It explains why the van was hit and why Alejandro survived while others died. Paula's story also draws from the broader logic of spiritual warfare, in which divine and demonic forces engage in perpetual struggle over human activity. She spoke of satanic possession. "Many people," she explained, "when they want to do something, it's not their idea alone, it's not their thinking; there's someone very powerful among them that makes them do things." Because of the constant machinations of the devil, people must seek out divine protection. It is important to pray for loved ones in the United States "because there too, although they're inside [the United States] there's much danger, there are many accidents there, in the road, on the plane. . . . When the enemy wants people, well, this plane falls and many people say, 'No, well what happened. . . . Everything was ok, but why did it fall?'"

Paula suggested that it is crucial to turn to God not only to ensure salvation, but also to ensure ongoing protection in this world. Drawing the focus of our conversation back to the border, I expressed frustration at U.S. efforts to keep people out of the country by erecting walls. I asked Paula whether such actions were in accordance with divine will. "No," she answered. "This is the will of the devil. Of the enemy. Why? Because the enemy wants to alienate people." Later, Paula offered an alternate interpretation. Whether the *gringos* decide to place more barriers at the southern periphery of the United States, or whether they decide to open the borders, their actions will be an expression of God's will.

While Paula's narrative gives a clear sense that God and the devil actively intervene in human affairs, the relative influence of divine, demonic, and human agency is less clear in her broader reflection on border enforcement. As I spoke with her, I had the sense that Paula was actively formulating her thoughts throughout the course of our conversation. Unlike the Protestant stories about the town's "conversion" and socioeconomic development, there does not appear to be a single narrative structure in place about evangelicals' experiences of crossing the border. The lack of clarity might also be due to Pentecostalism's pragmatic approach toward the obstacles and trials of daily life.[12] Paula's words indicate that although both divine and demonic forces are at work at the border, it is not our role take a God's eye view. God alone is judge. Although people cannot see and understand everything, they can act. They can navigate the sea of benevolent and hostile forces in Mexico and the United States by choosing to accept the salvation offered by God through Christ. They can call upon divine aid to protect themselves and others.

Alejandro, like his aunt, emphasizes God's power at the border. The theme of salvation is so central to his story that the hostile encounter with Border Patrol agents pales in comparison. Much as sociologist Pablo Vila[13] has observed among Pentecostals in Ciudad Juárez and El Paso, Alejandro places far greater emphasis on the spiritual border between sin and salvation than on the political boundary between nations. When I asked him about his feelings regarding the immigration agents involved in the accident, he quietly responded that he did not blame anyone, for God was in control. When, at his father's urging, I offered to put Alejandro in touch with border human rights groups, he declined. There would be justice, he said, but justice would come from God alone. As he reflected more, he told me that as he lay recovering he had begun to sense that someday soon there would be no borders. God was going to do away with such things, for the end times were coming soon.

The Rule of Law and the Law of Love

Alejandro declined the opportunity to press for earthly justice. At the same time, by accepting the authority of a God powerful enough to wipe away borders and put an end to human history, he refused to allow the Border Patrol agents who chased him to have the last word. Other Pentecostals offered a more straightforward critique of U.S. border policy. Referencing the Tower of Babel, Marta stated that the border is a product of human pride. "I believe that God didn't make any borders," she explained. "In the beginning, there was only one race, right? But when man wanted to be clever, and wanted to be larger than God . . . what did they make, a tower, right?" God responded by creating different languages. "That's why there are—Americans, Mexicans. God made it like that, but I think for God, there should be no borders." Although ethnic and linguistic divides are the result of divine punishment, Marta affirms that God's will is that human beings be united in love.

Christian opponents of undocumented immigration in the United States often draw attention to the notion of authority outlined in Romans 13:1, which states that people should be "subject to the governing authorities," for "[t]he authorities that exist have been established by God."[14] Opponents also refer to 1 Timothy 1:8, which states, "the law is good if one uses it properly."[15] El Alberto's Pentecostals regularly pray for local, state, and national leaders, and they stress the importance of obedience to authority. They embrace the biblical literalism and moral conservatism of many of their North American peers. They overcome the contentious issue of their own undocumented travel not by shunning or ignoring the rule of law, but by reframing it. They state that those who truly disobey authority are not the migrants who cross the border to the United States, but rather the government officials who put harmful laws in place. Both Marta and Pastor Elpidio suggested that those who formulate U.S. immigration policy have strayed from God's will. Pastor Elpidio explains:

As a pastor, I respect the laws. Because the Bible teaches us that we have to submit ourselves to the authorities. But also, I believe we know that among the leaders, they always create laws. And, some of the laws are good for us, and others affect us badly. So, on that end of things, I see that those [immigration] laws have affected many people, many families.

In a similar manner, Marta states, "The authorities are certainly chosen by God. But God sent the prophets to give us commandments, and God's commandments . . . from Genesis to Revelation, tell us that we must love our neighbor." Marta pointed out that Mexico, too, is guilty of closing its doors to Central Americans. "Just as the United States does to us, Mexico is doing to others."

Much as Alejandro looks toward a near future when God will do away with all borders, Pastor Elpidio suggests that the continuing stream of immigrants northward is divinely sanctioned. "Although they've tried to put up borders, and make walls, and everything else, but the U.S. government itself has seen that it hasn't been able to stop the people. . . . Here, the leaders of this earth put their laws in place. And they put up their borders. But for God, there are no borders." Elpidio explained that "we're just praying to God, that God will do something. . . . Because maybe with our own words we can't change the thinking and the decisions of the leaders. So all we can do is ask God."

That His Face Will Shine

If changes in U.S. border policy were to come, Pastor Elpidio indicated, they would come not as a result of political protest, but as a result of prayer. In the summer of 2008, I witnessed a vivid example of prayer in action. Days after I first heard Alejandro's testimony, Bethel's congregation held a group fast at his house.

As seen in chapter 4, Pentecostals in El Alberto occasionally fast as a means to connect with God. Part petition, part discernment, and partly an act of communion with the divine, fasting imbues prayer with extra authority and power. The act works through the body to sharpen the spirit and increase the likelihood that one's prayers will be heard. While fasting is one of the daily strategies through which evangelicals maintain meaningful cross-border ties, in this case the act served as a corrective ritual for a migration experience gone terribly wrong. By weaving sacred story into the fabric of immediate events, the rite worked to alter participants' sense of the possible, shaping not only their beliefs but also their concrete, flesh-and-blood orientation toward the problems at hand.

Preparations for the *ayuno* began early in the morning, as relatives and church members gathered outside of Alejandro's house. Dozens of chickens had been killed, and giant buckets of maize had been soaked and ground for tortillas. Women cleaned the chickens and boiled them over open fires. They made tortillas by the dozen for the shared meal that would follow. Rows of plastic lawn chairs had been placed in the dusty yard, and the pastor set up his electric keyboard to lead the attendees in song.

From the beginning of the service, Pastor Elpidio made clear that the purpose of the fast was to bring about a state of communion with God that would help restore Alejandro to health. About ten minutes into the service, after a period of song, he read the biblical account of Moses's encounter with God on Mount Sinai:

> Moses was there with the LORD forty days and forty nights without eating bread or drinking water. And he wrote on the tablets the words of the covenant: the Ten Commandments. When Moses came down from Mount Sinai with the two tablets of the Testimony in his hands, he was not aware that his face was radiant because he had spoken with the LORD.[16]

In the sermon that followed, the pastor drew several explicit comparisons between Moses's ascent at Sinai and the actions of the congregation that day. Just like today's worshippers, Moses had fasted and prayed. Today's effort, as in Moses's case, would bring the worshippers closer to God. Pastor Elpidio drew attention both to the difficulty of fasting and to its transformative power. "Fasting isn't an easy thing; fasting weakens the body," he insisted. "But how important fasting is! . . . Through fasting we can receive many miracles from God." He directed worshippers' attention to the length of Moses's time on Sinai. Although the worshippers today would fast for one day rather than forty, and although "we're not on a mountain, we're at a house," he insisted that they had come together with "a single purpose: to pray for the health and the life of our brother Alejandro. And do you believe that God can answer us? . . . God can do it."

During the fast that day, Pastor Elpidio carefully orchestrated a series of biblical images in such a way as to stir new possibilities to light. Part of the efficacy of ritual symbols lies in their ability to condense multiple meanings into a single form. Symbols are also iconic: they fuse abstract realities with the concrete stuff of daily life. When done effectively, ritual action can transform the abstract, unarticulated possibilities of a situation into a tangible form that can be observed and shared by all. Thus, as Nancy Munn puts it, symbolic acts "come to 'work back' upon the individual imagination with the authority of external reality."[17] By stating that the fasters were gathered at a house rather than a mountain, Pastor Elpidio brought the imagery of Sinai into close association with the space at hand. Participants listened to the story of Moses's fast as their own stomachs began to growl and as they smelled the chickens boiling nearby. This was no dry, disembodied reading of a text, but rather an attempt to fuse a sacred story with immediate reality. Most importantly, the presence of Alejandro's paralytic body at the front of the group kept his recent ordeal in constant view.

Pastor Elpidio implied a parallel between Alejandro and Moses. Much as Moses had undergone a different ordeal that brought him closer to God, Alejandro had endured the trauma of near death and, as he told it, come into closer contact with the divine. The Ten Commandments that Moses received "weren't just for him, but also for the people of Israel. And they were not only for the people of Israel, but rather they are the word of God for us as well." Similarly, Alejandro's near-death encounter would touch the lives of others. Alejandro had returned to the world as living proof that direct contact with God was possible, yet with his body broken and his face somber. The *ayuno* was an attempt to set things right. At the very least, it was an attempt to draw into view an ultimate horizon against which the difficulty of his accident would not have the final word. Moses had descended from Mount Sinai with a face so radiant it shone. "He had been there for forty days and forty nights," the pastor explained, "and as a result it says his face changed! He was a different Moses!" As a result of today's fast, the pastor told Alejandro, "your face [too] will change. It will be different."

In the vision of the border that emerged that day, the U.S.-Mexico frontier is but an earthly stage in which forces of good and evil struggle over the fate of the individual soul. Powerless to change immigration policy on their own, the best that people can do is to seek divine guidance and choose the path of salvation. Yet Pentecostal beliefs involve more than an otherworldly dismissal of immigration as a matter of concern. Submitting themselves to the authority of a God for whom there are no borders, Pentecostals embrace the undocumented journey as their right and travel with a sense of divine protection. As Robin Globus Veldman[18] demonstrates, conservative evangelical Protestant discourse serves to heighten worshippers' attention to certain concerns while "draining" other concerns of their ultimate significance. By dismissing the authority of divisive U.S. border enforcement laws, Pentecostals help carve out an acceptable space for continued migration. At the same time, fasting and other forms of worship ensure that their reflections on migration remain firmly grounded in collective reality. The fast following Alejandro's accident was a form of physical conditioning that instilled participants with a new sense the possible. By replicating, in part, the conditions that had brought about divine revelation on Mount Sinai, participants sought to make God's powers of protection and healing palpable in the here and now. They wove sacred narrative into the space outside this particular house, on this particular day, among this gathering of neighbors and friends, transforming the tragic accident into a catalyst for experiencing the reality of divine presence. Some participants had already crossed the border themselves or were contemplating the journey. As they did so, they would carry with them the sense of possibility that was generated on that day.

Pentecostals are not the only people in El Alberto who draw upon religion in conjunction with the migration journey. Catholics, too, set aside a moment near the beginning of each worship service to pray for relatives in the United States. When loved ones depart for the United States, one Catholic man explained, "we turn them over to God daily. . . . We ask God to give them the freedom to pass. . . . And yes, we've seen that there have been results." A youth leader at El Alberto's Catholic church states that migrants occasionally ask for a mass as a blessing before traveling north. Throughout the Valle del Mezquital as a whole, communities hold special masses in honor of migrants during their annual patron saint festivals. The local diocese has even issued a pamphlet offering spiritual guidance to potential migrants and their families. Catholic theological interpretations of the U.S.-Mexico border parallel Pentecostal perspectives. Agustín, for example, the Catholic man quoted throughout chapter 2, states that "God has no borders, anywhere. For us God is great, on a global level. He's the very first father we have."

Although an in-depth comparison between Catholic and evangelical approaches to migration is beyond the scope of this book, these observations indicate that the belief that "God has no borders" is not unique to Pentecostalism, and that evangelicals are not the only ones who seek divine protection for their journeys to the United States. It is also important to note that not all who have a "born-again" experience go on to become core members of a congregation. When I returned to El Alberto in 2011, Alejandro had recovered sufficiently to be able to drive a car. He and his wife were no longer attending services at Bethel. When I asked about the family, Pastor Elpidio simply said, "We're praying for them." The brevity of his words may have something to do with the evangelical narrative convention of downplaying details that might undermine a sense of God's efficacious presence in human life.[19] Yet the instance also indicates that conversion may not be the most adequate model for understanding religious adherence. As Henri Gooren argues, people often undergo various levels of religious affiliation and disaffiliation throughout their lives.[20] While not all of those who come in contact with Pentecostalism become members of a church, they may nevertheless absorb Pentecostal ideas into their daily experiences. The very fact that Alejandro immediately drew upon a Pentecostal salvation narrative as he struggled to put words to his vision of the afterlife speaks to the significance of the religion within the collective imagination of the town.

We have seen that Pentecostalism is relevant to all dimensions of the migration experience, from the strains of fostering transnational family ties to the trials of crossing the border and seeking work in the United States. Even so, the challenges and tradeoffs of transnational life have become so pronounced that even the resources of faith are not always enough. Not only have deaths at the border increased, but those who succeed in reaching United States do not necessarily find the American

Dream on the other side. Rather, they often find themselves in a situation of permanent marginality, living as outsiders within a country that welcomes their labor while denying their full belonging as human beings. Alejandro's border accident is merely one among many critical moments that have stirred forth questions about whether there might be a better way to live.

As seen in the group fast at Alejandro's house, Pentecostals continue to draw upon their faith as they absorb the shocks of migration. They continue to look past the limited timelines and authority structures of this world by seeking eternal salvation in the beyond. But they are also joining with their neighbors to seek solutions outside of the religious realm. The final section of this book turns to the Caminata Nocturna project and the underlying Mexican Dream it embodies. As discussed in chapter 2, the residents of El Alberto share a deeply rooted tradition of collective participation. This tradition cuts across religious differences, for it is grounded in the ties of kinship and shared cultural history. It is this shared history that they look to as a source of strength and resilience as they strive to generate sustainable local alternatives to migration.

PART III

7
The Night Hike

After the border accident that inspired the Pentecostal fast outside of Alejandro's house, a crowd of people from El Alberto and surrounding communities gathered at the base of the Gran Cañón in honor of the man from the community who did not survive. The decision to light luminaries on the canyon walls came naturally, for the town's members had been lighting the torches on a weekly basis for nearly four years as part of the Caminata Nocturna. The community began this "Night Hike" as a response to the increased danger of crossing the U.S.-Mexico border. They also began the endeavor in an effort to counteract the ill effects of migration upon the youth of the town. By opening their canyon area to tourists and sharing their own experiences at the border, they seek to raise awareness about the difficulties facing those who must leave their home countries in search of work. They also seek to earn money and create jobs. Although tourists purchase tickets for the virtual journey, the Caminata Nocturna is far more than an entertainment show.

The very same border danger that has spurred Pentecostals to fast and pray for divine protection has also prompted residents of El

Alberto as a whole to develop the Caminata. From a strictly evangelical perspective, the undocumented journey is just one of many possible catalysts for the only passage that truly matters in human life: the passage from an unsaved state to a state of salvation.[1] Pentecostal theology presents the border, like the rest of the "things of the world," as merely a temporary stage for a deeper spiritual struggle between God and Satan. Yet Pentecostals' lives are not defined by the religious sphere alone. Keeping their sights partly on the afterlife and the impending end of days, they also join hands with Catholics and other non-evangelicals to seek creative, this-worldly alternatives to migration. Their ecotourism project celebrates the human power to bring about social change. Using rigorous embodied action, the Caminata Nocturna enactment urges participants to join one another in demanding a new future for Mexico. It urges tourists and the youth of El Alberto alike to set their sights not on the United States, but rather on the "Mexican Dream"—the dream of a future in which migration will no longer be a necessity.

Laying the Foundations

When asked about their reasons for developing the Caminata, residents of El Alberto speak of the dangers that migrants encounter at the U.S.-Mexico border. Yet they also voice concerns about the effects of migration upon the young people in their town. Evangelicals, especially, explain that migration has disrupted the family, producing a generation of young people vulnerable to drugs, alcohol, and gang life. They explain that the youth have lost touch with tradition.

Early migration from El Alberto began as an effort to survive. Once people began working in the United States, the material circumstances of their daily lives changed dramatically. Those who once trekked back and forth to Ixmiquilpan selling firewood with their parents managed, a mere generation later, to provide their own children with houses, televisions, and automobiles. By the year 2008, all but two of the town's homes were made of cement. Nearly all of them had electricity, over 76 percent had running water, and more than half of the town's homes contained a television.[2] Today the children eat better, have better clothing, and enjoy greater access to education than their parents did. However, there exist deep tensions between the generations. While many among the first wave of migrants who traveled to the United States in the 1980s managed to obtain legal residency, younger generations of migrants travel under harsher conditions and with less hope for legal authorization. As those born to the first generation of migrants reach adulthood, many worry that the quest to provide their children with a better way of life has backfired.

Some parents fear that their children do not appreciate the hardships that they once endured. Patricia, a U.S. resident and a mother of three, explains that she first went to the United States as an undocumented immigrant in the 1980s and was able to secure papers in 1988. She now lives in Phoenix, where she attends a Pentecostal church with her family. Her children attend public school. Patricia states that she and her husband seek to impress upon their children the sacrifices required to get them where they are today. "I tell my children, 'Right now you're not suffering, you have everything, you have school, and no, we suffered a lot.' . . . We're giving them everything so they won't have to suffer like we did." One man, who had returned to El Alberto from Las Vegas in 2007 to complete the year of service that is required for ongoing membership in the community, explained that "it is a mistake when parents think they have to give their children everything." Rather than leaving one's children behind to search for better opportunities, he insisted, potential migrants would be wiser to stay in their places of origin, work hard, and give their children what they can. "Because [the children], too, are going to learn that they have to work in order to live, to survive. But we don't think like that."

Others express similar sentiments. Noé, who served as *delegado*, or town leader, several years past, explained that children often turn out rebellious when their parents provide them with everything. "The parents are at fault," he stated, "and the kids are in the streets, doing what they will, they don't learn a thing." Fortunato, an evangelical man quoted in previous chapters, explains, "When a child doesn't have the love of his parents—all the riches in the world don't mean a thing." Residents of El Alberto are also concerned about the fate of the youth who were born in the United States and have never set foot in their parents' town. As Fortunato observes:

> They no longer know the culture of the place they were born. They don't know their dialect, their mother tongue. They have no idea what a

community is. . . . Maybe one day after their parents die, they're going to show up and we won't know who they are! . . . They've left behind their roots . . . who we are, who we were, how our ancestors lived. Now they're going to live without roots.

Residents of El Alberto developed the Caminata Nocturna in an effort to protect the youth from the many dangers of migration and, at the same time, pass along their town's cultural heritage. In Noé's words, "We don't want to lose our origin. We don't want to lose our culture. We don't want to lose our way of thinking. . . . We want for the people from here, from El Alberto, to have employment."

Well before the Caminata Nocturna was concocted, the residents of El Alberto already owned and operated the small water park that draws upon the natural hot springs prevalent in the area. Once the town's members built the road that runs by the canyon on its way to Ixmiquilpan, they began to consider the possibility of bringing tourists there, as well. Salustio[3] was *delegado* at that time. He recalls that the canyon was dense with plant growth and virtually impassable, and so the town leaders began by clearing a path. Their first idea was to offer boat rides to the tourists who came from Mexico City and the surrounding region to use the water park. Salustio recalls seeing a television commercial for boat rides in the Grand Canyon while he was working in the U.S. Southwest. The town leaders named the area the Gran Cañón, superimposing the globally renowned tourist site onto the local landscape. They first welcomed tourists to the area during *Semana Santa*, or Holy Week, of 2004. But the river current soon proved too strong for the rowboat they had purchased. In a last-minute improvisation, one of the town officials built up a section of the river so that tourists could be taken across it in a pickup truck. The experiment was a success. From then on, members of the community began to develop the canyon area. They bought a motorboat, set up a rappel station, and made a zip-line. The next project was the Caminata Nocturna.

Salustio's nephew is the man who died in the border accident of 2008. Salustio observes that the purpose of the Caminata is "to explain to the people how you suffer. Well, one goes in search of a better life. But perhaps there are people—they don't achieve that better life. Because it ends there in the middle of their path. In the desert, or in the mountains." When the first Caminata was staged in 2004, no one from the community had yet perished at the border. Yet the residents of El Alberto decided to light torches in the canyon in memory of all those migrants from Mexico who, as Salustio put it, "didn't make it, or those who turn back, or those who return back, but already—already dead."

The first Caminata Nocturna was preceded by about four months of planning and discussion. A local activist from Ixmiquilpan, who first arrived in El Alberto as a tourist earlier that year, played a key role in the initial planning stage. Since then, he and his wife—along with an ecotourism specialist from a nearby town—have given invaluable contributions of time, effort, and talent to the Caminata and other projects. It is the members of the community as a whole, however, who have nurtured the initial idea of the Caminata and brought it into fruition. Virtually every decision regarding the ecotourism park must pass through the town's General Assembly, a governing body consisting of representatives from each household.[4] Salustio explains that the initial planning stages lasted a long time, for there was much discussion in General Assemblies about which aspects of their own migration experiences the town's members would include, and in what ways. The process was "somewhat difficult, because many said, 'Let's do it like this . . . but another says 'let's go to this place' . . . so we'd start to discuss, then we'd put it to a vote."

For the first trial, the town's members targeted the student market. They went from classroom to classroom at the university in Ixmiquilpan promoting the event. Dozens of students and professors agreed to come. A date was set, tickets printed, and the day arrived. That night the group walked until nearly four in the morning. At the close of the event they were met with a free campsite, firewood, beer, and a sumptuous barbecue in the style typical of the Valle del Mezquital: meat slowly roasted between agave leaves, over hot stones buried in the earth. Participation grew. The Caminata now attracts over a thousand participants a year. Today's border simulations are not always as rigorous as the initial one. The first Caminata "was a greater sacrifice," Salustio recalls. Nevertheless, the tourists rarely know what awaits them when they pay the 250-peso ticket for the event. Those working in the park pitch the simulation simply as a nighttime hike that deals with "a migrant's experience." Soon, though, tourists are enveloped in an experience that is well beyond what they imagined. The following is a composite description based on the eight Caminatas I observed during the summers of 2007 and 2009.

The Caminata

The first Caminata in which I participated began well after sundown in a clearing outside the sixteenth-century church of San Alberto. About forty people mingled in excitement, wearing dark clothing and carrying flashlights and headlamps. All but myself were Mexican citizens. While most of the participants were young—students or professionals in their twenties and thirties—there was also a handful of families, including several young children. The mood was half-playful, half-solemn. Families waited together in the dark. Teenagers joked and lit cigarettes. Some formed nervous huddles, giggling in anticipation.

Suddenly, a figure wearing a ski mask, dark sweater and camouflage pants evocative of Zapatista attire[5] appeared near the wall by the churchyard. He was soon joined by several others in similar attire. The mysterious arrival—who later introduced himself as Poncho[6]—told us that he was to be our guide and gathered us into a circle. He insisted that on this night, we would begin to recreate the bonds of brotherhood that had been lost among Mexicans. He spoke of physical perseverance and the benefit of a positive mentality. He also spoke of the difficulty that lay before us.

The opening speech set people on edge, priming them to expect the unexpected. The guides' dark ski masks were similarly unsettling. According to one of the guides, who was himself long familiar with the hardships of undocumented border crossing, such concealment is intended to invoke the uncertainty and lack of control that immigrants experience when they place themselves in the hands of a *coyote* or *pollero*. As crossing the border has grown more difficult over the last few decades, people have come to rely increasingly on the services of these paid guides, whose fees reach several thousand dollars. Using a *coyote* usually involves great risk, for one cannot be sure of the guide's honesty. As this guide explained, real *polleros* don't wear masks. "But it's as if they did. Because ... you've never seen that face, you don't know what that person's like. If that person's good or bad. . . . You are going to trust that person without knowing his face."

Giving themselves over to the care of guides whose faces they could not see, the group set off into the night. Murmurs, whispers, and stifled giggles mingled with the steps of eighty feet as tourists traveled around the church, down a steep embankment, and onto the road. The guides spun an atmosphere of creative improvisation into the event, throwing in humor and toying with the line between magic and banality. They took us past cornfields that had been tended by their grandparents and past quiet, night-enshrouded cows that mooing Border Patrol actors later wove jokingly into the narrative over their megaphones.

Although a playful element would persist throughout the Caminata, at this moment the group was overtaken by fright. Scarcely five minutes into the Caminata, as we crossed a bridge over the Rio Tula, sirens and lights sounded in the distance. Laughter and conversation ceased as tourists grabbed their children's hands, raced across the bridge, and fell to their stomachs in the gravel by the roadside. Taken off guard and against my own expectations, I began to cry. There was an immediate, visceral humiliation to being thrust to the ground and finding oneself on the receiving end of a gaze of surveillance, whether real or enacted. Adrenaline set in.

The reality that we had left behind persisted beneath the atmosphere of chase. Purple, green, and pink disco lights from the festival celebrating the closing of the school year in El Alberto converged with the receding flash of red and blue patrol lights on the treetops. Dance music rumbled on in the background. Yet these sights and sounds posed little threat to the Caminata. The "Border Patrol" chase was not an illusion that could be broken but rather a genuine physical event that had produced actual effects in our bodies.

Once the Border Patrol vehicles were out of sight, we scrambled down a steep embankment to the river. As the guides ushered us from hiding place to hiding place by the riverbank, costumed Border Patrol agents shined spotlights from the road above. They called out through megaphones in English and then Spanish with simulated, American-English accents. "Listen," they yelled, "We know you're there! *¡No vayan al otro lado; es muy peligroso!*"[7] As the agents exited their vehicles and descended toward the riverbank, the guides pushed us into a hollow space beneath a cluster of bushes. I felt myself packed in with other bodies. My leg began to cramp. I could not operate my voice recorder because my elbow was lodged against someone's back.

At that point—and this scene was repeated, in various forms, during each Caminata I observed—the Border Patrol agents staged a violent confrontation with another group of "migrants," actually volunteers from El Alberto hiding in the bushes a dozen feet away from the tourists. The Border Patrol actors landed upon these "migrants," drew them out by force, and began to question them and bark orders in mixed Spanish and English.

From the tourists' limited vantage point, the impression was of muffled violence and confusion. I glimpsed wrestling figures. I heard rustles, yells, and groans. During another enactment one Border Patrol agent, played by a man who had spent a good deal of time in the United States, shouted "You stupid Mexicans!" in between punches and groans. Once, a deafening staccato of gunshots—actually firecrackers—produced gasps among the hidden tourists. One of the apprehended migrants may have been "killed," but it was impossible to see. We could see only his body, a dull mass on the ground. "It's not real," a mother whispered to her child. But by that time, the reality of being pressed against the bodies of others in the darkness rendered disbelief difficult to maintain.

Enacting Border Militarization

The struggle that tourists observe from the bushes represents a worst-case scenario. Nevertheless, the tension of the encounter, as well as the physically demanding natural landscape in which it is embedded, reflect concrete changes in U.S.-Mexico border enforcement over the last few decades. We have seen that wide-scale U.S. migration from El Alberto began in the mid-1980s and that the town's members began to lay the groundwork for the Caminata in 2004. The time frame is significant, for it was during the early 1990s that the U.S. "prevention through deterrence" strategy prompted more and more undocumented migrants to attempted perilous desert routes to the United States. As one Caminata guide said, reflecting upon his experience, "It's like I tell you, it's a lot of suffering. . . . When I went the first time, well, yes it's really dangerous;

I had to endure about a day or two days of hunger there in the desert." Another spoke of how it had rained for six hours straight as he and his companions crossed the desert. It was cold, he said. They were soaked to the bone and all they could hear for hours on end was the "sssshh, ssssshh, sssshh" of rain falling on the sand. On another occasion, snow had fallen. Having no blankets, the group hugged one another to keep warm.

When I asked a guide which elements from his own experience he incorporates into the Caminata, he replied, "The danger. The danger—we try to do it in such a way that the people react." When a thunderstorm struck during the first Caminata I participated in, the guides pressed us onward for a good two hours through the underbrush. We crossed a steep sided irrigation channel and continued along a riverbank. By the end of the event, everyone was soaked from head to toe. I came down with a nasty cold the next day. During another, drier Caminata, as Border Patrol actors made intermittent appearances on the road above, tourists dashed from hiding place to hiding place, nettles, mud, and snapping branches pressing upon their bodies.

The physical extremity of the Caminata infuses the event with a sense of intensity that borders on reverence. But it is the interaction with hostile, weapon-toting Border Patrol actors that lends the greatest intensity to the event. When El Alberto residents first entered the international migration scene, a trend of border militarization was well underway. As Timothy Dunn argues, from the late 1970s through the early 1990s, the United States gradually began to apply the doctrine of Low Intensity Conflict to its southern periphery.[8] This Cold War strategy was originally developed as a means to control foreign civilian populations through the use of advanced technology and close collaboration between police and military institutions. As the "War on Drugs" and the Central American refugee crisis of the 1980s brought heightened attention to the U.S.-Mexico border, the U.S. government began to apply the doctrine to its home soil. The boundary between civilian and military law enforcement blurred as Border Patrol agents took on an increasingly militaristic role and as the INS acquired equipment formerly used in Central America and Vietnam.[9] The trend of border militarization continued as the 1996 Illegal Immigration Reform and Immigrant Responsibility Act (IIRIRA) created thousands of additional Border Patrol positions at the country's southern frontier.

As El Alberto residents' first forays into the United States escalated into a fully established pattern of transnational migration, the town's members thus encountered a border zone marked by a heightened presence of Border Patrol agents and sophisticated surveillance technology. The militarized climate increased after 9/11, when the U.S. government placed INS under the direction of the Department of Homeland Security.[10] Although it was not the first time that the rhetoric of fighting terrorism had influenced border politics, the intensification of anti-terrorism concerns after 9/11 resulted in increasingly restrictive conditions for immigrants.

Residents of El Alberto are acutely aware of the changing nature of border enforcement in recent years. In 2007, when I asked one of the Caminata guides if he had noticed any changes in border security over the last decade, he replied, "Five years ago there wasn't much security, like now. Before, people could pass quickly, they didn't suffer, people didn't die. And now yes, now every year a hundred, two hundred, three hundred die, because, well, there's a lot of security." While riding one night in the Ford F-150 that doubles as a Border Patrol vehicle, I asked a Border Patrol actor whether the real officials are as violent as their enacted counterparts. "When they're not on camera," he answered. "When there are cameras, they don't touch you. When there's no one else around, when they can't be seen, they treat you badly. They'll beat you with the butt end of their flashlights."

Not all of the immigrants whom I interviewed had experienced negative encounters with Border Patrol agents. Some had had no contact with them whatsoever. Yet at the heart of each Caminata lies a profanity-laden, gunshot-spiked struggle between "migrant" and "Border Patrol" actors. That scene of struggle condenses the abstract, technologically advanced state of the U.S. border militarization into a tangible human interaction. Although not necessarily representative of every crossing experience, it embodies a terrible possibility that lurks at the margins of each attempt. Hidden within the bushes, the tourists witness violence as experienced, in reality or in fearful imagination, by undocumented immigrants on the border. The event does not merely show the tourists something through a careful orchestration of symbols. Tourists observe the struggle after having been persecuted, with adrenaline coursing through their veins. Although the experience may communicate something to them, it also does something to them.

The wrestling match between "migrants" and Border Patrol actors is merely the overt expression of a subtler undercurrent of dehumanization that persists throughout the entire Caminata. From the first moment that tourists throw themselves on the ground by the bridge, they find themselves on the receiving end of a harsh gaze of government surveillance. Border Patrol vehicle lights frame the town of El Alberto, claiming ownership of the open spaces, the roads. While the *migra* are active, loud, and aggressive, the tourists are quiet. They hunch, cower, and hide in the dark, between the roadside and the riverbank. The Border Patrol agents carry technology. They have handcuffs, a megaphone, spotlights, and vehicles. The tourists have nothing. Their few possessions often become damaged or lost.

When the Border Patrol agents first speak to the tourists, they do not do so face to face. They do so from above. Their voices and their lights descend from the road to the tourists' hiding places. They speak to the tourists through megaphones, in voices magnified by technology. Some speak in English; others in broken Spanish with simulated English accents. One young female tourist remembered that simulated language barrier as the most distressing part of the Caminata. When the Border Patrol agents told the migrants to come out of their hiding places, she remembered, "They try to speak Spanish, knowing that they . . . aren't aware of what they're saying, right? I wanted to reflect on that. In a real situation it must be very distressing, because it's someone who doesn't master your language, doesn't know what they're saying, and . . . any moment they can shoot you."

Throughout the Caminata, tourists experience the alienation of cowering in the darkness like hunted animals and being spoken to in a language that is not their own. One tourist felt the dehumanization most vividly when a group of actors posing as a drug gang ordered the group to the ground and demanded money. Some felt the most impacted by the simple experience of getting their clothes dirty. It was after the first steep descent to the riverside, when tourists stepped ankle-deep in mud, that these participants realized that the Caminata was truly going to inconvenience them. As one participant, an accountant from Mexico

City, put it, "When you start to see that you're getting in the water, jumping over puddles, getting you skin muddy, getting wet . . . it's ugly." Another remarked, "You think you're going to go hiking on flat ground and everything, and the first thing that happens is you step into the mud, and you say damn! You know what, now my clothes are dirty."

Some tourists are upset by the physical intensity. "It was hard-hitting," a young woman told me. "I didn't expect it to be so real." Those who plan and implement the Caminata, however, insist that in order for the experience to make an impact, it must be difficult, and the difficulty must be unexpected. One tourist who was initially furious about the Caminata's physical demands told me that she would be willing to come back. She would even bring her family, because "good experiences are those that mark you, you share them with the people who are around you, right?"

The simulation immerses tourists in a disorienting nighttime landscape and forces them to give up control over their customary ways of being. As the tourists run, hide, and stumble in the darkness to escape "Border Patrol" agents, the boundaries between themselves and the natural world break down. Nature rasps at the margins of their bodies, penetrating the space between their toenails and their toes. They take home its bruises. It takes their sweat, their footprints, and sometimes even their cell phones. When I returned to the riverside during daylight hours, I found a trail of lost shoes, earrings, and water bottles. The ground was thick with footprints. Paths had been worn by the thousands of feet that had passed through the undergrowth. The effects of the Caminata were inscribed in space, much as the major crossing zones of the U.S.-Mexico border bear the marks of repeated human passage.

Pursuit by "Border Patrol" agents also forces people to interact with one another in new ways. During my first Caminata, the group at times transformed into a herd. Although I knew that the danger was not real, I felt myself pushing, like an animal in flight, toward the center of the group. I observed that people began reaching out to one another, tightening their family groups and improvising others. I heard families taking head counts. A child asked, "And my mom? Where's my mom?" One family, seeing me alone, invited me to walk with them. Strangers grabbed hands with strangers to help one another under low-lying branches. The guides discouraged us from using flashlights, and we began to listen and feel our way through the night. One moment found us packed together in a tunnel, over three-dozen bodies wedged within rounded concrete walls. From our cylindrical chamber we could hear Border Patrol actors yelling from the road above in electronically amplified voices. The vibrations of the truck engines surged through the tunnel walls and through the columns of people packed into one tense, shifting body.

Beneath the veil of the game, the Border Patrol actors knew that we were there. We could hear them talking with our guides on their radios, in hñähñu. But that reality mingled with this one without breaking its surface. Like childhood play, the fiction had become palpable and elastic. One woman later told me that she had thought of her uncle while hiding there. He had hidden in a tunnel once, too, at the real border.

When the Border Patrol agents were gone, we emerged from the tunnel into a desert dreamscape. The night was clear, and the blurred forms of cacti hovered, semi-animate, on the dark hillside. The way was rocky and uneven. Forged into one body in the tunnel, we stretched into a caterpillar-like filament, relaying whispered warnings down the line. "Careful—cactus spines!" "There's water here." "Watch out for that branch!"

We encountered the landscape in slow, shuffled sequence, partly through our own senses and partly through one another's guidance. After hiking for hours, the guides blindfolded us and carried us in the backs of pickup trucks for several miles. Our vision gone, a hush fell over the group. My attention to sound and feeling grew more acute. I heard my companions shift their weight. I heard the noises of the tires with each turn.

The trucks left the paved road and began a rocky descent. The vehicles came to a halt and the guides led us to the ground. I stumbled as someone placed my hand on the shoulder of the person ahead of me. We took small shuffling steps as we were led in a human chain into what I would later see was a large circle. Light flickered through our blindfolds, and we could smell fire. The long note of a conch sounded above. The guide instructed us to feel the earth beneath our feet, to listen to the sound of the water in the river nearby, to feel the air on our faces, and to sense the light of fire.

We removed our blindfolds to find ourselves at the base of the Gran Cañón. The canyon's walls were lit with torches, the same spectacle that would be witnessed after the border accident the following year. Beneath a flag held high against that backdrop of flames, we sang the Mexican national anthem yet again. The tourists and guides embraced one another. Some returned to their campsites, and others went up the hill to the restaurant's patio area. Huddled over steaming mugs of *café con leche* and *atole*, these bankers, students, business people, and computer programmers from the country's capital joined residents of El Alberto in an impromptu discussion about border issues, Mexican politics, and life in the United States.

Performative Dimensions of U.S. Border Enforcement

In the U.S. media, the U.S.-Mexico border is often portrayed as a dangerously unstructured zone, a desert wilderness shot through with human smugglers and dueling cartels. In the popular imagination the border is a space where nations meet their limits, where the concept of citizenship dissolves. The border is, as anthropologist Michael Kearney claims, a liminal zone. Like initiates, the migrants who cross it are "reduced to a categorical state of nonhuman—in this case an 'alien.'"[11] They surrender themselves to the care of *coyotes* that will, metaphorically, "either deliver them or eat them."[12] The border is a space of death, claiming the lives of hundreds each a year.

Although the roots of and the demand for undocumented immigration lie deep within Mexico and the United States alike—and although danger exists not only at the border but also in the entire migration corridor that extends to Central America—the richest imagery, the imagery most capable of inciting U.S. public reaction, lies within the border region. It is at the border that symbols of nationhood and human illegality most palpably coalesce. The fetish of the nation depends on the border for its being, and the fetish of the citizen draws its lifeblood from border soil. As we have seen, the U.S.-Mexico border often serves as a "political stage" that draws attention away from the larger, messier work of managing undocumented labor.[13] By diverting migrant traffic away from key media-visible cities during the mid-1990s, the INS replaced images of border chaos with images of order.[14] More recently,

Arizona governor Jan Brewer's unfounded words about "beheaded" bodies appearing at the border helped fuel popular support for S.B. 1070, which requires state law enforcement officials to inquire about the immigration status of those whom they encounter and suspect of being in the country without authorization. Border enforcement is not merely instrumental. It also has a performative dimension.

To borrow a definition from ritual theory, performance is "that kind of doing in which the observation of the deed is an essential part of its doing."[15] Instrumental action becomes performance when an audience is present, and when that audience's reaction matters. The Immigration and Naturalization Service had multiple audiences in the 1990s, and there are multiple audiences for Immigration and Customs Enforcement today, including American voters, Mexican officials, and migrants themselves. One performative task of border enforcement is to project an image of control to the American public. Another task is to instill fear and intimidation in immigrants themselves. U.S. border enforcement efforts employ symbolic imagery, transforming humans into aliens and flight vehicles into beasts. One of the latest pieces of technology employed by Border Patrol is the Predator-B. Also known as the "MQ-9 Reaper," the Predator B is a type of unmanned aerial vehicle, or drone, used for surveillance and bombing in U.S. military operations in Iraq and Afghanistan. Migrants have felt the gaze of these "hunter/killer" vehicles upon their backs.[16] They have also felt the gaze of helicopters, which they refer to as *moscas*, or "flies." In 2005, the U.S. Border Patrol sponsored a series of advertisements flooding Mexican televisions and radios with images of death. The campaign drew upon the tradition of folk ballads as well as images of village cemeteries to infuse the public imagination with a sense of danger.[17] Ironically, the U.S.-backed campaign was a response to increasingly fatal conditions that the U.S. Border Patrol itself had a hand in creating.

Migrants serve not only as audience members but also as props in the border enforcement drama, for their bodies are sites through which the concept of "illegal alien" is constructed and maintained. As Mae Ngai points out, the "alien" is a recent product, the result of a heightened post–World War I concern for international boundaries. In the aftermath of the war, human rights came to be framed primarily in terms of citizenship. At the same time, the war produced millions of refugees and other non-citizens. Though a genuine social and economic presence in society, the "alien" is "a person who cannot be and a problem that cannot be solved."[18] Today the U.S. government has periodic needs for undocumented labor, yet relegates immigrants to alien status in order to maintain control over their movement and justify their periodic expulsion from the country.[19]

Rendering humans into aliens requires substantial performative work. A promotional video on the U.S. Customs and Border Protection website offers a window onto how such work is done.[20] An immigrant on a stretcher is attended by Border Patrol agents. A father and child press their foreheads together tenderly as they are apprehended. While the video humanizes migrants to a certain extent, it also makes clear that the regulation and control of their humanity rests with government officials. Scenes of agents saving people's lives shift to scenes of tackling, chasing, and handcuffing. Yellow flowers in the background of the tackling scene reemerge in a section on "agricultural terrorism," subtly linking migrants with unwanted weeds. With its rapid succession of images and adrenaline-pumping soundtrack, the video is an acute expression of the dynamics of biopower, or the exertion of state control over human populations through the management of life itself. As Jonathan Xavier Inda argues, the exclusion of undocumented immigrants represents the bitter "underside" of biopower in the United States, for policy makers approach immigrant removal as "an essential and noble pursuit necessary to ensure the survival of the social body."[21] The militarization of the U.S.-Mexico border, by extension, rests on the assumption that the loss of immigrant life is merely an unavoidable byproduct of the necessary task of border control.[22]

Their lives alternately saved and seized by border enforcement agents, their bodies policed upon the border stage, undocumented migrants carry within their flesh the "contradiction of borders and boundaries in the age of global capital."[23] Today, discourse about national security also links immigrants with terrorism and crime, as seen in the growth of the immigrant incarceration industry. Through Section 287g, IIRIRA authorized the federal government to train state and local police forces in matters of immigration enforcement.[24] More recently, the Secure Communities Initiative has encouraged local and state law enforcement agencies to collaborate with federal agents for the purpose of identifying and deporting "criminal aliens" who "pose a threat to public safety."[25] In practice, the majority of the immigrants apprehended through these measures have not been dangerous "criminal aliens" but rather persons accused of minor misdemeanors. Nevertheless, their placement in detention facilities prior to deportation renders the line between immigration enforcement and the management of domestic criminals increasingly ambiguous. The growing criminalization of immigrants—or, as some scholars call it, "crimmigration"[26]— is a form of political performance that marks individuals "*as permanently undeserving*, rationalizing any consequences they may face during their lives."[27]

Subverting the Border Stage

In the theater of border enforcement, the U.S. maintains an illusion of bounded nationhood by criminalizing undocumented immigrants at the border line. What happens, however, when migrants tell the story? If the border is a political stage, as Peter Andreas has claimed, residents of El Alberto have crafted a stage of their own, seizing the power of frontier imagery for their own purposes. Much as Pentecostalism offers a new interpretation of the undocumented journey, the Caminata Nocturna wrests representational control from governments and news media and places it in the hands of those who have walked the desert trails with their own feet. While U.S. border enforcement policy objectifies migrants, the Caminata brings migrant voices front and center. It humanizes them.

The border simulation has served as a space for collective reflection not only among tourists, but also within the town of El Alberto itself. Although people have been processing aspects of the migration journey all along in their religious practices, the Caminata has allowed the town's members to express the difficulties and traumas of migration on a wider level. Before the Caminata, a former town leader told me, people rarely discussed the undocumented journey openly. Those who did put a good face on things, not wanting to worry others. During the planning stages of the simulation, however, stories began to emerge. The costumed officials, the simulated gunshots, the disorienting landscape, and the attacks by gangs are all drawn from El Alberto residents' flesh-and-blood experiences. I found through the course of my fieldwork that some young men who were reticent during interviews came alive in the Caminata as they donned Border Patrol garb and shouted and struggled with "migrant" actors. Others told me anecdotes from their own migration attempts as memories jostled to the surface during the simulation. When the tourists depart after some scenes of the Caminata, I have spotted small groups of women and children from El Alberto sitting in the background, serving as a second audience behind the audience of tourists.

The Caminata gathers together hundreds of migration experiences and presents them in a single, forceful vision. With a dynamic similar to that of the "socio-ontological" or religious narratives described by Anna Peterson, the enactment proposes an "alternative vision of the future" capable of transforming participants' sense of the possibilities that lay before them.[28] As a collective story, the Caminata tells us that border militarization has transformed the U.S.-Mexico divide into a dangerous place. It suggests that losing one's life during migration is a distinct possibility, and it suggests that beyond overt violence, there is another, more subtle form of violence at the border, the dehumanization that one experiences as an undocumented person. The Caminata brings to light "*el México que existe pero muchas veces no queremos ver*"—"the Mexico that exists but many times we do not want to see"—and it does so with prophetic force, seeking to motivate new forms of collective action.

If we simply read the Caminata to discover its meaning, however, we miss much of what it is and does. The Caminata is more than a storyline, more than narrative. Tourists are not simply audience members. They are participants. As Richard Schechner[29] has argued, no firm line separates theater from ritual. All performances are entertaining to some degree, and all performances act upon and transform those involved. Rather than interpret performances through the categories of "ritual" and "theater," it is more helpful to examine the particular balance of efficacy and entertainment within them. When entertainment dominates, there is a greater degree of separation between performers and observers. When efficacy dominates, the boundaries between actors and audience break down, causing those gathered to become a community.[30]

The Caminata is, on the one hand, packaged and marketed as entertainment. Tourists arrive within the context of vacation travels and weekend getaways. They purchase tickets and expect to be engaged. Their expectations and desires subtly shape the parameters of the event. One guide described changing the Caminata to accommodate occasional requests for a more rigorous experience. While the Parque EcoAlberto website solemnly entreats tourists to support their "hñähñu brothers," another page flashes the words "Make fun of the *migra!* Cross the border of extreme sport!"[31] Yet the border simulation is also efficacious. It shakes tourists out of the role of audience and makes them full participants in a performative event that borders on pilgrimage. As Victor and Edith Turner have suggested, "a tourist is half a pilgrim, if a pilgrim is half a tourist."[32] The self-transcendence that tourists seek in their travels evokes the *communitas* of religious travel, as tourists step out of the structures of daily life and encounter new surroundings. Like other forms of adventure travel, the Caminata appeals to tourists' thirst for authenticity amidst the perceived meaninglessness of postmodern life.[33]

Some Caminata tourists seek self-transformation. Some hope to educate their children about migration. Others hope to better understand what their own migrant relatives have endured. Others simply seek an adrenaline rush. Regardless of tourists' motivations, the Caminata works in and through tourists' bodies to generate a new, experimental social space out of the raw material of the migration journey. Undocumented border passage challenges migrants both mentally and physically. At the mercy of *coyotes* and the natural elements, migrants are pushed to new extremes. As they surrender to the experience, they discover survival resources they never realized they had. One Caminata guide, speaking of his own experiences at the border, explained, "I never prepare. I just go. Getting there, I don't even know whom I'm going to deal with. I don't know if that person is good or bad. I don't know if that person is going to cross me, or leave me in the desert. . . . You have to trust, whether or not you want to." For some, the experience provokes a heightened sense of reliance on God.

As residents of El Alberto recreate the danger and uncertainty involved in migration, they draw upon the same emotional dynamic that has driven some of them to convert to evangelical Protestantism. They seek to tap into, and amplify, the latent creative potential of the journey. The *migra* who chase the tourists do so not to keep them out of the United States, but rather to drive them into a new way of being. Rather than predatory *coyotes* who may "eat" their charges, the Caminata guides are compassionate trickster-clowns who use humor to push tourists out of their comfort zones.

At the start of the first Caminata I observed, a young tourist asked the guide named Poncho what would happen if the *migra* caught us. "Well, the thing I have to tell you is, they are authorized to use rubber bullets," he answered, sparking gasps and nervous giggles. When he led the group in singing the Mexican national anthem, flag held aloft, the guide urged people to sing louder, more forcefully. "We have to be dynamic," he shouted. "Ladies, you can tell how a guy is in bed by the way he sings. So sing like you mean it!"

If the Caminata is about the experience of immigrants who suffer, I asked later, why make light of it? Humor, Poncho answered, is one way to invigorate people, to render them receptive to the unexpected. "Most of the time, people go around with a layer of ice in front of their faces," he answered. "You have to break that ice."

On one occasion, after we had traveled by foot for about two and a half hours, Poncho gathered the group together. In a rousing speech, he urged us to realize our full physical potential by overcoming hunger and thirst.

"Are you hungry?" he shouted.

"No!" The tourists yelled back.

"Are you thirsty?" he shouted.

"No!" they replied. To which the guide reached into his backpack, opened a can of Coke, and drank it loudly in front of them. And burped.

"*Pues*, you told me you weren't thirsty, or I would have offered," he said.

I discussed the incident with another guide a few days later. In his young thirties, this man was no stranger to the undocumented journey. He explained that although the journey to the United States was difficult, life in rural Mexico had prepared him well. "The way life is here," he explained, "you go up in the hills, you go wherever. You don't get tired, and if you're hungry for two, three days, you put up with hunger. Because you're already used to it." More than a mere insult, the Coke-drinking incident contained a message of resilience, offering a playful counterpoint to treatments of hunger and thirst within Pentecostal fasting. Know when to put up with hardship, the prank suggested, and know when to gulp down a cold can of soda. Endure hunger but don't idolize it. Stay open to possibility.

A common complaint among tourists is that they are not told what to expect in the Caminata. They are not told to wear good sneakers and to bring raincoats. To give tourists such warning, the guide cited above insisted, would defeat the purpose of the Caminata. "We tell them, it's a simulation of how an immigrant suffers. You're going to go as an immigrant; do you think it's going to be a trip to the beach? . . . No. Because an immigrant suffers. An immigrant gets surprises." The Caminata embraces the ludic and the unexpected. Sometimes children from El Alberto join in the fun. During one Caminata that I observed, at least a dozen of the tourists were children. To better tailor the experience to that night's younger audience, four kids from El Alberto joined the team of guides. Dressed in white, they were introduced as "gringos" number one, two, three, and four. The little guides embraced their job with gusto. They herded the tourist-children along and reprimanded adult participants for turning on their flashlights. They danced ahead and climbed trees. They hid in bushes and snorted. They tackled our legs as we walked by. For a moment the border simulation became a goofy, magical game of tag.

The Caminata's paradoxical blend of playfulness, gravity, and danger is intentional. The guides use humor not to dilute or lighten the significance of the migration journey, but rather because play itself is efficacious. Play calls culturally accepted models of reality into question.[34] It frames things anew. Like ritual, the Caminata is a form of "work done playfully."[35] Although the simulation is not overtly religious, like ritual, it helps expand the sense of possible beyond the here and now, and strives to make palpable the presence of things unseen. The Caminata also fulfills the religious task of helping people to chart a shared course through space and time.[36] In the words of Charles Long, religions deal with "orientation in the ultimate sense," that is, "with the ultimate significance of one's place in the world."[37] Like Pentecostal worship, the Caminata proposes a new map of border space, and a new vision of relationships between human beings.

U.S. border enforcement renders humans into aliens as it inscribes separation on the land and in the mind. Border making also reverberates through Mexican society in the form of ethnic, regional, and class divides.[38] Pentecostals respond to these many barriers by celebrating the power of salvation and love to break through all human-made walls. Yet in the very act of rendering earthly borders obsolete, Pentecostalism imposes a new, rigid classification structure upon reality: a black-and-white divide between salvation and damnation, between life in Christ and life in *el mundo,* "the world." The Caminata Nocturna, like Pentecostalism, proposes a new interpretation of earthly borders. But rather than holding fast to moral absolutes, the Caminata accomplishes its work in the fertile darkness of anti-structural play. The border space of the simulation is something to be hurdled and crawled through, a rich loam teeming with rivers, sirens, and snorting beasts. Palms grasp palms; blisters and dirt grind into the skin. The boundaries of the body dissolve as humor stirs new possibilities to the fore. While the U.S.-Mexico border reifies, separates, and shuts out, the Caminata questions, opens, and destabilizes. While border enforcement draws a line between nations, the Caminata is messy, amorphous. The Caminata is also similar to Pentecostal worship in the sense that it fosters a sense of empowerment. For Pentecostals, however, spiritual empowerment comes from God. It is an open-ended benefit that allows people to make the most of the migration experience, regardless of whether or not they make it to the United States. In the Caminata, meanwhile, empowerment lies in awakening the innate collective potential of human beings so that they will rethink the patterns of migration in which they are immersed, and join together for change.

Poncho, the creative mind who for many years served as the main guide of the event, states quite openly that the reenactment is, for him, "a rite." The ritual quality is most vividly illustrated in the act of lighting torches. When he began to light fires upon the canyon walls during the first Caminata, Poncho recalls, others were reluctant to participate. But they gradually joined in, and "magic," he says, took over. A few years later, the simple gesture was so deeply established in the town that Protestants and Catholics alike used it for the interfaith memorial service in the canyon. Poncho is not the only one for whom the Caminata has near-religious significance. While chatting one afternoon outside a small store that doubles as a bar, I had asked a man from the community whether he identifies with a particular faith. At first he said that he does not. But then, as he reflected more over a pint of beer, he said, "I agree with what Don Poncho says in the Caminata." He explained that he is not a churchgoer, but believes that life consists of both good and bad. We all contain a hearty mixture of sinner and saint.

During the Caminata, tourists cross no wall, no fence, and no line. At the event's close, tourists realize that they have "made it," but not to the United States. Rather than concluding in a simulated Arizona, Texas, or California, the Caminata ends at the base of the torch-lit Gran Cañón. The canyon is a highly revered space for the residents of El Alberto, a place that they hope to preserve for future generations. By bringing the Caminata to a close in this location, residents of El Alberto draw attention to the importance of respecting one's place of origin. Rather than stand beneath a simulated Statue of Liberty or American flag, they gather to sing the Mexican national anthem. The true border that must be crossed, the guides insist, is not physical. The true border to be overcome is the boundary between the human and the inhuman, between *"los seres humanos"* and *"los seres inhumanos."* The Caminata seeks to break through the boundaries of race, class, and ethnicity that separate Mexican citizens from one another and prevent them from joining forces in pursuit of a better future.

Although it is advertised and packaged as a tourist event, the Caminata Nocturna is far more than entertainment. It is a rigorous, embodied event that uses creative performance to catalyze new understandings and generate new solidarities. It proposes a new map through which people might reorient themselves within Mexico and reconfigure their relationships with another. And it proposes a new vision for the future: the Mexican Dream. The next chapter outlines some of the many voices that have contributed to this vision of an alternate, migration-free future. We have seen that Pentecostalism in El Alberto is deeply intertwined with all dimensions of U.S. migration. Yet the town's tradition of collective participation provides an additional source of strength, resilience, and inspiration in the face of migration's many challenges. Pentecostals and non-Pentecostals find common ground in their community's Mexican Dream.

8

The Mexican Dream

Why do we have to leave our place? Our parents lived; they lived and worked with what they had. And they didn't die of hunger. Because life is survival, nothing more. You have to work to survive. To eat. If our parents, being poor, if they managed to survive, I think that we can too. In fact, that's the message that the Caminata Nocturna contains. . . . What we are trying to get across is that here, in Mexico, they can achieve their dream.
—Ramón, Caminata actor from 2007

The Caminata Nocturna's message is not for tourists alone. It is also directed toward the youth of El Alberto, many of whom serve as guides and actors in the border simulation for a year or more before making their own decisions about whether to cross the border to the United States. Countering the individualistic ethos of U.S. labor, the Caminata project seeks to foster a spirit of self-sacrifice, community participation, and respect for origins. It urges young people to realize that "here, in Mexico, they can achieve their dream." The border reenactment is but one among several projects through which the town's members aim to make the Mexican Dream a reality. In addition to the ecotourism park, El Alberto is home to a successful women's craft cooperative that sells hand-made agave fiber products to an international market. The town's members are also developing a water purification plant that will market low-cost, purified water to surrounding communities within the Valle del Mezquital.

This chapter takes a close look at the Mexican Dream that drives the Caminata Nocturna. A diverse range of voices, evangelical and non-evangelical alike, have contributed to the vision of an alternate future that is projected in the Mexican Dream. I argue that although these voices at times contradict on another, they also share important common ground. Residents of El Alberto embrace varied understandings of indigenous identity, along with different attitudes toward the past. They also embrace different interpretations of consumerism, migrant labor, and the ultimate horizon of human life. Nevertheless, evangelicals and non-evangelicals alike are bound together by a deep loyalty to their town and to their tradition of collective labor. They are also bound by their common concern for the wellbeing of future generations. The pursuit of Pentecostal salvation and the pursuit of the Mexican Dream, as we will find, are not mutually exclusive.

Life Is Survival

Ramón served as a guide and also as a Border Patrol actor in the Caminata Nocturna in 2007. That year, along with about sixty other men, Ramón had been called by the community to fulfill his *cargo*, a period of unpaid work that is required of all adult males in exchange for ongoing town membership. Ramón usually lives in the United States with his wife and children, and had returned to Mexico for the sole purpose of fulfilling the year of service. That summer, Ramón often gave the introductory speech at the start of the Caminata. Ramón does not identify as evangelical, although I learned later that members of his extended family attend Pentecostal churches in the United States. I cite his words at length, for he provides a revealing counter-narrative to evangelical portrayals of development, migration, and economic activity.

While Pentecostals draw upon divine power to buffer themselves against the many dangers encountered during migration, Ramón draws upon his cultural heritage to make a sharp critique of U.S. consumerism and of the systematic exploitation of migrant labor in the United States. He states that migration has altered people's notions of what it means to live a good life. Years of U.S. labor have transformed people's expectations and desires, trapping them in a cycle of alienated labor and consumerism that is gradually eroding both their bodies and their spirits. He also speaks of the pervasive loss of dignity experienced by undocumented migrants who, despite years of working in the United States, feel that they are never fully accepted in American society.

In his thirties at the time of the interview, Ramón explained that he initially did not want to travel to the United States, but his brother continually urged him to join him there. Ramón finally complied, mostly out of curiosity. "But I tell you, when I got there, I wasn't happy with it. Because I earned less," he laughed, "by doing harder work." In Mexico, Ramón had worked as a "steel guy," assembling steel girders at construction sites. The job was tough, he admitted, "but for periods of time only. And the work that I did [in the United States] was more difficult, because I was working with a pick and shovel. And I didn't know how to speak English." Ramón claims that although the experience was difficult, he learned from it. "It wasn't an offense for me. It was a way to learn how to be in a place, to say 'I've gotten here.'"

Ramón counters enchanted conceptions about the power of U.S. dollars. The problem, he says, is that "many people hear that . . . money [in the United States] doubles itself, so they automatically think that they can obtain it very easily. But no, they also have to start from the bottom up." He states that if the community does not continue to stage the Caminata, the youth will always want to travel to the United States in search of a better standard of living. "And like I tell you, they're not going to have it if they don't work. They have to work to have it. The same over there, as here."

The problem with migrant labor is not simply that saving money takes longer than expected. The problem is that one becomes locked into a cycle of work and consumption that gradually eats away at one's vitality. Although migration has helped lift El Alberto out of poverty, Ramón insists that working in the United States has also subjected people to a new type of impoverishment. He states:

> A Mexican who emigrates from here to there, at the age of fifty, physically he already looks very worn out. He looks worn out because he spends his whole life at work. Working, working, in the morning at work until the afternoon, and yes, he has everything that he wanted to have, a nice sofa, a nice house, a nice bed, some nice shoes, but he doesn't notice that physically, he wears himself out.

Ramón describes a moment of realization, when the hypothetical immigrant catches a glimpse of his own reflection in a mirror and pauses to think. As Ramón spoke, I could not help but wonder whether the immigrant he described was himself. "And if he stops to think, well, is the dream that he had really worth the effort? It's there that he finally realizes. And he says to himself"—Ramón whistled, as though in sudden realization—"'Well, yes I got things, but physically I'm already worn out.' And it's like he doesn't feel satisfaction, because maybe it's just material, but instead what gives a human being pleasure is that they live to be a hundred years old." True satisfaction lies in the simple ability to say "'as long as I'm healthy, that's ok.' That's a wise way of thinking."

Ramón's observations on work and consumerism illustrate the multiple levels of alienation that workers experience in a capitalist economy. In the double bind of alienation and commodity fetishism, products grow in value only to the extent that workers' humanity is diminished. As a worker spends time and energy creating objects of consumption, "the less," as Marx puts it, "belongs to him as his own."[1] Rather than the outward manifestations of time and energy well spent, products confront the worker from the outside as autonomous and alien powers. Ramón's hypothetical immigrant buys "everything he wanted to have" without realizing that his body is slowly deteriorating. He builds houses for others so that one day he will have enough money to buy a house of his own. Yet the value his labor instills in those houses saps him of his own life force and leaves its mark on his physique.

Those who work in the United States without documents experience an additional level of alienation, for they live under a stigma of illegality that serves to obscure their humanity and discredit the material contributions they make to their host country. "Many of the people who have already been away from their place of origin for maybe ten, twenty years," Ramón explains, "they've worked a lot, and yes they've achieved things, but they don't feel satisfaction, to be able to say, 'No, damn it, I did it, I succeeded, I feel proud.'" Instead, "they feel as though they never had the freedom to live in a place where their people understand them, their people accept them." On the contrary, they always live under "a scornful gaze, to call it that. Because people don't look favorably upon you." Although they work so that the U.S. economy "grows, strengthens, and represents a great country," even so, people in the host country "*no te mira con buenos ojos*"—they do not look upon you with "good eyes."

At the time of the interview, Ramón had worked for more than a decade in the United States, in a wide variety of construction jobs. His words suggest that immigrants experience the contradictions of the U.S. immigration system at a bodily level. Undocumented immigrants carry both a deep physical awareness of the material contributions their labor makes to the United States, and the nagging sense of a "scornful gaze" upon their backs. Ramón explains that U.S. citizens do not want to reflect upon the value of immigrant labor. "They don't recognize it, in other words." Although migrants manage to obtain material things, "they don't have a great satisfaction. . . . They're never going to have it. Why? Because they know that they were never looked favorably upon."

Just as U.S. citizens do not recognize the value of immigrant labor, the country's leaders turn a blind eye to the true history of the process through which their own country became strong. Ramón recognizes that the United States has, undoubtedly, "achieved a lot. But one could say that it has never achieved it alone, by its own people." Rather, "the leaders have brought many people, of the best people that the world has. . . . Whether they were American or not, all have participated so that [the country] can have the magnificence that it has."

Ramón's observations resonate with emerging scholarship on the dynamics of power within the current global "mobility regime," in which the selective control of mobility is done through social profiling that benefits some populations while facilitating the exploitation of others.[2] Ramón highlights the connection between migration and changing agricultural practices resulting from NAFTA. The goal of food production, he states, ought to be "so that human beings subsist. To live." Yet the desire for profit often leads to practices that run counter to that goal. In the United States, "the things they produce, they no longer give them the [proper] time. . . . It's done by means of chemicals, fertilizers, to produce like this, quicker," he said, snapping his fingers. "So obviously it's an abnormal process, abnormal. That's not good." Virtually in the same breath, he states that international migration is "a mistake." It is a mistake because emigrants are living "in the wrong place." They leave their places of origin, "in order to live better, let's say, to have a nice sofa, a nice bed, a nice house. And yes, they get it. But what is it that they're eating? Is it good or bad?" he laughed. The heavily processed foods consumed into the United States lead to poor health and premature death.

As Ramón's words indicate, it has become increasingly difficult as a result of NAFTA to produce one's livelihood through small-scale farming. The choice to migrate, like the choice to use chemical fertilizers, is heavily structured by the state and by capitalism. Ramón was not the only person in El Alberto who drew a connection between agricultural practices and human health. On one occasion, I spoke with a man in his eighties who stated that life in the past was easier—and healthier. "No, the plants we planted, we didn't have to put medicine on them," he explained, as he coaxed an unruly herd of sheep and goats into their pen. "Like tomatoes. They just grew. And now, everything we plant, it needs *medicina*. And the same with people: we didn't used to hardly ever get sick! Now, you have to go to the doctor, you have to pay. No, it's a bit difficult now."

The connection that these men draw between farming and health is not simply metaphoric. They recognize that working and eating are part of a single organic process. Just as chemical fertilizers produce rapid growth that robs the soil of its vitality, migrant labor produces short-term gains at the expense of long-term individual and collective well-being. In both cases, the mistake lies in having an accelerated expectation of productivity. Their observations express yet another level of alienation produced by wage labor, separation from nature. As Marx reminds us, "man *lives* on nature . . . nature is his *body*, with which he must remain in continuous intercourse if he is not to die."[3] The more people approach nature instrumentally, viewing it merely as a source of raw materials, the more they lose sight of the fact that nature itself is the source of their survival.

To return to Ramón's words in the opening quotation, "life is survival, nothing more." Ramón states that work ought to allow a person to live a long and healthy life. When the conditions of work run counter to that basic purpose, something is profoundly wrong. Drawing inspiration from those who came before, he states:

> People who lived very simply . . . our grandparents, ate simple food, basic food. But they reached seventy, eighty, ninety years old. And they kept themselves healthy. Today, there are about three people [in this

community] who are about a hundred years old. And for a human being to live a hundred years . . . for me, that's the most beautiful thing that a human being can achieve. To live a certain time.

The purpose of the Caminata Nocturna, Ramón explains, is to show young people that whether they stay in Mexico or travel to the United States, they must work hard. Whether they stay or go, they will face moments of suffering. The simulation subjects participants to difficult physical challenges in order to push their limits and to show them that they are capable of more than they imagined. "It's a way of showing them that physically, they can do it. . . . You suffer, but only for trying to live a dream," Ramón explains. Potential migrants can take the effort that they would have exerted in attempting to cross the U.S.-Mexico border and apply it to creating a future in Mexico.

Like the many evangelicals whose voices have resonated throughout the pages of this book, Ramón expresses deep concern about the dangers and drawbacks of U.S. migration. His thoughts on the effects of migration upon people's long-term vitality echo Pentecostals' prayers for the health of loved ones abroad, and his words about living under a "scornful gaze" recall evangelical suspicions of sorcerers who prey upon the spirits of those venturing far from home. Yet Ramón does not attribute migration's problems to spiritual causes, and he does not call for spiritual solutions. While Pentecostals call upon God to bless their loved ones with good jobs and financial wellbeing, Ramón unmasks the enchanted lure of dollars altogether by inviting people to embrace simplicity and live as their grandparents once did. He calls people to look to the past, and to learn from it.

Ironically, the same past that evangelicals often portray as impoverished, drunken, and sinful has become, in Ramón's vision, a source of wisdom, autonomy, and resilience that can offer the community's members guidance as they strive to create a new future. Several dramatic characters in the Caminata Nocturna can help us understand the varied visions of the past that inform the Mexican Dream. One is El Alberto's legendary first citizen, Don Beto, whose spirit of self-sacrifice and service counters the individualism of U.S. society. The others are a pair of self-described "Indians" who embody aspects of El Alberto's past while also representing members of Native American tribes through whose lands migrants from El Alberto have crossed at the U.S-Mexico border.

Crossing through "Indian Territory"

In 2009, a new set of characters joined the Caminata Nocturna. Those characters are Don Caco and Don Chaleque, a pair of wild-haired, barefoot "Indians" who receive the tourists with trepidation but ultimately offer them assistance. The first time I saw these self-described "*indios,*" the guides had just taken the group of tourists through a long tunnel. We stooped low to avoid the sharp wires protruding from the concrete above. As the last person emerged on the other side, the guides told us that we must proceed with caution, for we were now entering "Indian territory." After rounding a bend, we came upon a figure clothed in rough white cotton. He had long, disheveled black hair. His face was blackened with charcoal, and an animal skin flapped wildly upon his back. Scarcely had we taken in the image when the guides hurried us to the ground. The man began to shout. He lit a semi-circle of torches, revealing a ramshackle hut whose crooked angles twisted in the firelight. Gourds, clay pots, pelts, and animal skulls hung upon the gnarled branches.

The figure yelled brusquely at us in a language that I recognized as a simplified form of hñähñu. "*Hyudi!*" he shouted. "Sit!" the guides translated. The *indio* told us to avert our eyes. He was angry with us for passing through. Too many people had been crossing through this area, he said, and they were killing all of the animals. Soon another figure emerged from the hut, as wild and disheveled as the first. Raúl, the man who plays this second *indio,* later told me that his character's name is "Chaleque," and the other, "Don Caco."

"Eat!" Caco ordered Chaleque. He brought out several big, fat insects and laid them on the ground. "I like to eat these! They're my favorite food!" he explained, turning to the tourists. He made an exaggerated show of gobbling up the bugs. "We don't eat tortillas," Don Caco explained. In a charming non sequitur, he blurted out, "I have a pet crocodile!"

At first the *indios* made it clear that our presence was not welcome. We had invaded their territory and offended Doña Petra—a mysterious woman to whom they spoke, but whom we could not see. Eventually, however, they warmed up to our presence. Don Caco brought out a gourd of *pulque*—actually the sweet *agua miel* that is used to produce *pulque*—and instructed us to serve it to the weakest amongst us, for it would give them strength for the journey. Next, he brought out a piece of sheepskin bearing a roughly drawn map of El Alberto. The Catholic church rose prominently on the right-hand side. A river cut through the center of the map, crossed by two bridges. Four roads marked a rough rectangle around the place. The only other landmark was a collection of crosses marking the cemetery. There was no sign of either Pentecostal church. Pointing to a human figure standing near the upper left-hand edge of the map, Don Caco indicated where we were to travel and bid us on our way.

Although the characters of Don Caco and Don Chaleque come across as crude stereotypes, the actors' motivation is sincere. When I asked about their significance, the first answer I received is that the characters represent Native Americans who extend aid to migrants as they pass through reservation land at the U.S.-Mexico border. Indeed, in the 1990s, as the U.S. "prevention through deterrence" strategy drove immigrants away from urban areas and into the desert, tribal lands on the border became prime crossing regions. Two years before the *indios* show was invented, a former migrant from El Alberto, Eduardo, had described crossing through the 4,000 square mile Tohono O'odham reservation in southern Arizona. The Tohono O'odham are one among various Native American populations whose lands were "crossed" by the border when the United States gained vast reaches of territory from Mexico.[4] Eduardo recalls:

> The last time I went there, to the North, I suffered a lot. We didn't have anything to eat, nothing, we'd brought two packets of cookies, and there were seven of us.... We got to a place named Santa Rosa ... and we came upon some Indian houses.... I told them ... that we were hungry, and could they give us something to take with us. They gave us something to eat, a sandwich, and that was enough.

When the *indio* characters offer *agua miel* to tourists, they reenact the hospitality that some people from El Alberto have received at the hands of Native Americans on the border. The characters also voice the frustration of those who find themselves caught in the midst of an ugly drama of migration, border enforcement, and drug trafficking in the region today. Recently, as O'odham lands have become a prime corridor not only for migration but also for the drug trade, the region has attracted a heightened presence of Immigration and Customs Enforcement (ICE) officials who sometimes mistake tribe members for undocumented immigrants.[5]

Migrants from El Alberto and members of the O'odham nation share common ground as indigenous peoples whose options are severely restricted by nationally imposed spatial schemes. Yet the *indios* characters have an additional layer of significance. They represent not only Native Americans whom residents of El Alberto encounter at the U.S.-Mexico border, but also aspects of the town's own collective past. Through these characters, Raúl, along with Cirino, the man who plays Don Caco, seek to demonstrate how "Indians" lived in the years before development arrived on the scene. Rather than reject or distance themselves from those who went barefoot, drank *pulque,* and fought with machetes, the actors embrace their energy and resilience.

When I interviewed Cirino in 2009, he was occupying a service post at El Alberto's health clinic. By day, Cirino drove to and from the clinic, overseeing a renovation project and attending to other leadership responsibilities. By night, he donned a black wig, smeared his face with charcoal, and became Don Caco. The enthusiasm of Don Caco is never far beneath Cirino's skin. Once, Cirino stopped to offer me a ride as I walked along the road. His clothing was conservative and unassuming, but he tilted his head toward the back seat. "I've got my merchandise," he grinned. Looking in the rear-view mirror, I caught a glimpse of a black wig and an animal pelt peeking out of a cardboard box.

Cirino, who did not identify as belonging to a particular religion, was in his late fifties at the time of the interview. He does not know how to read or write, and speaks Spanish with a heavy hñähñu accent. He uses performance to bring the *indios* to life. The recording I made of our interview was difficult to follow, for he moved about as he spoke, acting out his stories. "One of my neighbors says, 'Why, you're working, you're coming up with many ideas, and you don't know how to write?' 'No, but I have my mind' I told him. . . . My mind is working, but not just for myself—for my community." Cirino explains that the *indios* scene is a way to preserve a living memory of the past. He states:

I had the idea [to show how] we lived before, because before there was no road, nothing like that, no hanging bridge, nothing. Entirely on foot . . . one little path, see, a very narrow little path, like this! Let's go take the water out of the river to drink. . . . I'd like for the people to see . . . the Indian who was here, the original people here before. So that [people] wouldn't forget.

Cirino traces his inspiration for the role to conversations he had with his grandfather when he was a child. In the evenings, when he and his grandfather would sit together after a long day's work, Cirino used to ask him how people once lived. "'Pure fighting,' his grandfather would answer, 'pure machetes.'" Cirino states that he represents the *indio* in a rough manner because, quite simply, that is how people in this region once lived. Likewise, Raúl explained, "The Indian that exists here is very bad and doesn't like to associate with people from the city. That's why we act like this and we're bad, although there are good and bad." Raúl extends this morally ambiguous description to the man whom he credits with uniting the town in years past. Even the highly esteemed Eulogio Barrera, he says, "was a person who was sometimes good, and sometimes bad."

Rough, dirty, and unshod, the *indios* are characters of ambiguous moral fiber. Yet it is through these unlikely persons—through the voice of those from the past who were "sometimes good, sometimes bad"— that Raúl, Cirino, and others have chosen to convey a message to tourists and to members of their own community. The *indios* embody a strong local knowledge and a fierce commitment to place that is integral to the Caminata's anti-emigration effort. When the *indios* shout "do not cross" to the tourists passing through, past and present time, border space and local space converge in their warning. They invite participants to reflect, simultaneously, on the local and international repercussions of their actions. Rather than accuse the tourist "migrants" of violating a national boundary, the *indios* accuse them of violating customary norms of engagement with the natural world. They reach through the subverted border space of the Caminata Nocturna to offer tourists a new map, the hand-drawn, sheepskin map that is grounded in local, experiential knowledge—and with that, they bid the tourists on their way.

The bellicose, insect-devouring *indios* are but one expression of a varied and contested ethnic identity in El Alberto. Within their ecotourism project, residents of the town consciously craft images of their indigenous identity as they present themselves to the outside world. Different faces of this identity can also be seen in the architecture of the park. Like Don Caco's hut, the tourist cabins in the Gran Cañón are inspired by the cactus-walled dwellings once typical of the region. Yet the structures could not be more different. The *indios'* skull-strewn shack evokes the "hovels" described by representatives of the Patrimonio Indígena del Valle del Mezquital in the 1950s.[6] By contrast, the cabins for which tourists pay a thousand or more pesos a night combine rustic authenticity with *feng shui* precision. They are a performance in their own right, complete with track lighting and elaborately embroidered linen pillows.

Visits by politicians and the media also call for selective performances of indigenous life. When MTV came to El Alberto several years ago, the town assembly instructed everyone to dress "*de indígena*," donning the traditional white cotton clothing common in years past. Some expressed resentment at having to dress like "Indians." Others told me that they wore the clothing gladly, for they are proud of their heritage. On another occasion, representatives of the water purification company Bonafont were greeted by women in embroidered blouses performing traditional dances. When I showed the video in Phoenix to several people from El Alberto, they were surprised, for they knew that a few of the dancers were Pentecostals whose faith strictly prohibited such activities. "They look like turkeys," one elderly evangelical man observed matter-of-factly. I also observed dueling masks of indigenous self-representation during a planning meeting for the 2007 anniversary celebration of the Gran Cañón. The celebration brings hundreds of visitors and serves as a promotional strategy for the ecotourism park. Committee members decided to pool their resources to provide chickens, goats, and soft drinks for the event. Each participant would also provide one traditional dish, such as squash-blossom empanadas. There was much joking as they debated what counted as "traditional" fare. One young man burst out, "Pizzas! I'll bring some pizza." Another chimed in, "I'll bring blood!" Traditional Valle del Mezquital fare includes a dish made of blood, and pizza is far from foreign to members of this community.

They are at once more "civilized" and more "savage" than a sanitized, tourism-packaged version of indigenous identity would allow.

In the "*indios*" show staged by the characters Don Caco and Don Chaleque, aspects of El Alberto's past that have been obscured by the evangelical storyline burst forth with a bold and celebratory vengeance. Indeed, it was Raúl himself, the man who plays Don Chaleque, who once strongly objected to my decision to focus primarily on Pentecostalism within this book. I suspect that many Pentecostals, in turn, are not entirely comfortable with the way he and Cirino portray the "*indios*" within the Caminata Nocturna. Nevertheless, Pentecostals do embrace some aspects of the past, finding within it a source of motivation for the Mexican Dream. Evangelicals and non-evangelicals alike take pride in their town's tradition of collective labor, as embodied by another character from the Caminata Nocturna, Don Beto.

Don Beto: Work, Community, and the Ties That Bind

During the start of each Caminata, the guides tell the tourists the story of El Alberto's first citizen. Years ago, the tale goes, the town was little more than a few huts in the sticks. There were no roads, no running water—"*ni padres ni madres.*"[7] Folks went barefoot. Outsiders rarely arrived in the town. Yet there lived in the hills a man named Don Beto who would offer water, food, and a resting place to those passing through. While the tale of Don Beto mentions the same poverty and isolation found in Pentecostal narratives of the past, this version emphasizes harmony. Don Beto was an ideal first citizen whose selfless love undergirds El Alberto's collective labor system and inspires the hospitality shown to tourists today.

"Many will ask themselves, 'Who is Don Beto?'" observed Poncho at the start of one Caminata. "Don Beto is the classic character who gave us our cultural and historical identity. . . . He tells us, 'You have to be honest. You have to be sincere, you have to be of your word, and you have to be *de bigote,*'" that is, "of one's mustache." In the past, Poncho explained, "a funny way to make a promise was to pull out a mustache hair. When you pull out a mustache hair, what happens? It hurts! So it's like giving your word. . . . It's an agreement, you have to fulfill it." Poncho states that residents of El Alberto must struggle to overcome the stereotypes that have portrayed them as ignorant "Indians," and they must do so by drawing their cultural heritage of sincerity and cooperation to the fore. Similarly, Mexican citizens must overcome the country's reputation of crime and corruption by fostering a spirit of brotherhood in the country as a whole.

At first I was skeptical of the figure of Don Beto. Surely the mustache-toting founder was little more than an anecdote invented for tourists. But then I was told that character is indeed rooted in local tradition. Raúl, a Catholic, insisted that Don Beto and the patron saint of the community are one and the same, as Beto is the Spanish nickname for Alberto. Ricardo, a Pentecostal, elaborated, saying that more than a patron saint, Don Beto was an actual person. When I asked him whether Catholics and Protestants alike share this view, he answered that they do, for "it has nothing to do with religion. It's our past." Ricardo explains that the town was founded not by Don Beto alone but also by his wife, Doña Chona, and his sister-in-law, Doña Petra. These individuals lived "long ago. In the beginning. Before the church was here—thousands of years ago." I had my suspicions, however, for I knew that San Alberto was a patron saint of recent origin.

At the start of one Caminata, Poncho explained that death had taken Don Beto by surprise, "but he came back from the other side to leave us something very important. Perhaps many won't be able to understand it, for it's a marvelous thing we have, the ability to create tradition." My suspicions that Don Beto exists merely in the realm of efficacious fiction were confirmed one night as I helped a friend in the town make desserts for a visit from the state of Hidalgo's Secretary of Tourism. While the meal would consist of traditional fare, she wanted the dessert to be creative, fusing local products with global cuisine. We devised cheesecake with prickly pear topping and chocolate cake with pomegranate icing.

"We'll tell them it's an original recipe from Don Beto's wife," I joked as I spread the fuchsia icing on the cake.

"Oh, now you're catching on," she laughed. "That it's all made up."

Don Beto is no ancient founder figure. He was concocted six years ago at the start of the Caminata. When Ricardo, Poncho, and others speak of Don Beto, however, their animate, joyful creativity suggests that the story is no lie—and that the spirit he represents cuts across religious differences. There is something deeper to Don Beto than a mere tourist diversion. For Ricardo, an evangelical, that "something deeper" is his desire to reach out to the youth, for his own son and nephew have battled drug addiction and been imprisoned in the United States. Don Beto represents the culture of work that runs deep in El Alberto and is stronger, some say, than religious difference. Many look to the tradition of collective labor that he embodies as a necessary antidote to the social dislocation facing young people. By requiring all young men to serve for a year, the town's members seek to instill in them lasting values that will help keep them from harm's way.

Whether or not they realize it, the space that tourists cross through during the Caminata Nocturna brims with evidence of the collective work projects that have been transforming El Alberto ever since the town was "united" after emerging from its period of interreligious conflict. The simulation crosses through decades-old irrigation channels and hidden pathways that link plots of land farmed by generations of families. The Border Patrol trucks double as utilitarian vehicles during the day, as town leaders use them to haul supplies and drive throughout the roads announcing upcoming town meetings. The event also utilizes the bridge, tunnels, and paved road that the community's members have built during group work parties known as *faenas*.

Ricardo helped oversee the construction of one of the main roads that now runs through town. As he told me about the work process one afternoon, he paused to enter his house and returned with three photographs. The pictures showed a vision of solidarity: men, women, and children alike wielding picks and shovels, clearing the brush to make way for the bulldozer that would prepare the ground for the road. Ricardo explained that the road exists today because of the sweat and toil of each person depicted there. They were paid not in money but in the knowledge that their efforts would benefit generations to come. Noé, another former *delegado*, explained that the members of the town have "worked . . . like one single woman, like one single man. . . . If since 1985 this community had not worked, had not put in its time, El Alberto would not be like it is today." The projects are carried out not merely for the sake of those present, but also so that those yet to come will "see that we have worked, and we have built a lovely community."

Although they profess different religious faiths, these men express a moral, even an aesthetic understanding of work that conventional North American notions of productivity cannot fully encompass. Even the "Protestant ethic" that has played such a role within U.S. public life does not account for the sense of unity these men express. More than a utilitarian activity carried out in exchange for wages, work in El Alberto helps generate the social fabric itself. Whereas immigrants to the United States work as outsiders under the unshakeable shadow of a "scornful gaze," those who work in El Alberto help forge the ties that make the place a community and, in turn, earn a sense of belonging within it. As within other indigenous societies in the Americas, work is the medium through which people forge bonds of reciprocity, cultivate harmonious relationships, and mold young people into fully functioning adults.[8] It is through work that one earns full adult membership in the community.

The community, or *comunidad*, is a unit of collective land ownership that is legally recognized by the Mexican government. Within a *comunidad*, those who can demonstrate "prior, longstanding, community-based use of the land and waters" are deemed the rightful owners of a place.[9] Individual members of a *comunidad* have access to shared natural resources, but they are not permitted to sell land to outsiders. In El Alberto, families manage their own plots of land, yet people have shared rights to pasture grounds, waterways, and the ecotourism park. Town membership also guarantees burial rights in the local cemetery and the right to participate in the town government. The town is governed by a rotating system of committees. Decisions are also reached through large, town-hall style meetings. Held roughly once a week, these General Assemblies require the attendance of at least one representative per household. Sometimes the discussions, which are conducted almost entirely in hñähñu, can be quite heated. All who wish to are given time to voice their opinions, although I have seen long-winded participants ushered out of the spotlight with a chorus of "enough, enough, let's move on!" While General Assemblies encourage active, grass-roots participation, they also have a coercive dimension, for excessive absences result in a fine. Fines also result when a household fails to send a representative to scheduled *faenas*, or communal work parties. *Faenas* strengthen social solidarity by demanding that one sacrifice one's time, energy, and comfort for the good of the group. As one male in his early thirties put it, "We have to do *faena* and sometimes we have to work all afternoon and all night. We have to do it. And, 'No, I'm hungry,' well, all of us are hungry, what are we going to do? And we have to do it." Parents encourage their children to participate in *faenas* in order to learn the value of hard work.

The *cargo*, or year of service, is another form of traditional labor in El Alberto. Successful completion of the year of unpaid work allows young men to be considered full members or "citizens" of the town upon reaching adulthood. They must then fulfill additional service posts every six to eight years to avoid losing community membership rights. While women are appointed to certain part-time service posts, the full year of service is generally reserved for men, with the exception of single mothers who are heads of households. Such is not the case in all communities of the region. Some have even been governed by female *delegadas* as migration opens up new spaces for women's participation.[10]

Unlike the traditional Mesoamerican *cargo* system, which combines civil and religious duties, *cargos* in El Alberto are purely secular. The energy people invest in them, however, can assume a near-transcendent quality, and for Pentecostals and Catholics alike. While fulfilling a *cargo*, one is constantly at the beck and call of the community. On one occasion, I observed a *comité* member operating construction equipment as part of a road-building project early in the morning. Later that day I spotted him running messages for the town leader, and that night he served as a guide in the Caminata until three in the morning. All told, he had completed a twenty-hour workday. Others confirmed that such a schedule was not uncommon. The relentless demands of the year of service can result in significant sleep deprivation. In 2008, two town authorities became so tired after serving back-to-back shifts that they suffered a car accident in which one of them broke his neck. Younger men participating in the year of service for the first time speak of the work with a mixture of pride and resentment characteristic of new recruits in boot camp.

The year of service demands such sacrifice, in part, because it is a means through which the boundaries of group membership are forged and contested. In recent years, members of the community have begun to test religious leaders' loyalty by requiring that they, too, complete the year of service. When I was last in El Alberto, both Marcos and Pastor Isaías had served a *cargo,* and Pastor Elpidio had just been called to do so. The year of service was a sensitive subject of debate during my first visits to El Alberto because of the increased difficulty of undocumented U.S. travel. Those who were in the United States without papers risked losing everything if they should return to Mexico to fulfill the requirement. Their choice had increasingly become a choice between life in America and membership in the *comunidad,* with long-range implications for themselves and their family members. By 2011, the community had decided for the first time to allow U.S. immigrants to name a substitute for their year of service. This solution will likely produce new inequalities, as those in the United States pay relatives in El Alberto thousands of dollars in exchange for the substitution. For years, however, the service obligation has functioned as a powerful leveling mechanism for the inequalities that result from migration. The year of service demands time, labor, and physical presence. Large, shiny pickups with license plates from Arizona, Nevada, Utah, and beyond are a common feature in the landscape of El Alberto. Yet the owners of the trucks who are fulfilling their years of service must put these status symbols to the service of the Caminata and pay for the gas that they use to haul tourists from point to point in the park.

El Alberto's labor requirement acts as a stringent test of loyalty, as participants give long days and sleepless nights in service to their town. But the service year also functions, in a more mundane way, to foster long-lasting relationships between neighbors. Working in the ecotourism park reproduces, in part, the social dynamics of the traditional Mesoamerican *milpa* agriculture. In a *milpa* system, people work small, varied plots of land in cooperation with relatives and neighbors. The goal is not to produce a single cash crop for profit, but to produce a wide variety of foods and medicinal herbs that households need for their survival. The system works by making efficient use of myriad inputs that would otherwise go to waste, such as household and animal byproducts, "dawn weeding hours, after-school hours," and culturally specific knowledge of vegetables, flowers, and herbs.[11] More than a system of food production, the *milpa* is a center of focus through which ties of reciprocity are forged and maintained, and through which inheritance patterns are channeled.[12] Because of the system's "fundamentally anti-entrepreneurial character," *milpa*-based practices work against individual advancement.[13] Noé, for example, compares the nature of *milpa* work in El Alberto to the climate of life in the urban United States. In the city, he explained:

> You even have to buy tomatoes, onions, everything, and without money. But here, . . . I'll go with one of my relatives or a neighbor, I help them pick tomatoes today, and tomorrow I go with another neighbor, I'll pick *chiles*, and next week I go with another and I'll harvest maize, and they give me maize, they give me beans, they give me tomatoes, *chile*—and look, . . . I have salsa, I eat tortillas made 100% by hand. What more could I ask?

Today, there is simply not enough arable land for the *milpa* system to function as the primary base of subsistence. Land conflicts in the Valle del Mezquital have increased as the region's population has grown.[14] El Alberto's ecotourism park offers a partial solution to this dilemma. It provides not only a source of income, but also a shared venue in which people can work together and forge relationships of reciprocity. The year of service helps to inculcate a communal, egalitarian ethos that counters the individualism of wage labor in the United States.

While the Caminata Nocturna is a thrilling experience for tourists, for those who must repeat the same Caminata week after week for a year, the event can become mundane. Even so, the Caminata provides them with opportunities for social interactions that otherwise may never occur. During several Caminatas, I accompanied the Border Patrol actors on their shift. Bursts of activity were followed by long periods of waiting. The young men helping out with the Border Patrol acting sat in the back of the vehicle, text-messaging their girlfriends and yawning from time to time. The Caminata was, for them, an inconvenience. It required that they sit cramped in the back of a truck with uncles and older neighbors while their friends attended dances in nearby towns. Yet there are also moments of camaraderie and spontaneous humor. During one shift I observed, the crew shared tamales and sodas. Later in the night the group broke into peals of laughter when my knee hit the siren button by accident and a man who had fallen asleep during a patrol shift startled and drove off. Over the course of a year, such minor, seemingly insignificant occurrences accumulate into a body of shared experiences that help forge lasting bonds of town citizenship.

In Mexican communities with a high rate of U.S. migration, a young person's first undocumented border crossing journey acts as a rite of passage. That is, crossing into the United States for the first time is so physically challenging, and involves such a deep transformation of one's personal identity, that it helps mark the transition to adulthood.[15] As we have seen, Pentecostals instill the life-crisis of border crossing with new significance, interpreting the border experience as one trial within a deeper drama of salvation. Likewise, the year of service acts as another rite of passage for young people in El Alberto, whatever their religious persuasion. The rigor of the work rivals the exertion of the undocumented journey, and the length of the period gradually helps mold young people into adults who will eventually become responsible for the collective welfare of their community. As Leonardo puts it, service in the Caminata and other town activities helps pass along to youth "that heart, that mentality, of not abandoning the town."

Mapping Local Territory

The spirit of cooperation and commitment to place that is embodied in the fictional character of Don Beto is not merely a matter of sentimentality. It is also a matter of survival. The right to exist as a *comunidad* and manage land on their own terms is a right for which indigenous people have shed blood, both in El Alberto and in Mexico as a whole. During the late nineteenth century, massive numbers of the rural population were transformed into debt peons with little option but to work on *haciendas*.[16] The resulting conflict between landowners and peasants gave rise to the Mexican Revolution, which culminated in the redistribution of land as *ejidos*—a type of communally owned land—and *comunidades*. Residents of El Alberto stress the importance of maintaining harmony within their town, for struggles have demonstrated that strength, power, and protection depend upon unity. They have watched neighboring communities gradually lose their autonomy after opening their land for sale to outsiders, and they refuse to let the same happen to them. As neoliberal reforms result in growing national neglect of Mexico's rural areas, the pressure to emigrate continues. A government-issued sign posted in the window of the *secundaria* in 2009 provides a fitting illustration of the social expectations facing young people today. The sign states, "If you're thinking of going to the United States, do not forget the following documents," including a vaccination card and Mexican identification. Concerned parents state that their students would rather seek money in the North than pursue scholarships and continue their studies at home. Others state that even when students manage to secure scholarships, their post-graduation employment options remain limited.

Although they are still deeply involved in U.S. migration, residents of El Alberto seek to preserve their autonomy by inculcating young people with the values of loyalty and collective service. They also defend the physical boundaries of the community, as suggested by the sheepskin map that Cirino shows tourists in the Caminata Nocturna. Cirino's role as a mapmaker extends beyond the border simulation. He occasionally takes young people from El Alberto on excursions in the hills to show them the town's boundaries. As he explains, "Some young people still don't know where the territory of El Alberto is. . . . That's why I'm helping them. . . . We're covering the route so they find out where it is." Cirino's knowledge of the territory is the type of knowledge that cannot be shared through words alone. As Keith Basso reminds us, "wisdom sits in places"—land triggers memories and stories for those who know it well.[17] During one *faena*, a group of people from the community made an excursion to the town's border and worked all day to clear the brush from and reinforce the worn stone markers that indicate boundaries of the *comunidad*. Later Ricardo showed me photos he had taken of the event. He spoke with the same mixture of enthusiasm and pride that he exhibits while speaking about his evangelical faith, or while brainstorming new ideas for the Caminata Nocturna.

It may seem ironic that a community whose members have long crossed the U.S.-Mexico without documents should take such pains to reinforce the boundaries of their own town, and that they should do so, literally, in stone. Yet it is partly the dislocation brought about by migration that causes the community's members to guard their own geographical borders with such precision. To recall the sermon about evil symbols described in chapter 5, we can see Pastor Elpidio acting as a mapmaker, as well, arming worshippers with a global vision of space and time that will help them better navigate the many dangers of mobility. Cirino's boundary marking serves a parallel and complementary purpose. At times, these two forms of mapmaking—the global, Pentecostal version and the local, place-based version within the Mexican Dream—converge. In 2009, a decades-long territorial conflict with the neighboring community of La Estancia erupted in an exchange of bullets. The dispute concerned a section of land that borders the swimming pool area of Parque EcoAlberto. A year later, the town's members gathered near the site of the conflict for a memorial service, echoing the event following the border accident described in the opening pages of this book. Pastor Elpidio, Pastor Isaías, and Don Marcos joined forces to lead members of all three churches, Catholic and Protestant alike, in prayer. The community has repeated the gesture each year since.

Residents of El Alberto have spilled blood, even risked their lives, while crossing the U.S.-Mexico border. That they have also spilled blood while defending the boundaries of their hometown points to the fierce dedication behind their pursuit of the Mexican Dream. El Alberto's members recognize that migration is so deeply established that change will take time. Their struggle for the Mexican Dream is a struggle that occurs in the midst of, and in tension with, the ongoing commitments of transnational life. Even Ramón, whom I have quoted extensively in this chapter, knew that he would soon risk the undocumented journey to rejoin his family in Las Vegas. Ramón states that although he must continue to cross the border, he helps stage the Caminata Nocturna in the hope that future generations will not be compelled to follow. "Nothing can be obtained easily. . . . Achieving a good standard of living will take a process. It will mean that those who are here now will have to work so that others who come after will have that privilege of living better." A life free of dependence on migration, he notes, is a still just a dream. Nevertheless, "when someone has a dream and wants to realize it, it can be done." Despite their religious differences, and despite the challenges that await them, residents El Alberto continue to fight for their dream.

Conclusion

El Alberto is not the only community of the Valle del Mezquital region that has witnessed its first border crossing fatality in recent years. A young man from the neighboring community of El Dadho put it bluntly: "They go to the North, and they come back as ashes." Despite recent claims that the economic recession in the United States has led to a decrease in Mexican immigration, border deaths have not abated. Over 250 deaths were recorded along the Arizona-Sonora section of the border in the 2009–2010 fiscal year, 183 deaths the year following, and nearly 100 in the first half of the 2011–2012 fiscal year. The Arizona-Sonora section of the border alone witnessed over two thousand deaths from the year 2000 to the beginning of 2012. These numbers represent only those bodies that have been found, and do not include missing persons whose remains are unaccounted for.[1]

The explicit logic of U.S. border enforcement policy is that greater security measures will decrease the flow of "illegal immigrants," drugs, and other unauthorized materials across the boundaries of the United States. The effects of border enforcement upon migration patterns, however, are far from straightforward. We have seen that the "prevention through deterrence" strategy of the mid-1990s simply drove people toward more remote crossing areas, resulting in an increase in the annual migrant death rate. More recently, the buildup of fencing, technology, and additional enforcement agents at the U.S.-Mexico border has perpetuated the trend of driving migrants toward potentially deadly, remote routes.[2] Yet border enforcement is only one dimension of U.S. immigration policy. Throughout American history, immigrants have alternately been welcomed to the United States or selectively targeted and expelled.[3] The 2012 Supreme Court decision on Arizona's S.B. 1070 was yet another manifestation of this pattern. In this decision, the Court upheld one of the most controversial portions of the bill, which authorizes state law enforcement officials to investigate the immigration status of people they suspect to be in the country without documentation. As over a dozen states debated similar legislation, and as the rise of a growing immigrant detention industry accompanied increased collaboration between federal and local law enforcement agents, the border remained one of the most visible and volatile points of interaction between unauthorized migrants and the state.

While the obvious rationale behind U.S. border policy is that greater enforcement will slow the flow of undocumented passage, migrants are far more than individually calculating actors, and the border is far more than a simple, utilitarian barrier. As soon as border enforcement touches human lives, it becomes an object of the collective imagination. The impact of the border extends from the most intimate embodied experience to the realm of nightmares, stories, and dreams. In the collective imagination of El Alberto, the border is and has been many things. In the 1980s it was a place of adventure, the setting for a game of hide-and-seek with Border Patrol agents who often turned a blind eye to people's passage. In today's migration, expectations of possibility are shot through with danger. For some, the border is a literal and biblical desert, where migrants call upon divine aid. For others, it is a battleground within a global process of spiritual warfare. Armed with the blood of Christ, Pentecostal migrants cross that battlefield impervious, in their eyes, to physical and spiritual attack. Multiple notions of space collide at the border, as the lived-in territory of border tribes clashes with U.S. territorial schemes, at the same time that Mexican migrants seek passage. The imagined border space of the Caminata

Nocturna is populated not only by migrants and Border Patrol agents but also by gang members, drug traffickers, and the *"indios"* Don Beto and Don Caco, whose ambiguous mixture of hospitality and hostility calls to mind El Alberto's past. Indeed, the significance of the border in El Alberto's collective imagination runs deeper still, for it is embedded in the life cycle, touching upon the most intimate of biological processes. Fetuses are shaken in the womb as their mothers clamber down border fences or are transported in the back of lurching *migra* vehicles. Children cross the border as they transition into adulthood, seeking to expand their options as did parents, aunts, and uncles before them. And the border is part of that final transition, death. In the most extreme cases, it takes bodies in and sends them forth as ashes. Other bodies emerge from the border alive but broken or paralyzed, with eyes and hearts that have seen the beyond.

This book has argued that Pentecostals in El Alberto have long drawn upon religious beliefs and practices to prepare for and make sense of the dangers they encounter at the U.S.-Mexico border. They have also drawn upon their faith throughout the many other challenges of living and working across borders. They do so as relational, embodied beings whose notions of progress and prosperity can be traced back to their early efforts to overcome poverty. This book has also argued that the challenges of migration have become so pronounced in recent years that even religion does not provide sufficient solutions. Rather, residents of El Alberto have found new hope within their border crossing simulation and in the vision of the future articulated in the Mexican Dream. The pages that follow take a closer look at how Pentecostal beliefs and motivations dovetail with the Mexican Dream. They also offer some concluding observations about the contributions this case study can offer to the larger literature on religion, migration, and the U.S.-Mexico border.

Salvation, Migration, and the Mexican Dream

While early evangelical conversion in El Alberto was driven by spiritual concerns, it was also driven by the simple desire to live a better life. People turned to the new religion to overcome illness and sorcery, to quit drinking, and to help bring irrigation and development to their town.

However, neither the new religion nor socioeconomic development conquered all of people's woes. Shortly after the initial period of wide-scale religious conversion, migration emerged as a separate, parallel effort to survive. At first, the material changes brought by U.S. migration were so dramatic that religious narratives of those years recede into the background. Yet migration produced challenges of its own. Today people suffer from the strain of being separated from loved ones across an international border. They find themselves precariously dependent upon relatives who are, in turn, subject to the fluctuations of the U.S. economy. Migration has produced broken families. It has led to drug addiction and delinquency among youth. Migration has also produced new forms of danger, from the physical risk of the undocumented journey to the diffuse, pervasive dangers of technological mobility.

The economic changes that El Alberto has witnessed over the past few decades have been so rapid that the memory of poverty still lurks close at hand. In little more than a generation, migration has brought people the ability to buy processed foods and automobiles and electronic goods. But although their feet are covered and their bellies are full, their social worlds are far from stable. Today their worries center not on how to keep infants alive or how to coax crops from sparse soil, but rather on what to do in the event that U.S. relatives are laid off, teenagers are exposed to drugs and street culture, or the lives of loved ones are snapped short at the U.S.-Mexico border. The relatively predictable suffering of the past has been replaced by pervasive uncertainty. Survival is still a matter of concern, but survival has also become more complicated as people's lives have become more deeply enmeshed within the global economy.

On the one hand, Pentecostalism has thrived amidst the many difficulties produced by migration. Prayer and worship have become intertwined with earning and consuming, as the religion helps people navigate the disparities of wealth and poverty they encounter in a transnational context. Yet conditions have become so difficult that some have begun to step back and reexamine their goals and achievements. Recall Ramón's hypothetical immigrant, who finally stops to ask himself whether his pursuit of the American Dream has been worth the effort. It is there that the person finally realizes, Ramón explains, that material pursuits do not bring satisfaction—that the point of life is, quite simply, "to live." While migration and Pentecostal conversion alike were fueled by the desire to overcome material hardship, the Mexican Dream takes a different approach. It proposes new ways for people to "intensify joy and confront suffering" in the face of migration's challenges.[4] Before exploring the relationship between Pentecostalism and the Mexican Dream, however, it may be helpful to make some concluding remarks about the role of Pentecostalism in U.S. migration. Only by understanding the extent to which the quest for salvation has become intertwined with the quest for U.S. earnings can we appreciate the full implications of the Mexican Dream.

Pentecostalism is often perceived as excessively otherworldly, emphasizing individual salvation rather than the pursuit of large-scale social change. However, throughout these pages, we have seen countless examples of another side to the religion: a fierce non-dualism in which body and spirit are inseparable. In years past, much of Pentecostalism's appeal for indigenous converts lay in the religion's engagement with bodily experiences of illness, conflict, and healing. More recently, tensions between Pentecostalism's non-dualist and otherworldly dimensions have rendered the religion uniquely suited to the challenges of migration. Pentecostals' lives are, on the one hand, thoroughly intertwined with economic and material processes. The religion treats matters such as finding a job, increasing one's earnings, and using digital technology as valid sites for the workings of the Holy Spirit. Yet Pentecostals also look upon the world with wary eyes, for the Holy Spirit is not the only agent at work. Satan is also an active presence in human life, ever seeking to discourage, disrupt, and destroy. Thus despite their deep immersion in the world—or, perhaps, because of it—Pentecostals strive to attain spiritual purity in their bodies, churches, and homes. A pastor in the United States once compared *cristianos* to salmon swimming upstream, against the currents of a sinful society. Pentecostals draw upon divine healing and spirit exorcism to cleanse and protect their bodies from the exposure to spiritual harm that they face each day as they venture forth to earn a living. They maintain a distinct religious culture within their congregations and within their families by rejecting drinking and dancing and by looking upon non-Christian entertainment with a wary eye. Near-compulsory attendance at lengthy worship services reinforces the sense that Pentecostals' primary stock is not in this realm.

Pentecostals' partial rejection of *el mundo*, the world, can be read in part as a protest against the genuine suffering that they and others have experienced within the context of migration. The sobs people emit during nightly prayers for relatives in the United States indicate a deep ache of separation. Claims that Satan wishes to divide people and destroy families speak to the social divisions produced by migration. Claims that the U.S.-Mexico border is, like the Tower of Babel, the product of human pride, speak to a deep desire for an alternate world order. Nevertheless, from a strictly evangelical perspective, there is very little that human beings can or ought to do to bring about social change. Within Pentecostal teachings, the ultimate power to bring about wide-scale change rests with God. Individuals can appeal to God through fasting and prayer. They can also tend their own moral soil. As a result, Pentecostals have become master adapters. Immersed in problems larger than themselves and which they did not cause, *cristianos* respond by fine-tuning their own souls. When the world shows them hardship, they fast. When the world stirs up bitterness in their hearts, they forgive. Faced with illness and impurity and accident and injury, they lay on hands and heal. And when the world presents them with grueling work hours and unsavory coworkers, they take these as opportunities to strengthen their own patience and sense of character.

From a Marxian perspective, Pentecostalism may well appear disempowering, an opiate that spins fibers of self-deception as people mold themselves into ideal migrant workers within an exploitative binational system. Pentecostalism offers people access to similar congregations within whatever city they find themselves, thus helping them establish a sense of belonging as they chase fleeting jobs across the continent.[5] By providing access to fluid, transportable spiritual networks, the religion helps people adapt to a global regime of flexible accumulation.[6] Ricardo, for example, told me that one of the first things he did when he found construction work in Washington State was to locate a Spanish-speaking evangelical church. "Wherever you go, you can find them," he explained. Pentecostalism helps married couples cope with geographical separation by binding them in close-knit congregations that guard against infidelity. The religion buffers people against the chaotic, unpredictable dimensions of mobility by arming them with the weapons of spiritual warfare. Pentecostalism helped facilitate the transition from the abject poverty of a few decades past to a cycle of production, consumption, and desire that some fear is spiraling out of control today. By providing a sense of stability to laborers in motion, the religion has helped keep cities of the U.S. Southwest stocked with construction workers who build rows of new mansions, even as others sit vacant nearby.[7] The religion has inspired U.S. missionaries to reach out to residents of El Alberto while paying little heed to the root causes of migration, just as El Alberto sends its own missionaries to the regions of Mexico whose indigenous populations travel to Hidalgo to do the agricultural work left undone by those in the North.[8] The religion has helped people find encouragement and peace as they occupy the bottom rungs of the U.S. economy, and it has helped diffuse potential outrage when lives and limbs are lost at the U.S.-Mexico border.

From the perspective of the saved, however, the religion brings immeasurable empowerment. Pentecostalism provides an alternate system of authority that counters the social divisions and spatial schemes of nation-states. The religion helps inspire El Alberto's residents to demand options that their grandparents never dreamed of. It has allowed people like to Alejandro to state with confidence that "someday soon, there will be no borders." Adherents describe a profound increase in self-esteem following their conversions. An *hermana* described knowing that all women are like queens and princesses in God's eyes. A Pentecostal man in Phoenix who comes from El Alberto's neighboring town of El Dexthi once described the great joy he feels in knowing that he is "a precious jewel in God's hands." He recalls that as a recent convert in the United States, he would often repeat to himself the biblical words, "for God did not give me a spirit of fear, but of power, and love, and self-discipline," until the words had penetrated to his core. Pentecostalism teaches people how to drop negativity and bitterness from their lives like hot coals as they foster a greater capacity to forgive. Contrary to Marx's notion that religious people project their own best qualities outward onto the divine, Pentecostals in El Alberto and the United States draw upon their faith to more vividly grasp their own worth in the face of life's challenges.

The result of this spiritual alchemy is to produce individuals whose hearts have been worn until they are supple and whose self-esteem has been tested until it has grown strong. Believers state that the benefits of Pentecostalism extend even further. From an evangelical perspective, faith does not simply help people overcome hardship. Rather, faith transforms hardship into a catalyst for salvation. To recall Pastor Elpidio's words, migration "pushes us, too, to depend more on God. . . . So, to depend on God is the most beautiful thing. Wherever one may go." Pentecostals view migration as but one of many possible life events that can help bring about spiritual change. The net result is something greater and richer than the mere removal of hardship would entail.

No matter how effectively Pentecostalism responds to migration's many difficulties, however, challenges arise frequently enough that the desire for change is never wholly quenched. I think of Natalia, a young evangelical woman from El Alberto who was caught and held in a U.S. detention facility after attempting to cross the border to the United States. As a young teen, Natalia had remained in Mexico when her parents left for the United States to earn enough money to finance her younger sister's eye operation. Natalia recalls how weak she had been when faced with the task of cleaning her sister's eyes. I think of a recent conversation with Natalia in which she was disheartened by her deportation, disheartened by a minor accident that left her unable to work for several months, and disheartened by the death of a close friend whose cancer could not be cured by prayer.

Faced with repeated challenges such as these, residents of El Alberto have begun to ask whether there might be another way to seek a better life. As we have seen, a popular refrain among evangelicals is that when the religion first arrived in their town, it "opened people's eyes." Pentecostals claim that their religion lifted them out of ignorance and isolation. It helped them gain critical insight onto their oppressed position within Mexico. The religion brought clarity, for it was not the faith of the Spanish colonizers but rather the religion of the land of opportunity in the North. Nevertheless, some people now state that their eyes had remained closed to a new type of oppression, the voluntary bondage of migrant labor and consumerism. The blindfolds used to cover tourists' eyes at the close of the Caminata Nocturna represent the disorientation migrants feel at the hands of their *coyotes*. On a deeper level, the blindfolds also refer to the blindness of those who have become conditioned to accept migration as an inevitable step in life. The Caminata Nocturna is an attempt to "open people's eyes" to the deleterious effects of migration and to make them aware of the many ways in which U.S. labor is sapping away their power. In the words of Fortunato, a Pentecostal man who also serves as a guide in the Caminata Nocturna, the point of having participants wear blindfolds and then remove them is to open their eyes to the fact that "Mexico can change. Mexico will be different. And we don't need to walk to many places to be able to survive. Rather, jobs can be created here itself."

Like Pentecostalism, the Caminata Nocturna uses embodied action to bring about change. Much as Pentecostals fast and lay on hands to access the Holy Spirit, the Caminata Nocturna uses physical action to impact people at the level of flesh and blood. The border reenactment shows city people who "don't know how to walk" what it is like to suffer a bit, to get blisters, and to go hungry. Like Pentecostal beliefs, the Mexican Dream that underlies the Caminata Nocturna expresses a deep dissatisfaction with the status quo. The project is grounded in the assumption that the whole business of crossing the border and risking one's life to pursue material things in the United States is not as it should be. But the Mexican Dream calls for a new set of solutions. The Mexican Dream calls people's attention back to the basic priority of living in harmony with other human beings and with the natural world. It calls people to take a second look at the impoverished past they once sought to escape through migration and conversion, and to learn from it.

Ramón, the visionary spokesperson behind the Caminata Nocturna whose words I recounted in detail in the last chapter, does not articulate his critique of migration in terms of a supernatural struggle or in terms of a stark polarity between good and evil. Rather, he speaks about the importance of relationships. He speaks about cultivating respect for origins, and about paying attention to how one's actions affect other people and the natural world. The problem, in his view, is not that Satan divides people or that people must be saved from their inherently sinful natures. Rather, the problem is that people are living and working incorrectly. Migrant labor is the wrong kind of work because it damages the body. It is the wrong kind of work because is unbalanced, because it is unsustainable, and because it is pursued for the wrong ends.

To summarize Ramón's reflections, all good things in life take time and effort. There are no quick fixes, and money does not double itself.

Part of the trouble with migrant labor in the United States is that rapid profits are produced for the employers, at the expense of immigrants. Ramón states that people must not sacrifice quality in exchange for rapid growth or expect the land to produce faster than it is able to. He states that true satisfaction is found not in material gain but rather in the act of living itself. To live well is not to amass things. It is to be strong and healthy, to reach an advanced age. The most beautiful thing a human being can achieve is "to live to be a hundred years old." Finally, the point of work is to produce sustenance so that one might live. Done correctly and with the right intent, work ought to foster meaningful relationships and a sense of connection with the fruits of one's labor. Work should build rather than erode community. It should not produce waste.

In Ramón's view, understanding one's origin is the key to making wise choices and treating others well. "Because the important thing is origin," he explains. "Who you are, where you're going, . . . and what it is you're going to do. Are you doing good for people, or are you doing bad? Everything consists of origin." Traveling to the United States is a mistake because it requires that one negate one's origins. Yet opponents of immigration in the United States have also made the mistake of forgetting that they share the world with others. Looking down upon immigrants "is like thinking that only I am here in the world. And that's incorrect, because all of us are here in the world." By respecting where one came from, one can better remember the profound interdependence of human life.

Ramón is not the only one to speak of the importance of origins. References to the past are woven throughout the Caminata Nocturna, expressing a sense of stability amidst the very same global economic change and cultural mobility with which Pentecostalism wrestles. While Pentecostalism provides people with spiritual support as they follow fleeting jobs across the continent, the Caminata highlights what Manuel Castells calls the "space of places" as an antidote to the rootlessness of contemporary life.[9] The event begins outside the sixteenth-century church of San Alberto and closes at the bottom of a canyon whose name—the Gran Cañón—playfully roots global geography in local space. The guides point out the legends behind specific trees and riverbanks. They lead tourists through the territory of the *indios* who chastise them for disrespecting the local fauna, and they incorporate the story of that legendary "first settler," Don Beto. Little matter whether the story is of ancient or recent invention. What matters is the urge to reference particularity, rootedness, and tradition.

Like Pentecostalism, the Mexican Dream provides people with maps of space and time. It also charts out guidelines for human action. The sense of time and space embodied in the Mexican Dream, however, contrasts markedly with evangelical cosmology and sacred history. We have seen that Pentecostals make a strong distinction between pre- and post-converted states. Highlighting the flawed nature of the past allows them to emphasize the dramatic nature of the changes involved in salvation. Evangelicals do not necessarily blame themselves for the poverty they experienced in the past. Nevertheless, they are far more likely to look to the future for solutions. What matters is not so much who one is and where one came from as whether one is saved and where one is heading. A worship song frequently sung at Bethel's affiliated church in Phoenix offers a clear illustration. "*Vamos adelante, sin mirar atrás!*" the lyrics urge. "Let's go forward, without looking back!" Evangelicals fix their eyes on the end of history when Christ will return and the saved will be separated from the damned once and for all. This premillenarian vision lies in stark contrast to the creation story mentioned in chapter 2, which offers humans' continued existence as evidence that God has no reason to destroy us as he did the dwarf and giant races that came before. Within the Mexican Dream, as within this traditional creation story, the past does matter. The past matters because it contains the key for living well today. The past is a source of wisdom and resilience, and the future lies in human hands.

On one level, the Mexican Dream calls for a day when all people will be able to make a viable living without leaving their places of origin. But on another level, the Mexican Dream calls for a change that is even more wide reaching. Whereas Pentecostalism calls people to heed their own spiritual wellbeing as they buffer themselves against the dangers of mobility, the Mexican Dream calls people to extricate themselves from the web of migration and consumption that holds them captive. Whereas Pentecostal worship seeks to control the potential danger of commodities and the media, the Mexican Dream seeks to unmask commodity fetishism altogether. In the eyes of Pentecostals, spiritual struggle occurs throughout the course of earthly life, yet the end result—salvation—trumps all worldly priorities. Ramón, however, presents us with the possibility that life, life itself, is the point of things. He calls people to look toward the past as they return to a type of work that existed before dollars, work that was the energy exerted, through one's hands and feet, to obtain food. There is a compelling simplicity to this vision, for the possibility that it proposes would involve opting out of the logic of consumption and desire that helps hold the unbalanced system of labor migration intact.

The irony of the Mexican Dream is that even as people strive for it, their lives remain deeply intertwined with the United States. Yet the project is not merely a naïve attempt to recapture a complex cross-border reality safely within the container of the nation-state. The dilemma that the Caminata poses—the choice of whether or not to migrate—is shorthand for a larger and more extensive decision-making process that members of El Alberto face on an ongoing basis. Thus, the question is not whether the town's residents will be involved in migration in coming years, but rather to what extent they will be, and to what extent they will manage to create a better future for the generations to come.

Futures on Earth and in Heaven

One might ask why Pentecostals, with their concern for individual salvation and their belief in the fast-approaching end of days, would throw their efforts behind the collective, this-worldly goals outlined in the Mexican Dream. Yet human beings are creative creatures, capable of combining ideologies and practices in ways that help them face the paradoxes at hand. I recall a conversation with Paula, a woman whose views on migration and on Pentecostalism I have cited frequently throughout this book. As we sat over mugs of *café con leche* at her kitchen table, Paula spoke with joy and conviction about the workings of the Holy Spirit. As sometimes occurs in interviews, I felt chills. Paula began to speak of the end times. I had been telling her that I had a hard time understanding the notion that the end of the world is coming soon.

Paula explained that the Lord will come instantly—in the blink of an eye. Women will be standing at their *molinos* grinding corn, and one will be taken and the other will not. People will be working in the fields, and some will be taken, and others left behind. Her words drifted into a haunting tune. "*Como un relámpago*," she sang, "like a flash of lightning, like a flash of lightning—that's how the Lord's return will be!"

Paula's striking apocalyptic vision meshes with the landscape of her town, incorporating everyday, productive activities that, in her eyes, will one day be cut short. She explained that the end days will arrive soon. In the meantime, she is doing everything in her power to ensure that she will be one of the chosen. "Because how wonderful it will be to be there with the Lord, to take delight in him there!"

As Paula painted the contours of this apocalyptic scene, I recalled the uncanny joy with which she had once compared the life of a Christian to that of an animal that knows that its life belongs to the one who raised it, nurtured it, and might at any moment choose it for slaughter. And I thought how uncanny it was that a person so dedicated to the communal life of El Alberto should embrace so individualistic and otherworldly a vision. Paula is a pillar of Templo Bethel, but she is also a pillar of her community. She is the former president and driving force behind the craft cooperative that brings extra income and a measure of self-sufficiency to women from El Alberto and several other neighboring towns. As treasurer of the Gran Cañón, she occupies one of the most significant public positions held by a woman in El Alberto. She works tirelessly to improve the shared life of her brothers and sisters both within the church and without. Yet her face glows as she speaks about the end days.

Paula's vision of life swiftly interrupted reflects the reality of migration, in which separation from loved ones is frequent, deportations from the United States can be as random as lightning, and the ache for reunification is persistent. But there is more to her words than a mere separation anxiety projected onto the religious realm. It is Paula's very awareness of the precariousness of life that inspires her to strip back the veil of everyday reality, ground herself in the certainty of the eternal, and give of herself so that others may live well in the time that remains to them.

"Many people say that the important thing is here," Paula explained, in this world. However, "we are living like passengers. It's as though we've rented here, as though we've rented a house. . . . But where the second life is, is in eternity." Paula states that her faith inspired her to create the women's cooperative. "I can say that I made the cooperative . . . for the time that the Lord gives me to be here. To see, to work, . . . to eat in this life that I live. In the meantime." Yet she stresses that she does not work for her sake alone. "I am going to have another life, a second life with the Lord, and so because of that, that's precisely why I thought of doing this—so that the rest who come after me will live better."

Here limited characterizations of evangelical other-worldliness must be called into question. Paula's individualistic vision of salvation inspires her to pursue the very goals that lie at the core of the "Mexican Dream." Her words are echoed by evangelicals like Ricardo, who finds in the Caminata Nocturna a solution to the social ills plaguing the youth. Fortunato also finds inspiration for the Mexican Dream in his faith. I once observed Fortunato preach at an evening service at Templo Bethel, and then duck out early to don a black ski mask and serve as a guide in the Caminata Nocturna later on. I asked him why he helps with the project, if the end of the world is close at hand. "Ah," he answered. "As long as the Lord has not yet come . . . we have to struggle for the sake of the young people, to have a better life. . . . Because God himself said that we have to work. We're going to eat, but by the sweat of our brow! . . . God can't give things if we don't work."

Pentecostal faith and the Mexican Dream intersect not only in the lives of individuals, but also within the congregation as a whole. Pentecostals have drawn upon their faith to cross the U.S.-Mexico border, yet they have also draw upon their faith to bless and reinforce the borders of their own community—as seen in the annual interfaith service held at the site of a boundary conflict with a neighboring town. Moreover, Pentecostals have joined Catholics and non-evangelicals in publicly blessing their community's ecotourism projects. During a worship service at Templo Bethel, Pastor Elpidio showed the congregation a series of photographs depicting a prayer service he had helped lead at the Gran Cañón. The prayer marked the inauguration of several new tourist cabins. Pastor Elpidio pointed out the pastor of Sinaí and the leader of the Catholic church in the photographs, indicating the value of interreligious harmony. He explained that it was important to pray for El Alberto, for God was doing great things within the town. Rather than draw attention away from human efforts to create change, he indicated that those efforts are infused with a sense of divine purpose. His words grounded the evangelical notion of progress within the particular geography of his hometown, further reinforcing the notion that El Alberto is a "divinely blessed town."

Concluding Thoughts

Through their ecotourism projects and through their religious devotion, residents of El Alberto are claiming both the right to migrate and the right to stay home. If their actions seem contradictory, it is because the economic regime in which the residents of the town are immersed is itself fraught with contradiction. It is a system that propels people to cross borders at the same time that it criminalizes undocumented travel. It is a system fraught with global forces that seek to control the mobility of indigenous people's bodies, while also restricting their ability to live in and manage their ancestral lands.

In a recent International Tribunal of Conscience in Mexico City, delegates of the Global Alternative Forum of Peoples in Movement urged the international community to recognize migration as a universal human right. Yet participants also urged members of the international community to protect people's right *not* to migrate, as well as their right not to be forcibly displaced. As these delegates made clear, we cannot adequately support people in their efforts to cross borders in search of work if we do not also work to transform the political and economic conditions that cause them to leave home in the first place. By celebrating the dynamic, boundary-crossing dimensions of religion, scholars of religion and migration have emphasized the first half of this equation, yet they have given insufficient attention to the latter. It is necessary to understand the role of religion in mobility, yet we must also recognize, as Arturo Escobar reminds us, that "there is an embodiment and emplacement to human life that cannot be denied."[10] Throughout this book, I have sought to draw attention to both dimensions of migrants' struggle. Religions facilitate movement and territoriality alike, and they do so in ways that do not always coincide with the spatial schemes of nation-states.

Throughout these pages, I have also sought to highlight the ways in which religious narratives and practices both draw upon and shape embodied experience. To draw from Thomas Tweed's definition, religions are both "organic and cultural," that is, they are at once intimately embodied and socially shared.[11] Religious beliefs and practices reflect the fact that most humans have two eyes, two hands, and two feet. Likewise, religions within a community that is facing high levels of migration are likely to reflect the physical experiences that migration demands. In El Alberto, the hunger and exhaustion that migrants experience in the desert find direct expression in Pentecostal practice. Pentecostals draw metaphoric connections between thirst for water and thirst for the Holy Spirit. The act of ritual fasting recreates the involuntary experience of hunger that some have experienced while crossing the desert and that others have experienced as part of the poverty that drove them there. These religious practices also have a historical dimension. As Pentecostal migrants cross the U.S.-Mexico border, they draw upon physical memories of survival, protection, and prosperity that can be traced to the days when development projects were beginning to transform the material conditions of their town and converts were first beginning to receive from God the visceral gift of divine healing. They travel as members of a community that, as they see it, God has led out of poverty and into the light of salvation and abundance. They carry inherited miracle stories that reinforce their conviction that the goals they pursue are in accordance with divine will.

As people draw upon Pentecostal worship and prayer amidst migration, the religion helps them confront and overcome hardship. But that is not all Pentecostalism does. Evangelical believers in El Alberto state that their religious experiences during migration push them beyond the level of ordinary existence and into a deeper and more vivid spiritual life. That dynamic of transformation does not remain within the realm of individual experience alone. Through collective, creative action, people seize the difficulty of the migration journey and put it to work in new ways. For Pentecostals, the undocumented journey is fodder for ritual innovation. It is also fodder for evangelization, as miracles at the border are fashioned into salvation narratives. The same loss of control that has deepened some evangelicals' faith at the border has also lent creative force to the Caminata Nocturna—a performance that has been described by one of its core participants as a "rite." As scholars interested in religion and migration, we must begin to look beyond questions of how religions help people to overcome hardship by also examining how the challenges involved in migration help to fuel religious innovation, growth, and change.

Finally, the case of El Alberto challenges us to rethink the metaphors we use as we attempt to describe transborder religious expressions. While I have drawn upon transnational, global, and borderlands perspectives throughout this book, these approaches do not wholly encompass the reality I wish to describe. To apply a transnational lens, as Peggy Levitt explains, is to recognize that "some social processes happen inside nations while many others, though rooted in nations, also cross their borders."[12] Borderlands scholars, meanwhile, examine the dynamics of encounter as experienced by those who dwell in geographical or cultural peripheries. Luis León, for example, writes of the "religious poetics" through which Mexicans and Mexican-Americans negotiate the many spaces of *nepantla*, or "in-betweenness," that they encounter in Mexico City and the United States.[13] While I am indebted to transnational and borderlands theorists, I also believe that additional metaphors are needed to capture the unique quality of Mexican migration to the United States. No matter how careful we are to avoid the pitfalls of methodological nationalism, it is difficult to avoid portraying migrants as the exception—that is, as the sole agents of border crossing in an otherwise bounded world, who use religion to make sense of their own unique mobility. As we see in the case of El Alberto, Mexican migrants to the United States are not the exception. Rather, their religious lives reflect the entire texture of a deep and extensive interdependence between the two countries. As residents of El Alberto draw upon Pentecostalism, they draw upon a religion that is neither Mexican nor American, but rather multinational and relationally constituted from the start. Early Pentecostal revivals in the United States were accompanied by near-simultaneous outpourings of the Holy Spirit in Mexico and throughout Latin America.[14] The first stirrings of Pentecostalism in Kansas and Los Angeles rapidly traveled south across the border with Mexican migrant workers who soon founded their own churches. By that time, Protestantism had already gained a hold in the country, as Mexican leaders sought to build alliances with North American missionaries and investors who could help challenge the cultural dominance of Catholicism and usher in a new development agenda. In El Alberto, Pentecostalism found fertile soil in the very same material conditions that helped spur U.S. migration. The religion emerged amid cultural and economic shifts that were not bound within nations.

Mexico and the United States are linked together in innumerable ways: through their geographical proximity, through trade, and through mutually influential political actions. The religions that migrants and their loved ones draw on are an integral part of that relationship. As Douglas Massey, Jorge Durand, and Nolan Malone argue, U.S.-Mexico migration has, at least until the 1990s, functioned like a piece of "well-ordered machinery."[15] They suggest that the interaction between U.S. border policies and Mexican migration patterns produced a system with inertia of its own. The binational machinery is made of distinct cogs and wheels, but it is wired together so closely and so intricately that many of its parts have become inseparable. The metaphor is a good one, for it suggests that there is a reality and a substance to that system. It implies that those who travel to the United States do so within a broader context, a context that preexists them. To take a more organic approach, we might borrow from Martin Buber to recognize that all people's lives are "inscrutably included within the streaming mutual life of the universe."[16] We might recognize the United States and Mexico as bound together in a single, albeit exploitative, whole. Rather than ask how religions transcend the space between nations, we might ask how attention to people's religious practices can help us better glimpse the social, material, and economic structures at work beneath the constructions of the border and of the nation-state. The goal is not to envision a utopian world without borders, but rather to examine the underlying textures of power that extend throughout the continent, to explore how religions are intertwined with those power relations, and to ask how they might be transformed.

GLOSSARY OF SPANISH AND HÑÄHÑU TERMS

atole (Spanish): traditional Mesoamerican beverage made of corn
ayuno (Spanish): a religious fast
bādi (hñähñu): literally, "one who knows"; a hñähñu ritual specialist among the Sierra Otomí
bracero (Spanish): temporary contract laborer invited to work in the United States under the Bracero program beginning in the early 1940s
brujo/bruja (Spanish): witch
Caminata Nocturna (Spanish): Night Hike
cangandho (hñähñu): type of stone statue occasionally found in farm fields and believed to have been created by ancestors
cargo (Spanish): a responsibility or post fulfilled in service to the town
casa culto (Spanish): literally, "house service" or "home service"; an evangelical worship service held in a home
castillo (Spanish): "castle"; term used for a type of firework display popular in Catholic festivals
cholo (Spanish): slang term for gang member
comunidad (Spanish): community; in Mexico, a distinct legal entity referring to a group of people, usually indigenous, who are granted shared rights to a parcel of land based on their prior, customary use

comité (Spanish): committee; in El Alberto, also used as a title for those fulfilling service posts

costumbre (Spanish): traditional Mesoamerican religious and cultural practices

coyote (Spanish): paid border-crossing guide

culto (Spanish): church service

delegado (Spanish): town leader appointed by the General Assembly; serves for one year

ejido (Spanish): a type of collectively owned property established by the Mexican government

epazote (Spanish): a pungent herb native to Mexico and used for flavoring

faena (Spanish): collective work party in which members of a community gather to accomplish a task, such as repairing a road

hechicero (Spanish): sorcerer

hermano/hermana (Spanish): brother/sister; term used among evangelicals to refer to fellow members of the faith

iglesia (Spanish): church

malos aires (Spanish): "evil winds" or "bad airs"; in Mexican folk healing, these are believed to bring illness upon those who encounter them

mayordomo (Spanish): Catholic festival sponsor

migra (Spanish): slang for U.S. immigration officials

milpa (Spanish): Mesoamerican form of small-scale agriculture

mosca (Spanish): "fly"; slang for Border Patrol helicopter

nahual (Spanish): human-animal double common throughout Mesoamerican religions

nopal (Spanish): edible pad of the prickly pear cactus

pollero (Spanish): literally "poulterer"; a *coyote* or border-crossing guide

pulque (Spanish): an alcoholic beverage made of fermented agave nectar

quelite (Spanish): lambsquarters, an edible green

ropa de manta (Spanish): a rough cotton fabric or muslin

secundaria (Spanish): three-year secondary school that is roughly equivalent to middle school in the United States, usually attended by students aged 12–15

verdolaga (Spanish): purslane, an edible green

wema (hñähñu): in traditional hñähñu religion, the bones of giant ancestral beings believed to have the power both to cure people and to send illness

zaki (hñähñu): life force within hñähñu religion

NOTES

Notes to the Introduction
1. Hagan, *Migration Miracle*.
2. Tweed, *Crossing and Dwelling*.
3. Bourdieu, *Outline of a Theory of Practice*.
4. Levitt, *God Needs No Passport*, 12.
5. van Gennep, *The Rites of Passage*; Turner, *The Forest of Symbols*.
6. Hondagneu-Sotelo et al., "There's a Spirit that Transcends the Border."
7. Durand and Massey, *Miracles on the Border*.
8. Hagan, *Migration Miracle*.
9. Ibid.; Hondagneu-Sotelo, *Religion and Social Justice for Immigrants*.
10. Campese, "Beyond Ethnic and National Imagination."
11. Hagan, "Religion and the Process of Migration."
12. Miller Llana, "Mexicans 'Cross the Border.'"
13. Suarez Chávez, *Entrenamiento Para Migrantes*.
14. Tweed, *Crossing and Dwelling*, 54.
15. Ibid., 54.
16. Smith, *To Take Pace*, 104.
17. Glick-Schiller, "Transmigrants and Nation-States."
18. Immigrant workers in the Bracero Program, a U.S. immigration measure that brought millions of Mexican contract laborers to the United States from its initiation in 1942 through the end of the program in the 1960s. Andreas, *Border Games*, 34–35.
19. Butler, Wacker, and Balmer, *Religion in American Life*, 312–14.
20. Bowen, *Evangelism and Apostasy*, 41.
21. Espinosa, "Borderland Religion."
22. INEGI, "Censo de Población y Vivienda 2010."
23. Ibid.
24. INEGI, "Censo de Población y Vivienda 2010." The census states that 76 percent of the people age three and over in the community spoke an indigenous language in 2010. Although the census does not specify which indigenous language was spoken, I am not aware of any cases of people speaking indigenous languages other than hñähñu.

25. Pérez Aguilar, *Diagnóstico Situacional de Salud*.
26. Fournier García and Mondragón, "The Native Aristocracy," 47.
27. Ramsay, personal email correspondence, April 21, 2010.
28. Ibid.
29. Peña de Paz, "El Agua y Poder"; López Pérez, "Composición del Sujeto Social."
30. Olivar Vega et al., "Relaciones Interétnicas e Intraetnicas," 182.
31. Dow, *The Shaman's Touch*, 17.
32. Crummett and Schmidt, "Heritage Re-Created," 441.
33. Fournier García and Mondragón, "The Native Aristocracy."
34. Ibid., 50.
35. Ibid., 51.
36. Ramsay, personal email correspondence, April 21, 2010.
37. Crummett and Schmidt, "Heritage Re-Created," 441.
38. INEGI, "Censo de Población y Vivienda 2010."
39. Steigenga and Cleary, *Conversion of a Continent*.
40. INEGI, "Panorama de las Religiones en México en 2010."
41. Dow, "The Expansion of Protestantism in Mexico," 830.
42. INEGI, "Panorama de las Religiones en México en 2010."
43. Bowen, *Evangelism and Apostasy*.
44. Durand, Massey, and Capoferro, "The New Geography of Mexican Immigration."
45. Ibid., 2.
46. Ibid., 18.
47. Ibid., 15.
48. Fox and Rivera-Salgado, *Indigenous Mexican Migrants*, 247.
49. Ibid., 244.
50. Crummett and Schmidt, "Heritage Re-Created," 437.
51. Ibid.
52. Fox and Rivera-Salgado, *Indigenous Mexican Migrants*, 12.
53. Ibid., 19.
54. Andreas, *Border Games*; Andreas and Biersteker, *The Rebordering of North America*; Dunn, *The Militarization of the U.S.-Mexico Border*.
55. Schechner, *Performance Studies*; Grimes, *Beginnings in Ritual Studies*; Driver, *Liberating Rites*.
56. Underiner, "Playing at Border Crossing."
57. Badone and Roseman, *Intersecting Journeys*; Turner and Turner, *Image and Pilgrimage in Christian Culture*; Coleman and Eade, *Reframing Pilgrimage*; Swatos, *On the Road to Being There*.
58. Rivera-Garay has commented upon this dynamic (personal communication, 2009).
59. Williams, Steigenga, and Vásquez, *A Place to Be*.
60. Inda, "The Value of Immigrant Life."

Notes to Chapter 1

1. Pérez Aguilar, *Diagnóstico Situacional de Salud*, 1.
2. Peña de Paz, "El Agua y Poder"; López Pérez, "Composición del Sujeto Social."
3. Fournier García and Mondragón, "The Native Aristocracy," 50.
4. Schmidt and Crummett, "Heritage Re-Created," 408.
5. Rueda Vallagrán, *Patrimonio Indígena*, 45 (my translation).
6. Ibid., 49.
7. Ibid., 12.
8. Mariz, *Coping with Poverty*.
9. Ibid.
10. Turner, *The Ritual Process*.
11. Burdick, *Looking for God in Brazil*.
12. Bowen, *Evangelism and Apostasy*.
13. Thompson, *The Making of the English Working Class*.
14. Bastian, *Protestantismo y Sociedad*, 84–85.
15. Ibid., 141.
16. Ibid., 162.
17. Bowen, *Evangelism and Apostasy*, 41.
18. Ramírez, *Bodas de Oro*.
19. Ibid., 26 (my translation).
20. Ibid., 28.
21. Ibid., 26.
22. Ibid., 127.
23. Bastian, *Protestantismo y Sociedad*, 212.
24. Garret Ríos, "Modernidad y Conversión Religiosa."
25. Rueda Vallagrán, *Patrimonio Indígena*, 12.
26. Ramírez, *Bodas de Oro*, 127 (my translation).
27. Smilde, *Reason to Believe*.
28. Actual name.
29. Wright, "The Art of Being Crente," 233.
30. Cahn, *All Religions Are Good in Tzintzuntzan*, 169.
31. Weber, *The Protestant Ethic*.
32. Ibid., xiii.
33. Willems, *Followers of the New Faith*.
34. Martin, *Tongues of Fire*.
35. Ibid., 284.
36. Dow and Sandstrom, *Holy Saints and Fiery Preachers*.
37. Chance, "Changes in Twentieth-Century Mesoamerican Cargo Systems."
38. Dow and Sandstrom, *Holy Saints and Fiery Preachers*, xi.
39. Smilde, *Reason to Believe*.
40. Ibid., 145.
41. Pitarch, "La Conversión de los Cuerpos."
42. Ibid., 10.

43. Opas, "Different but the Same."
44. Mariz, *Coping with Poverty*.
45. Pitarch, "La Conversión de los Cuerpos," 9.

Notes to Chapter 2
1. Lastra, *Los Otomíes*, 327.
2. Edgerton, *Theaters of Conversion*, 167.
3. Sanchez Vásquez, *Los Elementos Rituales*, 181.
4. Ibid., 174 (my translation).
5. Ibid., 153–54.
6. Harvey, *Animism*.
7. Lastra, *Los Otomíes*, 326.
8. Sanchez Vásquez, *Los Elementos Rituales*.
9. Lastra, *Los Otomíes*, 326.
10. Sanchez Vásquez, *Los Elementos Rituales*, 203.
11. Ibid., 204.
12. Frías, "Otilia Corona."
13. Norget, *Days of Death*, 223–34.
14. Actual name.

Notes to Chapter 3
1. Rivera Garay, personal email correspondence, September 30, 2011.
2. Actual name.
3. Hondagneu-Sotelo, *Doméstica*.
4. Bastian, *Protestantismo y Sociedad*, 11.
5. Andreas, *Border Games*, 37.
6. Ibid., 34–35.
7. Fox and Rivera-Salgado, *Indigenous Mexican Migrants*, 2.
8. Blecker, "NAFTA and the Peso Collapse," 1.
9. Fox and Rivera-Salgado, *Indigenous Mexican Migrants*, 3.
10. Andreas, *Border Games*, 35–37.
11. Massey, Durand, and Malone, *Beyond Smoke and Mirrors*.
12. Ibid., 4.
13. Massey, Rugh, and Pren, "The Geography of Undocumented Mexican Migration," 137.
14. Ventura, "Learning from Globalization-Era Las Vegas."
15. Garret Ríos, "Modernidad y Conversión Religiosa," 65.
16. Sanchez Vásquez, *Los Elementos Rituales*, 239–40.

Notes to Chapter 4
1. Actual name
2. Harvey, *The Condition of Postmodernity*.
3. Ibid., 147.

4. González de la Rocha, *The Resources of Poverty*.
5. González de la Rocha, "From the Resources of Poverty."
6. Ibid., 81.
7. Kirby, "Is Globalisation Good for Us?" 2.
8. Vásquez and Friedmann Marquardt, *Globalizing the Sacred*.
9. Bastian, *Protestantismo y Sociedad*.
10. Ibid., 214.
11. I have noticed Old Testament themes taking on an even more prominent role in the worship songs common in Bethel's affiliated congregation in Phoenix.
12. Jeannerat, "Of Lizards, Misfortune, and Deliverance," 258.
13. Robbins, "On the Paradoxes of Global Pentecostalism."
14. Garrard-Burnett, "Stop Suffering?" 221.
15. Ibid.
16. Comaroff and Comaroff, "Millennial Capitalism."
17. Vásquez, "The Global Portability," 273.
18. Cunningham, "Nations Rebound?"; Vásquez, "The Global Portability."

Notes to Chapter 5
1. Sanchez Vásquez, *Los Elementos Rituales*.
2. Ibid., 226 (my translation).
3. Appadurai, "Disjuncture and Difference."
4. Whitehead and Wright, *In Darkness and Secrecy*.
5. Lastra, *Los Otomíes*, 328.
6. Sandstrom and Sandstrom, *Traditional Papermaking*, 141.
7. Ibid.
8. Ibid., 130.
9. Sanchez Vásquez, *Los Elementos Rituales*, 181.
10. Ibid., 191.
11. Lastra, *Los Otomíes*, 329.
12. Dow, *The Shaman's Touch*.
13. Sanchez Vásquez, *Los Elementos Rituales*, 165.
14. Garret Ríos, "Modernidad y Conversión Religiosa."
15. Galinier, *The World Below*, 200.
16. Dow, *The Shaman's Touch*, 49.
17. Ibid., 62–73.
18. Ibid., 135–50.
19. Galinier, *The World Below*, 68.
20. Nutini and Roberts, *Bloodsucking Witchcraft*.
21. Ibid., 128–29.
22. Whitehead and Wright, *In Darkness and Secrecy*, 1–19.
23. Ibid., 7.
24. Ibid., 15.
25. Hosea 4:6 (NIV).

26. My translation.
27. Taussig, *The Devil and Commodity Fetishism*.
28. Much as Paul H. Johnson has shown in his study of Protestant revivals and social change in nineteenth-century Rochester, NY. Johnson, *A Shopkeeper's Millennium*.
29. Meyer, "Commodities and the Power of Prayer."
30. Ibid., 248.
31. Appadurai, "Disjuncture and Difference."
32. Ibid., 56.
33. Ibid., 30.
34. Robertson, "Glocalization"; Vásquez and Friedmann Marquardt, *Globalizing the Sacred*.
35. Garrard-Burnett, "Stop Suffering?" 227.
36. Ephesians 6:12 (NIV).
37. Garrard-Burnett, "Stop Suffering?" 229.
38. Jenkins, *The Next Christendom*.
39. Wagner, *Warfare Prayer*; Wagner, *Confronting the Powers*.
40. Jorgensen, "Third Wave Evangelism," 446–47.
41. Ibid., 447.
42. Vásquez, "The Global Portability," 283.
43. Ibid., 279.
44. Note the allusion to seven years of famine described in Genesis.

Notes to Chapter 6

1. Smith, "Religion and Ethnicity in America," 1175.
2. Neville, "*Rites de Passage.*"
3. Grimes, *Deeply into the Bone*.
4. Eschbach et al., "Deaths during Undocumented Migration."
5. Andreas, *Border Games*, 108.
6. Eschbach et al., "Deaths during Undocumented Migration," 12–13.
7. McCombs et al., "Border Deaths Database."
8. Hagan, *Migration Miracle*, 158.
9. van Gennep, *The Rites of Passage*.
10. Hagan, "Religion and the Process of Migration."
11. Smilde, *Reason to Believe*, 143.
12. Wacker, *Heaven Below*.
13. Vila, *Border Identifications*.
14. NIV.
15. NIV.
16. Exodus 34: 28–28 (NIV).
17. Munn, "Symbolism in Ritual Context," 593.
18. Globus Veldman, "How Conservative Christians Talk about Climate Change."

19. Smilde, *Reason to Believe*.
20. Gooren, "Conversion Careers in Latin America."

Notes to Chapter 7
1. Vila, *Border Identifications*.
2. Pérez Aguilar, *Diagnóstico Situacional de Salud*.
3. Actual name.
4. Rivera Garay, "El Parque EcoAlberto."
5. Underiner, "Playing at Border Crossing."
6. Actual name.
7. "Don't go to the other side; it's very dangerous!" (my translation).
8. Dunn, *The Militarization of the U.S.-Mexico Border*, 3.
9. Ibid., 69.
10. Andreas and Biersteker, *The Rebordering of North America*, 7.
11. Kearney, "Borders and Boundaries of State and Self," 84–85.
12. Ibid., 85.
13. Andreas, *Border Games*, 9.
14. Ibid., 108.
15. Driver, *Liberating Rites*, 81.
16. United States Air Force, "MQ-9 Reaper."
17. Marosi, "Border Patrol Tries New Tune."
18. Ngai, *Impossible Subjects*, 5.
19. Kearney, "Borders and Boundaries of State and Self," 82.
20. U.S. Customs and Border Protection, "This is CBP."
21. Inda, "The Value of Immigrant Life," 135.
22. Ibid., 149.
23. Comaroff and Comaroff, "Naturing the Nation," 649.
24. Rodríguez, "Migration in an Era of Restriction."
25. U.S. Immigration and Customs Enforcement, "Secure Communities."
26. Bosworth and Kaufman, "Foreigners in a Carceral Age," B102.
27. Escobar, "Neoliberal Captivity," 73.
28. Peterson, "Religious Narratives and Political Protest," 30–31.
29. Schechner, *Performance Studies*.
30. Ibid., 72.
31. Parque EcoAlberto, "Caminata Nocturna."
32. Turner and Turner, *Image and Pilgrimage in Christian Culture*, 20.
33. Badone and Roseman, *Intersecting Journeys*, 6.
34. Turner, "Body, Brain, and Culture," 233–34.
35. Driver, *Liberating Rites*, 99.
36. Tweed, *Crossing and Dwelling*.
37. Long, *Significations*, 7.
38. Vila, *Border Identifications*.

Notes to Chapter 8
1. Marx, Engels, and Tucker, *The Marx-Engels Reader*, 72.
2. Shamir, "No Borders?"
3. Marx, Engels, and Tucker, *The Marx-Engels Reader*, 75.
4. Luna-Firebaugh, "The Border Crossed Us," 60.
5. Eckholm, "In Drug War, Tribe Feels Invaded."
6. Rueda Vallagrán, *Patrimonio Indígena*, 12.
7. Literally, "neither mothers nor fathers"—used here as slang for "nothing at all."
8. Overing and Passes, *The Anthropology of Love and Anger*; Opas, *Different but the Same*, 290–91.
9. Alcorn and Toledo, "The Role of Tenurial Shells," 127.
10. Rivera Garay, "La Negociación de las Relaciones de Género."
11. Annis, *God and Production*, 37.
12. Alcorn and Toledo, "The Role of Tenurial Shells," 38.
13. Annis, *God and Production*, 38.
14. Olivar Vega et al., *Visiones de la Diversidad*, 188.
15. Marosi, "Border Patrol Tries New Tune."
16. Alcorn and Toledo, "The Role of Tenurial Shells,"127.
17. Basso, *Wisdom Sits in Places*.

Notes to the Conclusion
1. Coalición de Derechos Humanos, "Arizona Recovered Human Remains Project."
2. McCombs, "No Signs of Letup."
3. Ngai, *Impossible Subjects*.
4. Tweed, *Crossing and Dwelling*.
5. Vásquez and Friedmann Marquardt, *Globalizing the Sacred*.
6. Harvey, *The Condition of Postmodernity*, 141–72.
7. Streitfeld, "Building is Booming."
8. Raesfeld, "Jornaleros Agrícolas."
9. Castells, *The Rise of the Network Society*, 13.
10. Escobar, *Territories of Difference*, 7.
11. Tweed, *Crossing and Dwelling*, 66.
12. Levitt, *God Needs No Passport*, 23.
13. León, *La Llorona's Children*.
14. González and González, *Christianity in Latin America*, 283.
15. Massey, Durand, and Malone, *Beyond Smoke and Mirrors*, 4.
16. Buber, *I and Thou*, 16.

BIBLIOGRAPHY

Alcorn, Janis B., and Víctor Manuel Toledo. "The Role of Tenurial Shells in Ecological Sustainability: Property Rights and Natural Resource Management in Mexico." In *Property Rights in a Social and Ecological Context: Case Studies and Design Applications,* ed. S. Hanna and M. Munasinghe, 123–40. Washington, DC: The World Bank, 1995.

Andreas, Peter. *Border Games: Policing the U.S.-Mexico Divide.* Ithaca, NY: Cornell University Press, 2000.

Andreas, Peter, and Thomas J. Biersteker. *The Rebordering of North America: Integration and Exclusion in a New Security Context.* New York: Routledge, 2003.

Annis, Sheldon. *God and Production in a Guatemalan Town.* Austin: University of Texas Press, 1987.

Appadurai, Arjun. "Disjuncture and Difference in the Global Cultural Economy." In *The Anthropology of Globalization: A Reader,* ed. Jonathan Xavier Inda and Renato Rosaldo, 46–64. Malden, MA: Blackwell, 2008.

Badone, Ellen, and Sharon R. Roseman. *Intersecting Journeys: The Anthropology of Pilgrimage and Tourism.* Urbana: University of Illinois Press, 2004.

Basso, Keith H. *Wisdom Sits in Places: Landscape and Language among the Western Apache.* Albuquerque: University of New Mexico Press, 2007.

Bastian, Jean Pierre. *Protestantismo y Sociedad En México.* México, D.F.: CUPSA, 1984.

Blecker, Robert A. "NAFTA and the Peso Collapse: Not Just a Coincidence." Briefing Paper, Economic Policy Institute, Washington, DC, 1997. Available online at http://www.epi.org. Accessed March 16, 2012.

Bosworth, Mary, and Emma Kaufman. "Foreigners in a Carceral Age: Immigration and Imprisonment in the U.S." *Stanford Law & Policy Review* 22, 1 (2011): B101–26.

Bourdieu, Pierre. *Outline of a Theory of Practice.* Cambridge, UK: Cambridge University Press, 1977.

Bowen, Kurt. *Evangelism and Apostasy: The Evolution and Impact of Evangelicals in Modern Mexico.* Montreal: McGill-Queen's University Press, 1996.

Buber, Martin. *I and Thou.* Edinburgh: T. & T. Clark, 1950.

Burdick, John. *Looking for God in Brazil: The Progressive Catholic Church in Urban Brazil's Religious Arena.* Berkeley: University of California Press, 1996.

Butler, Jon, Grant Wacker, and Randall Herbert Balmer. *Religion in American Life: A Short History.* New York: Oxford University Press, 2008.

Cahn, Peter. *All Religions are Good in Tzintzuntzan: Evangelicals in Catholic Mexico.* Austin: University of Texas Press, 2003.

Campese, Gioacchino. "Beyond Ethnic and National Imagination: Toward a Catholic Theology of U.S. Immigration." In *Religion and Social Justice for Immigrants,* ed. Pierrette Hondagneu-Sotelo, 175–90. Piscataway, NJ: Rutgers, 2007.

Castells, Manuel. *The Rise of the Network Society.* Malden, MA: Blackwell, 1996.

Chance, John K. "Changes in Twentieth-Century Mesoamerican *Cargo* Systems." In *Class, Politics, and Popular Religion in Mexico and Central America,* ed. Lynn Stephen and James Dow, 27–42. Washington, DC: Society for Latin American Anthropology Publication Series, American Anthropological Association, 1990.

Coalición de Derechos Humanos. "Arizona Recovered Human Remains Project," 2012. Available online at http://derechoshumanosaz.net/projects/arizona-recovered-bodies-project. Accessed July 12, 2012.

Coleman, Simon, and John Eade. *Reframing Pilgrimage: Cultures in Motion.* London: Routledge, 2004.

Comaroff, Jean, and John L. Comaroff. "Millennial Capitalism: First Thoughts on a Second Coming." *Public Culture* 12 (2000): 291–343.

Comaroff, Jean, and John L. Comaroff. "Naturing the Nation: Aliens, Apocalypse and the Postcolonial State." *Journal of Southern African Studies* 27, 3 (2001): 627–51.

Cunningham, Hilary. "Nations Rebound?: Crossing Borders in a Gated Globe." *Identities: Global Studies in Culture and Power* 11 (2004): 329–50.

Dow, James. *The Shaman's Touch: Otomí Indian Symbolic Healing.* Salt Lake City: University of Utah Press, 1986.

———. "The Expansion of Protestantism in Mexico: An Anthropological View." *Anthropological Quarterly* 78, 4 (2005): 827–50.

———. "The Sierra Ñähñu (Otomí)." In *Native Peoples of the Gulf Coast of Mexico,* ed. Alan R. Sandstrom and E. Hugo García Valencia, 231–54. Tucson: The University of Arizona Press, 2005.

———, and Alan R. Sandstrom. *Holy Saints and Fiery Preachers: The Anthropology of Protestantism in Mexico and Central America.* Westport, CT: Praeger, 2001.

Driver, Tom. *Liberating Rites: Understanding the Transformative Power of Ritual.* Boulder, CO: Westview Press, 1998.

Dunn, Timothy J. *The Militarization of the U.S.-Mexico Border, 1978–1992: Low-Intensity Conflict Doctrine Comes Home.* Austin: CMAS Books, University of Texas at Austin, 1996.

Durand, Jorge, and Douglas S. Massey. *Miracles on the Border: Retablos of Mexican Migrants to the United States.* Tucson: University of Arizona Press, 1995.

———. *Crossing the Border: Research from the Mexican Migration Project.* New York: Russell Sage, 2004.

Durand, Jorge, Douglas S. Massey, and Chiara Capoferro. "The New Geography of Mexican Immigration." In *New Destinations: Mexican Immigration in the United States,* ed. Víctor Zúñiga and Rubén Hernández-León, 1–20. New York: Russell Sage, 2005.

Ebaugh, Helen Rose, and Janet Saltzman Chafetz, eds. *Religion Across Borders: Transnational Immigrant Networks*. Walnut Creek, CA: AltaMira Press, 2002.

Eckholm, Erik. "In Drug War, Tribe Feels Invaded by Both Sides." *New York Times*, January 25, 2010, A1.

Edgerton, Samuel. *Theaters of Conversion: Religious Architecture and Indian Artisans in Colonial Mexico*. Albuquerque: University of New Mexico Press, 2001.

Eschbach, Karl, Jacqueline Hagan, and Nestor Rodríguez. "Deaths during Undocumented Migration: Trends and Policy Implications in the New Era of Homeland Security." *In Defense of the Alien* 26 (2003): 37–52.

Escobar, Arturo. *Territories of Difference: Place, Movements, Life, Redes*. Durham, NC: Duke University Press, 2008.

Escobar, Martha D. "Neoliberal Captivity: Criminalization of Latina Migrants and the Construction of Irrecuperability." Ph.D. diss., University of California, San Diego, 2010.

Espinosa, Gastón. "Borderland Religion: Los Angeles and the Origins of the Latino Pentecostal Movement in the U.S., Mexico, and Puerto Rico, 1900–1945." Ph.D. diss., University of California, Santa Barbara, 1999.

Fournier-García, Patricia, and Lourdes Mondragón. "The Native Aristocracy and the Evolution of the Latifundio in the Teotihuacán Valley, 1521–1917." In *Beyond the Hacienda: Agrarian Relations and Socioeconomic Change in Rural Mesoamerica*, ed. Neil L Whitehead, Rani T. Alexander, et al. Durham, N.C.: Duke University Press, 2003.

Fox, Jonathan, and Gaspar Rivera-Salgado. *Indigenous Mexican Migrants in the United States*. La Jolla, CA: Center for U.S.-Mexican Studies and Center for Comparative Immigration Studies, UC San Diego, 2004.

Frías, Luis. "Otilia Corona: Un Año Enterrada en Su Patio." *Criterio*, December 2009. Available online at http://www.criteriohidalgo.com/notas.asp?id=466. Last accessed July 30, 2012.

Galinier, Jacques. *The World Below: Body and Cosmos in Otomí Indian Ritual*. Boulder: University Press of Colorado, 2004.

———. "Ancestros Transnacionalizados: Memoria Histórica y Nuevos Modelos de Identificación de las Migraciones Otomíes." Paper presented at the XI International Colloquium of Otopame Studies, St. Petersburg, Florida September 14–18, 2009.

Garrard-Burnett, Virginia. "Stop Suffering? The Iglesia Universal del Reino de Dios in the United States." In *Conversion of a Continent: Contemporary Religious Change in Latin America*, ed. Timothy J. Steigenga and Edward L. Cleary, 218–38. New Brunswick: Rutgers University Press, 2007.

Garret Ríos, María Gabriela. "Modernidad y Conversión Religiosa Entre Los Otomíes De Ixmiquilpan, Hidalgo." M.A. thesis, Universidad Nacional Autónomo de México, Mexico City, 2006.

Geertz, Clifford. *The Interpretation of Cultures: Selected Essays*. New York: Basic Books, 1973.

Glick Schiller, Nina. "Transmigrants and Nation-States: Something Old and Something New in U.S. Immigrant Experience." In *Handbook of International Migration:*

The American Experience, ed. Charles Hirschman, Josh Dewind, and Philip Kasinitz, 94–119. New York: Russell Sage, 1999.

Globus Veldman, Robin. "How Conservative Christians Talk about Climate Change." Paper presented at the Association for Environmental Studies and Sciences Annual Meeting, Santa Clara, California, June 21–24, 2012.

González, Ondina E., and Justo L. González. *Christianity in Latin America: A History.* New York: Cambridge University Press, 2008.

González de la Rocha, Mercedes. *The Resources of Poverty: Women and Survival in a Mexican City.* Oxford, UK: Blackwell, 1994.

———. "From the Resources of Poverty to the 'Poverty of Resources'? The Erosion of a Survival Model." *Latin American Perspectives* 28, 4 (2001): 72–100.

Gooren, Henri. "Conversion Careers in Latin America." In *Conversion of a Continent: Contemporary Religious Change in Latin America,* ed. Timothy J. Steigenga and Edward L. Cleary, 52–72. New Brunswick, NJ: Rutgers University Press, 2007.

Grimes, Ronald. *Beginnings in Ritual Studies.* Columbia: University of South Carolina Press, 1995.

———. *Deeply into the Bone: Re-Inventing Rites of Passage.* Berkeley: University of California Press, 2000.

Hagan, Jacqueline Maria. "Religion and the Process of Migration: A Case Study of a Maya Transnational Community." In *Religion Across Borders: Transnational Immigrant Networks,* ed. Helen Rose Ebaugh and Janet Saltzman Chafetz, 75–91. Walnut Creek, CA: AltaMira Press, 2002.

———. *Migration Miracle: Faith, Hope, and Meaning on the Undocumented Journey.* Cambridge, MA: Harvard University Press, 2008.

Harvey, David. *The Condition of Postmodernity: An Enquiry into the Origins of Cultural Change.* Oxford, UK: Blackwell, 1989.

Harvey, Graham. *Animism: Respecting the Living World.* New York: Columbia University Press, 2005.

Hendricks, Tyche. "On the Border: For the Tohono O'odham, the U.S.-Mexico Border is a Recent and Difficult Development." *San Francisco Chronicle,* December, 2005. Available online at http://www.sfgate.com/news/article/ON-THE-BORDER-For-the-Tohono-O-odham-the-2558506.php#photo-2701679. Last accessed July 30, 2012.

Hondagneu-Sotelo, Pierrette. *Doméstica: Immigrant Workers Cleaning and Caring in the Shadows of Affluence.* Berkeley: University of California Press, 2001.

———. *Religion and Social Justice for Immigrants.* New Brunswick, NJ: Rutgers University Press, 2007.

———, Genelle Gaudinez, Hector Lara, and Billie C. Ortiz. "There's a Spirit the Transcends the Border: Faith, Ritual, and Postnational Protest at the U.S-Mexico Border." *Sociological Perspectives* 47, 2 (2004): 133–59.

Inda, Jonathan Xavier. "The Value of Immigrant Life." In *Women and Migration in the U.S.-Mexico Borderlands,* ed. Denise A. Segura and Patricia Zavella, 134–60. Durham and London: Duke University Press, 2007.

INEGI (Instituto Nacional de Estadistica, Geographia e Informacion). "Hablantes—Principales Lenguas—1970-2005—Nacional," July 3, 2006. Available online at http://www.inegi.org.mx. Last accessed June 25, 2010.
———. "Censo de Población y Vivienda 2010." Available online at http://www3.inegi.org.mx/sistemas/iter/consultar_info.aspx. Last accessed July 25, 2012.
———. "Panorama de las Religiones en México en 2010." Available online at http://www.inegi.org.mx/prod_serv/contenidos/espanol/bvinegi/productos/censos/poblacion/2010/panora_religion/religiones_2010.pdf. Last accessed July 25, 2012.
Jeannerat, Caroline. "Of Lizards, Misfortune, and Deliverance: Pentecostal Soteriology in the Life of a Migrant." *African Studies* 68, 2 (2009): 251–71.
Jenkins, Philip. *The Next Christendom: The Coming of Global Christianity*. Oxford, UK: Oxford University Press, 2011.
Johnson, Paul E. *A Shopkeeper's Millennium: Society and Revivals in Rochester, New York, 1815–1837*. New York: Hill and Wang, 1978.
Jorgensen, Dan. "Third Wave Evangelism and the Politics of the Global in Papua, New Guinea: Spiritual Warfare and the Recreation of Place in Telefolmin." *Oceana* 75, 4 (2005): 444–61.
Kandel, William, and Douglas S. Massey. "The Culture of Mexican Migration: A Theoretical and Empirical Analysis." *Social Forces* 80, 3 (2002): 981–1004.
Kearney, Michael. "Borders and Boundaries of State and Self at the End of an Empire." *The Journal of Historical Sociology* 4, 1 (1991): 77–93.
Kirby, Peadar. "Is Globalisation Good for Us? Introducing the Concept of Vulnerability." Working Paper no. 129, Institute for History, International and Social Studies, Aalborg University, 2004.
Lastra, Yolanda. *Los Otomíes: Su Lengua y Su Historia*. México, D.F: Universidad Nacional Autónoma de México, Instituto de Investigaciones Antropológicas, 2006.
León, Luis. *La Llorona's Children: Religion, Life, and Death in the U.S.-Mexican Borderlands*. Berkeley: University of California Press, 2004.
Levitt, Peggy. "Redefining the Boundaries of Belonging: The Institutional Character of Transnational Religious Life." *Sociology of Religion* 65 (2004): 1–18.
———. *God Needs no Passport: Immigrants and the Changing American Religious Landscape*. New York: New Press, 2007.
Long, Charles H. *Significations: Signs, Symbols and Images in the Interpretation of Religion*. Aurora, CO: The Davies Group, 1999.
López Pérez, Sócrates. "Composición del Sujeto Social en el Valle del Mezquital." Paper Presented at the 53rd Symposium of the International Congress of Americanists, Mexico City, July 19–24, 2009.
Lorentzen, Lois Ann, Joaquin Jay Gonzalez III, Kevin M. Chun, and Hien Duc Do, eds. *Religion at the Corner of Bliss and Nirvana: Politics, Identity, and Faith in New Migrant Communities*. Durham, NC: Duke University Press, 2009.
Luna-Firebaugh, Eileen. "The Border Crossed Us: Border Crossing Issues of Indigenous Peoples of the Americas." *Wicazo Sa Review* (Spring 2002): 159–81.

Mariz, Cecília Loreto. *Coping with Poverty: Pentecostals and Christian Base Communities in Brazil.* Philadelphia, PA: Temple University Press, 1994.
Marosi, Richard. "Border Patrol Tries New Tune to Deter Crossers." *Los Angeles Times,* July 4, 2005. Available online at http://articles.latimes.com/2005/jul/04/local/me-bordersongs4. Last accessed July 30, 2012.
Martin, David. *Tongues of Fire: The Explosion of Protestantism in Latin America.* Oxford, UK: Blackwell, 1990.
Marx, Karl, Friedrich Engels, and Robert C. Tucker. *The Marx-Engels Reader.* New York: Norton, 1978.
Massey, Douglas S. *New Faces in New Places: The Changing Geography of American Immigration.* New York: Russell Sage, 2008.
———, Jorge Durand, and Nolan J. Malone. *Beyond Smoke and Mirrors: Mexican Immigration in an Era of Economic Integration.* New York: Russell Sage, 2002.
———, Jacob S. Rugh, and Karen A. Pren. "The Geography of Undocumented Mexican Migration." *Mexican Studies/Estudios Mexicanos* 26, 1 (2010): 129–52.
McCombs, Brady. "No Signs of Letup in Entrant Deaths." *Arizona Daily Star,* December 27, 2009, B1.
———, et al. "Border Deaths Database: Total Border Deaths by Calendar Year." *Arizona Daily Star,* March 31, 2011. Available online at http://azstarnet.com/news/local/border/html_c104ad38-3877-11df-aa1a-001cc4c002e0.html. Last accessed July 30, 2012.
Meyer, Birgit. "Commodities and the Power of Prayer: Pentecostalist Attitudes Toward Consumption in Contemporary Ghana." In *The Anthropology of Globalization: A Reader,* ed. Jonathan Xavier Inda and Renato Rosaldo, 247–69. Malden, MA: Blackwell, 2002.
Miller Llana, Sara. "Mexicans 'Cross the Border'—at a Theme Park." *Christian Science Monitor,* February 21, 2007, 1.
Moreno Alcántara, Beatriz, María Gabriela Garret Ríos, and Ulises Fierro Alonso. *Otomíes Del Valle Del Mezquital.* México, D.F: CDI, Comisión Nacional para el Desarrollo de los Pueblos Indígenas, 2006.
Munn, Nancy D. "Symbolism in Ritual Context." In *Handbook of Social and Cultural Anthropology,* ed. John J. Honigmann, 579–612. Chicago: Rand McNally, 1973.
Neville, Grace. "*Rites de Passage:* Rituals of Separation in Irish Oral Tradition." In *New Perspectives on the Irish Diaspora,* ed. Charles Fanning, 117–30. Carbondale and Edwardsville: Southern Illinois University Press, 2000.
Ngai, Mae M. *Impossible Subjects: Illegal Aliens and the Making of Modern America.* Princeton, NJ: Princeton University Press, 2004.
Norget, Kristin. *Days of Death, Days of Life: Ritual in the Popular Culture of Oaxaca.* New York: Columbia University Press, 2005.
Nutini, Hugo G., and John M. Roberts. *Bloodsucking Witchcraft: An Epistemological Study of Anthropomorphic Supernaturalism in Rural Tlaxcala.* Tucson: University of Arizona Press, 1993.
Olivar Vega, Beatriz, Beatriz Moreno Alcántara, and Gabriela Garret Ríos. "Relaciones Interétnicas e Intraetnicas de los Nähñu del Valle del Mezquital, Hidalgo."

In *Visiones de la Diversidad: Relaciones Interétnicas e Identidades Indígenas en el México Actual,* ed. Miguel A. Bartolomé, 177–223. Mexico: Instituto Nacional de Antropologia e Historia, 2005.

Opas, Minna. "Different but the Same: Negotiation of Personhoods and Christianities in Western Amazonia." Ph.D. diss., University of Turku, Finland, 2008.

Orsi, Robert. "Everyday Miracles: The Study of Lived Religion." In *Lived Religion in America: Toward a History of Practice,* ed. David D. Hall, 3–21. Princeton, NJ: Princeton University Press, 1999.

Overing, Joanna, and Alan Passes. *The Anthropology of Love and Anger: The Aesthetics of Conviviality in Native Amazonia.* New York: Routledge, 2000.

Parque EcoAlberto. "Caminata Nocturna," undated. Available online at http://parqueecoalberto.com. Last accessed April 12, 2007.

Peña de Paz, Francisco. "El Agua y Poder Local En El Valle Del Mezquital." Paper presented at the 53rd Symposium of the International Congress of Americanists, Mexico City, July 19–24, 2009.

Pérez Aguilar, Angélica María. *Diagnóstico Situacional de Salud 2008.* Ixmiquilpan, Hidalgo: Colegio de Estudios Científicos y Tecnológicos del Estado de Hidalgo, 2008.

Peterson, Anna L. "Religious Narratives and Political Protest." *Journal of the American Academy of Religion* 64, 1 (1996): 27–44.

Pitarch, Pedro. "La Conversión de los Cuerpos: Singularidades de las Identificaciones Religiosas Indígenas." *Liminar: Estudios Sociales y Humanísticos* 2, 2 (2004): 6–17.

Raesfeld, Lydia Josefa. "Jornaleros Agrícolas En El Valle Del Mezquital." Paper presented at the 53rd Symposium of the International Congress of Americanists, Mexico City, July 19–24, 2009.

Ramírez, Raymundo. *Bodas de Oro: Movimiento de La Iglesia Independiente Pentecostés.* Pachuca, Hidalgo: Libro Histórico, 1972.

Reyes, Belinda I. "U.S. Immigration Policy and the Duration of Undocumented Trips." In *Crossing the Border: Research from the Mexican Migration Project,* ed. Jorge Durand and Douglas S. Massey, 299–320. New York: Russell Sage, 2004.

Rivera Garay, María Guadalupe. "La Negociación de las Relaciones de Género en el Valle de Mezquital: un Acercamiento al Caso de la Participación Comunitaria de Mujeres Hñahñus." *Estudios de cultural otopame* 5 (2006): 249–66.

———. "Ecoturismo, migración y desarrollo comunitario: El caso de El Alberto." Paper presented at the 53rd Symposium of the International Congress of Americanists, Mexico City, July 19–24, 2009.

———. "El Parque Ecoalberto: Una Alternativa de Desarrollo Comunitario en una Comunidad de Migrantes en el Valle del Mezquital." Paper presented at the XI International Colloquium of Otopame Studies, St. Petersburg, Florida, September 14–18, 2009.

Robbins, Joel. "On the Paradoxes of Global Pentecostalism and the Perils of Continuity Thinking." *Religion* 33, 3 (2003): 221–31.

Robertson, Roland. "Glocalization: Time-Space and Homogeneity-Heterogeneity." In *Global Modernities,* ed. Mike Featherstone, Scott Lash, and Roland Robertson, 25–44. London: Sage, 2005.

Rodríguez, Néstor P. "Migration in an Era of Restriction." Paper presented at the XXX International Congress of the Latin American Studies Association, San Francisco, California, May 23–26, 2012.

Rouse, Roger. "Mexican Migration and the Social Space of Postmodernism." In *The Anthropology of Globalization: A Reader*, ed. Jonathan Xavier Inda and Renato Rosaldo, 157–71. Malden, MA: Blackwell, 2002.

Rueda Vallagrán, Quintín. *Patrimonio Indígena del Valle del Mezquital*. Pachuca, Hidalgo, México: Talleres Gráficos del Estado, 1951.

Sanchez Vásquez, Sergio. *Los Elementos Rituales del Paisaje Cultural en Ixmiquilpan, Hidalgo*. Ph.D. diss., Escuela Nacional de Antropologia e Historia, INAH, Mexico, 2003.

Sandstrom, Alan R., and Pamela Effrein Sandstrom. *Traditional Papermaking and Paper Cult Figures of Mexico*. Norman: University of Oklahoma Press, 1986.

Schechner, Richard. *Performance Studies: An Introduction*. London: Routledge, 2002.

Schmidt, Ella, and María Crummett. "Heritage Re-Created: Hidalguenses in the United States and Mexico." In *Indigenous Mexican Migrants in the United States*, ed. Jonathan Fox and Gaspar Rivera-Salgado, 401–15. La Jolla, CA: Center for U.S.-Mexican Studies, UCSD/Center for Comparative Immigration Studies, UCSD, 2004.

Shamir, Ronen. "No Borders? Notes on Globalization as a Mobility Regime." *Sociological Theory* 23, 2 (2005): 197–217.

Smilde, David. *Reason to Believe: Cultural Agency in Latin American Evangelicalism*. Berkeley: University of California Press, 2007.

Smith, Jonathan Z. *To Take Place: Toward Theory in Ritual*. Chicago: University of Chicago Press, 1987.

Smith, Timothy L. "Religion and Ethnicity in America." *The American Historical Review* 83, 5 (1978): 1155–85.

Steigenga, Timothy J., and Edward L. Cleary. *Conversion of a Continent: Contemporary Religious Change in Latin America*. New Brunswick, NJ: Rutgers University Press, 2007.

Streitfeld, David. "Building is Booming in a City of Empty Houses." *New York Times*, May 16, 2010, A1.

Suarez Chávez, Aida. *Entrenamiento Para Migrantes: Periodismo Cultural* (with photographs by Carlos Enrique Sevilla). Pachuca de Soto, Mexico: Consejo Estatal para la Cultura y las Artes de Hidalgo, 2011.

Swatos, William H, ed. *On the Road to Being There: Studies in Pilgrimage and Tourism in Late Modernity*. Leiden: Brill, 2006.

Taussig, Michael. *The Devil and Commodity Fetishism in South America*. Chapel Hill: University of North Carolina Press, 1980.

Thompson, E. P. *The Making of the English Working Class*. London: Penguin, 1991.

Turner, Victor Witter. *The Forest of Symbols: Aspects of Ndembu Ritual*. Ithaca, NY: Cornell University Press, 1967.

———. *The Ritual Process: Structure and Anti-Structure*. Chicago: Aldine Publishing Company, 1969.

———. "Body, Brain, and Culture." *Zygon* 18, 3 (1983): 221–45.

———, and Edith L. B. Turner. *Image and Pilgrimage in Christian Culture: Anthropological Perspectives*. New York: Columbia University Press, 1978.

Tweed, Thomas A. *Our Lady of the Exile: Diasporic Religion at a Cuban Catholic Shrine in Miami*. New York: Oxford University Press, 2002.

———. *Crossing and Dwelling: A Theory of Religion*. Cambridge, MA: Harvard University Press, 2006.

Underiner, Tamara L. "Playing at Border Crossing in a Mexican Indigenous Community . . . Seriously." *The Drama Review* 55, 2 (2011): 11–32.

U.S. Air Force. "MQ-9 Reaper," January 5, 2012. Printable fact sheet available online at http://www.af.mil/information/factsheets/factsheet.asp?id=6405. Last accessed July 30, 2012.

U.S. Customs and Border Protection. "'This is CBP': A Fast-Paced Video Glimpse of Border Security," 2008. Available online at http://www.cbp.gov/xp/cgov/newsroom/multimedia/video/border_security_video. Last accessed April 11, 2008.

U.S. Immigration and Customs Enforcement. "Secure Communities," undated. Available online at http://www.ice.gov/secure_communities. Last accessed November 15, 2011.

van Gennep, Arnold. *The Rites of Passage*. Chicago: University of Chicago Press, 1960.

Vásquez, Manuel A. "The Global Portability of Pneumatic Christianity: Comparing African and Latin American Pentecostalisms." *African Studies* 68, 2 (2009): 273–86.

———, and Marie Friedmann Marquardt. *Globalizing the Sacred: Religion Across the Americas*. New Brunswick, NJ: Rutgers University Press, 2003.

Ventura, Patricia. "Learning from Globalization-Era Las Vegas." *Southern Quarterly* 42, 1 (2003): 97–112.

Vila, Pablo. *Border Identifications: Narratives of Religion, Gender, and Class on the U.S.-Mexico Border*. Austin, TX: University of Texas Press, 2005.

Wacker, Grant. *Heaven Below: Early Pentecostals and American Culture*. Cambridge, MA: Harvard University Press, 2001.

Wagner, Charles Peter. *Warfare Prayer*. Ventura: Regal Books, 1992.

———. *Confronting the Powers: How the New Testament Church Experienced the Power of Strategic-Level Spiritual Warfare*. Ventura: Regal Books, 1996.

Warner, R. Stephen, and Judith G. Wittner, eds. *Gatherings in Diaspora: Religious Communities and the New Immigration*. Philadelphia, PA: Temple University Press, 1998.

Weber, Max. *The Protestant Ethic and the Spirit of Capitalism*. New York: Routledge, 2001.

Whitehead, Neil L., and Robin Wright. *In Darkness and Secrecy: The Anthropology of Assault Sorcery and Witchcraft in Amazonia*. Durham, NC: Duke University Press, 2004.

Willems, Emílio. *Followers of the New Faith: Culture Change and the Rise of Protestantism in Brazil and Chile*. Nashville, TN: Vanderbilt University Press, 1967.

Williams, Philip J., Timothy J. Steigenga, and Manuel A. Vásquez. *A Place to Be: Brazilian, Guatemalan, and Mexican Immigrants in Florida's New Destinations*. New Brunswick, NJ: Rutgers University Press, 2009.

Wright, Robin. "The Art of Being *Crente:* The Baniwa Protestant Ethic and the Spirit of Sustainable Development." *Identities: Global Studies in Culture and Power* 16 (2009): 202–26.

INDEX

Action: collective, 6; creative, 6; instrumental, 159; prayer in, 137–42
Agency: location of, 116; Meyer on, 113; of non-human beings, 107–8
Agricultural practices: health and, 172–74; of U.S., 172–73. See also *Milpa*
Agua EcoAlberto, 64
El Alberto: boundaries of, 188–89; Cipriano on, 35–37; community study of, 29; daily life in, 146–47; development of, 12, 22, 44–47; economy of, 2, 12, 168, 194, 205; governance of, 44, 46, 183–84; harmony in, 54, 64–67, 187; history of, 31–33, 49; housing situation in, 87–88; isolation of, 12; labor requirement of, 184–86; Las Vegas, NV and, 80–81; migration increase in, 126, 188; Otomí community, 1; Pentecostalism in, 2–4, 8–10, 12–14, 22–23, 30, 207–8; population of, 10; Protestantism in, 42; Raúl on, 55–56; religious transformation in, 13, 39–44, 47; as transnational social field, 8; violence in, 33–37
San Alberto festival, 19, 58, 63
Alcohol, 36; overcoming, 50; Pentecostalism and, 34
Alejandro (informant): border crossing of, 122, 132–33; religious transformation of, 122–23, 133; on salvation, 135–36
Alienation, 171
American Dream, 2, 83, 141–42, 194–95
American wake, 124–25
Andreas, Peter, 126; on border, as political stage, 161
Annunciation House, 4
Appadurai, Arjun, on imagination, 114
Ayuno. See Fasting
Aztec Triple Alliance, 11, 31
Azusa Street revival, 9

Bad air (*malos aires*), 107, 109, 210
Bādi (ritual specialists), 108, 110, 209
Balneario (swimming pool area), 10–11. See also Parque EcoAlberto
Barrera, Eulogio, 66–67
Base ecclesial communities (*comunidades eclesiales de base*), 63
Bastian, Jean Pierre, on Pentecostalism, 94–95
Bearing witness, in Pentecostalism, 65
Bethel, Templo, 18
Beto, Don, 174, 201; Caminata Nocturna and, 180–87; collective labor and, 182; creation of, 181–82; significance of, 182
Bible: hñähñu translation of, 38–39; *lluvia de versos* (rain of verses), 95; in Pentecostalism, 95
Biopower, 26
Body, as social product, 50–51
Border, as political stage, 162–64, 167; Andreas on, 161; collective imagination of, 192–93; making of, 165–66
Border crossing: accidents during, 122, 132, 134, 140; of Alejandro, 122, 132–33; Arizona-Sonora section of, 191; connotations of, 26; deaths, 141, 158, 191–92; early experiences of, 79–80; faith in, 204–5; as high-risk game, 21–22; as rite of passage, 187; significance of, 3; simulation of, 1–2, 7; spiritual rewards of, 129
Border danger, 124, 152–53, 158, 174; rise in, 24, 81, 145–46
Border enforcement: changing nature of, 154; explicit logic of, 191–92; "illegal alien" creation through, 165–66; performative dimensions of, 158–61; subverting, 161–67
Border militarization, 5, 14, 16; dangers of, 125–26, 162; death and, 160; enacting, 152–58; trend of, 153–54

>> 231

Border Patrol agents: in Caminata Nocturna, 151–52; encounters with, 154–55; heightened presence of, 154; language barrier of, 155; migrants confronted by, 154
Border policy: Inda on, 26; rationale behind, 192
Border politics, terrorism and, 154
Border reenactment. *See* Caminata Nocturna
Braceros (temporary contract laborers), 9, 29, 38, 77, 209
Brewer, Jan, 159
Brujo/bruja. *See* Witch
Buber, Martin, 208

Cahn, Peter, 47
Caminata Nocturna, 1–2, 55, 145, 209; blindfold significance in, 198–99; Border Patrol chase in, 151–52; characters in, 175–76; development of, 149; Don Beto and, 180–87; embodiment in, 199; expectations of, 165; humor in, 164–65; message of, 168; Mexican Dream and, 167–69; news article about, 6–7; opening speech of, 150–51; participants in, 150; Pentecostalism and, 25; performance of, 7, 22, 24–25, 162; physical extremity of, 153–54; play in, 165–66; purpose of, 148, 161–63, 167, 174; reality of, 155–56, 186–87; research into, 15–22; as ritual, 166–67; Salustio on, 148–49; self-transformation through, 163; tourist experience of, 150–58, 165
Cangandhos (stone statues), 209; Sánchez Vásquez on, 107
Capitalism, Protestantism and, 47–48
Cargo system (unpaid work, socio-religious structure), 48, 60–61, 66, 209; demands of, 184–85; Ramón's experience with, 169; as secular, 184
Casa cultos (home services), 88, 209
Castells, Manuel, 200–201
Catholic festival sponsor (mayordomo), 35, 64, 210
Catholicism, 22–23; Cipriano on, 35–37, 39; on *fiesta* system, 57–58; identity and, 13; migration and, 140–41; narratives of, 65; Pentecostal conversion and, 59–60; Pentecostalism and, 54–55; perspective on change of, 54–55; Post-Vatican II changes in, 60; poverty and, 41; on progress, 66–67; Tomás on, 36–37; transnational presence of, 63
Católicos (Catholics), 14
CEBs. *See Comunidades eclesiales de base*
Cholo (gang member), 119, 209
Christians (*Cristianos*), 14, 195–96
Cipriano (informant): on Catholicism, 35–37, 39; conversion of, 42–47; on El Alberto, 35–37; progress of, 45–46
Cirino (informant): inspiration of, 178; performance of, 177–78; on town boundaries, 188–89
Civic activities, in relation to religion, 20
Clausura (school closing festival), 7–8
Collective labor, 13, 23, 62; Don Beto and, 182; emergence of, 55; *fiesta* system compared to, 64–65; productivity compared with, 183; projects of, 182
Collective land ownership. *See Comunidad*
Collective organizing, 2, 26; culture of, 67; development and, 61
Colonia Cristiana del Calvario, 41
Comaroff, Jean and John, on economy, 100
Comité (committees), 183–84, 210
Commodity fetishism, 113, 171, 201
Communally owned land (*ejidos*), 187, 210
Communication, to U.S., 88–89
Communitas, 35, 163
Comunidad (collective land ownership, legally recognized indigenous community), 10, 93, 95, 187, 209; boundaries of, 188; membership in, 183–85; selective performance of, 179; significance of, 183; survival and, 187–89
Comunidades eclesiales de base (base ecclesial communities, CEBs), 63
Consejo Mexicano de la Bahía de Tampa (Mexican Council of Tampa Bay), 15
Consumerism, Ramón on, 169–71
Conversion: Catholicism and, 59–60; chain of, 42, 50; of Cipriano, 42–47; development and, 49; driving forces of, 47, 89, 104; embodied, 50–53; emergence of, 69, 193; indigenous motivations for, 31; migration and, 163; of Roberto, 105; Smilde on, 133; stories of, 31, 53; survival and, 50–53, 61, 193–94; Tomás on, 42, 50; witchcraft and, 104–5
Convivir (spend close time together), 18
Costumbre (custom), 57, 59, 89, 108–9, 210
Coyote (guide), 5, 24, 78, 88, 163–64, 210;

faith in, 132, 158; uncertainly associated with, 150–51
Creation myths, 57
Creative action, 6. *See also* Performance
Cristianos (Christians), 14, 195–96
Cross. *See* La Santa Cruz
Culto (church service), 210
Curanderismo (Mexican folk healing), 9
Customs (*costumbre*), 57, 59, 89, 108–9, 210

Dark shamanism, Wright and Whitehead on, 108–9
The dead (*los muertos*), 107
Death: during border crossing, 141, 158, 191–92; border militarization and, 160; rites, 124–25; as symbol of sacrifice, 24
Delegado (town leader), 45–46, 147, 182, 210
Department of Homeland Security, 4
Development: of Caminata Nocturna, 149; collective organizing and, 61; conversion and, 49; of El Alberto, 12, 22, 44–47; by PIVM, 48–49; religion and, 12–13; in Valle del Mezquital, 29, 31–33
Devil: Internet and, 117, 120; pact with, 102–3; Taussig on, 112. *See also* Satan
Devotional paintings (*retablos*), 6
Dollars, attraction of, 82–83
Domestic labor, 71–72, 74
Drones, in border enforcement, 159
Dunn, Timothy, on Low Intensity Conflict, 153
Durand, Jorge, 80, 208

Echeverría, Luis, 66
Economy: activities of, 71; Comaroffs on, 100; contradictions in, 100; of El Alberto, 2, 12, 168, 194, 205; flexible accumulation, 92; migration and, 83; Protestantism and, 49; of U.S., 171
Ejidos (communally owned land), 187, 210
Elpidio, Pastor, 88, 95, 98–99; on evil, 110–16; on fasting, 138–39; on God's will, 137; on immigration, 136–37; on migration, 127–28, 198; on *nahuales*, 103, 109; on prayer, 128–29
Embodiment, 22; in Caminata Nocturna, 199; conversion and, 50–53; Escobar on, 205; in Pentecostalism, 89–90, 95–96
Emilia (informant), 90–94
Empowerment: in Caminata Nocturna, 166; in Pentecostalism, 166

End times, 116; immigration realities and, 20; Paula on, 202–3
Escobar, Arturo, on embodiment, 205
Esquivel, Prudencio, 41
Evangélicos (evangelicals), 14, 18
Evil, 106; expressions of, 109; manifestations of, 102–4, 113–14; symbols of, 110–12
Evil eye (*mal de ojo*), 119

Faenas (traditional work parties), 41, 183–84, 188, 210
Faith: in border crossing, 204–5; in *coyotes*, 132, 158; Paula on, 134; salvation through, 198; undocumented journey and, 129
Fasting (*ayuno*), 6, 96, 130, 206, 209; as corrective ritual, 137–40; Elpidio on, 138–39; migration and, 98–99; prayer compared to, 97; preparations for, 138; as reciprocal exchange, 98–99
Fiesta system, 23, 52, 89; Catholicism on, 57–58; changes to, 55, 59–64; collective labor compared to, 64–65; dates of, 57; harmony and, 34; Norget on, 60–61; social subjugation and, 35–37, 39
Flexible accumulation, Harvey on, 92
Food: indigenous identity and, 179; migration and changes in, 69, 172–73; traditional, 72, 210–11. *See also* Fasting (*ayuno*)

Gang member (*cholo*), 119, 209
Gang membership, violence and, 93–94
Garrard-Burnett, Virginia, on prosperity theology, 99–100
Garret Ríos, Gabriela, on reciprocity, 107
General Agreement on Tariffs and Trade (1986), 93
Global Alternative Forum of Peoples in Movement, 205
Globalization: social effects of, 93–94; spiritual pressures of, 117–18
Glocalization, 114
Glossolalia (speaking in tongues), 9
God's will: Elpidio on, 137; Marta on, 137
Gooren, Henri, on conversion, 141
Gran Cañón, 10, 148, 167, 200. *See also* Parque EcoAlberto
Gringo (white person), 78–79
Guadalajara, migration to, 73
guide. See *Coyote*

Hagan, Jacqueline: on migration risks, 3, 126; on Pentecostal Maya migrants, 6
Harmony, 49; in El Alberto, 54, 64–67, 187; emergence of, 51–52; *fiesta* system and, 34; illness and, 52; lack of, 33–34; religion and, 66
Harvey, David, on flexible accumulation, 92
Healing stories, 51–52; causality logic in, 108–9; of youth, 118–19
Health, agricultural practices and, 172–74
Hechicero (sorcerer), 34, 210; witches as distinct from, 108
Heriberto (informant), on U.S. income, 81–82
Hñähñu: conquest of, 31; cosmos, 106–9; identity, 12; illness and healing to, 22; as preferred term, 11; religion among, 57, 106–7; resistance by, 11–12; traditional religious practices of, 34–35
Holy Spirit: active intervention in world of, 115; as currency, 98; healing and, 9, 52; workings of, 195
Holy Week (*Semana Santa*), 148
Household survival strategies, 92–93
Housing situation, in El Alberto, 87–88
Human-animal doubles (*nahuales*), 82, 106, 210; Elpidio on, 103, 109

ICIP. *See* Iglesia Cristiana Independiente Pentecostés
Identity, 124; Catholicism and, 13; hñähñu, 12; indigenous, 169, 179–80; Protestantism and, 13
Iglesia Cristiana Independiente Pentecostés (ICIP): founding of, 39–41; growth of, 12; historical study produced by, 31; organizational divisions within, 12–13. *See also* Pentecostalism
IIRIRA. *See* Illegal Immigration Reform and Immigrant Responsibility Act
Illegal alien, as term, Ngai on, 159–60
Illegal immigration, 26, 76–77, 191–92
Illegal Immigration Reform and Immigrant Responsibility Act (IIRIRA), 153–54, 160
Illness: causes of, 51, 62, 103, 104; harmony and, 52; to hñähñu, 22; non-dualistic approach to, 9, 22
Imagination, Appadurai on, 114
Immigrant detention industry, 160–61
Immigration: climate of in U.S., 25; Elpidio on, 136–37; local law enforcement and, 19–20; Neville on, 124–25; opponents of, 200; restrictions to, 79–80; trends in, 80–81; U.S. policies on, 76–77, 80, 136–37, 153–54. *See also* Illegal immigration; Migration
Immigration Act (1965), 77
Immigration and Naturalization Services (INS), 4, 125–26, 158–59
Immigration enforcement post-9/11, 4
Immigration officials. *See* Migra
Immigration Reform and Control Act (1986), 14, 80
Income. *See* U.S. income
Inda, Jonathan Xavier: on border policy, 26; on undocumented immigrants, 160
Indians (*indios*), representations of, 175–78, 180
Indigenous community. *See* Comunidad
Indigenous identity, 169, 179–80
Indigenous migration. *See* Migration
Indigenous population, Valle del Mezquital and, 11
Indigenous religiosity, within Pentecostalism, 22
Indios (Indians), representations of, 175–78, 180
Individualism, U.S. society and, 174
Inequality, structural, 79
INS. *See* Immigration and Naturalization Services
Inseguridad (lack of safety), 113
Instrumental action, performance and, 159
International Tribunal of Conscience, 205
Internet, Pentecostal interpretations of, 117, 120
Irrigation, 11, 32, 36, 61–62
Isaías, Pastor, 46–47; migration advice of, 128
Ixmiquilpan, Hidalgo, 10, 13; migration to, 70

Jackson, Michael, 111
Juárez, Chihuahua, 4

Kearney, Michael, on border crossing, 158

Labor: cycle of, 170; profits from, 200; requirement, 184–86; shortages, 77; systemic exploitation of, 74, 169; value of, 172. *See also Braceros*; Collective labor; Domestic labor

Labor migration. *See* Migration
Language: barrier, of Border Patrol agents, 155; Summer Institute of Linguistics and, 38–39; Tower of Babel and, 136; women and, 74. *See also* Otomí language
Las Vegas, NV, El Alberto and, 80–81
Leonardo (informant), 66
Levitt, Peggy: on religion, 3; on transnationalism, 207
Life crisis, migration as, 5, 187
Life force (*zaki*), 108, 211
Liminal zone, border as, 158
Limpias (spiritual cleansings), 108
Lived religion, 22. *See also* Religion
Local law enforcement, immigration and, 19–20
Long, Charles, on religion, 165
Love, as divine commandment, 136–37
Low Intensity Conflict, Dunn on, 153
Lucha libre (Mexican freestyle wrestling), 105
Lucita (informant): on religious division, 62–63; on religious transformation, 54

Mal de ojo (evil eye), 119
Malone, Nolan, 80, 208
Malos aires (bad air), 107, 109, 210
Marginality, 142
Mariz, Cecilia: on poverty, 33; on religion, 51
Marta (informant): father of, 104–5; on God's will, 137; on migration, 79, 131–32; recollections of, 72–74; on religion, 75
Martin, David, on Protestantism, 48
Massey, Douglas, 80, 208
Mateo (informant), on U.S. income, 81
Mayordomo (Catholic festival sponsor), 35, 64, 210
Mbonthi (region name), 11
Mestizo (of Native American and European ancestry), 38–39, 74
Metaphor, 130, 207
Mexican Council of Tampa Bay (Consejo Mexicano de la Bahía de Tampa), 15
Mexican Dream, 2, 4, 24–25, 124, 146; approach of, 195; Caminata Nocturna and, 167–69; as guidance for action, 201–2; Pentecostalism and, 193–204; struggle for, 189
Mexican Economic Miracle, 32, 71
Mexican folk healing (*curanderismo*), 9
Mexican freestyle wrestling (*lucha libre*), 105
Mexico: in 1940s to 1970s, 32; agribusiness in, 77; Ixmiquilpan, Hidalgo, 10, 13, 70; Pachuca, Hidalgo, 10–12, 39; Protestantism in, 37–39; U.S. and, 208
Mexico City, migration to, 70–76
Meyer, Birgit, on agency, 113
Mezquital, Valle del, 1; as arid region, 11, 31; development in, 29, 31–33; as indigenous population center, 11; land conflicts in, 186; mountain folklore in, 82–83; Pentecostalism in, 9; poverty in, 31–32. *See also* Patrimonio Indígena del Valle del Mezquital
Middle school (*secundaria*), 188, 211
Migra (U.S. immigration officials), 128, 131, 155, 163–64, 210
Migrant: Border Patrol agent confrontation of, 154; as expendable, 91; exploitation of, 74, 169; Pentecostal Maya, 6; risks for, 126–27; rural, 77; sacrifices of, 147; surrender by, 163; typical experiences of, 79–80, 92; working conditions of, 74. *See also* Undocumented migrant
Migrant women, resilience of, 5–6. *See also* Women
Migration: advice, 127–28; benefits of, 68–69; biblical desert metaphors and, 130; Catholicism and, 140–41; challenges of, 3, 5, 194; changing patterns of, 14; collective action and, 6; context of, 24; conversion and, 163; dangers of, 124, 174; early stories of, 70; economy and, 83; from El Alberto, 126, 188; Elpidio on, 127–28, 198; emergence of, 69–70; establishment of, 14; fasting and, 98–99; gendered dimensions of, 72–73; to Guadalajara, 73; Hagan on, 3, 126; homecoming from, 71–72; indigenous, 15; internal, 15, 29, 69–70, 76, 81; Isaías on, 128; to Ixmiquilpan, 70; jobs available from, 71; as life crisis, 5, 187; Marta on, 79, 131–32; to Mexico City, 70–76; NAFTA and, 15; negative influences of, 119–20; Pentecostalism and, 18, 22–24, 141–42, 192; poverty and, 170–71; progress and, 66; Ramón on, 169–70, 189, 199; realities of, 90–94; reincorporation following, 131; religion and, 2–10, 75–76, 126–27, 130; rise in, 23, 71; Roberto on, 71, 78; social networks and, 2–3; stories of, 161–67; survival and, 69, 194; as theologizing experience, 124–26, 131; theology of, 6; transnational, 154; trends in, 80–81; to U.S., 76–81; for women, 70–74. *See also* Immigration; Theology, of migration

Migration narratives, religion and, 23, 76, 81
Millenarianism. See End times
Milpa (type of agriculture), 56–57, 185–86, 210
Mobility: forms of, 104; protection from, 120–21
Mobility regime, 172
Morality, as embodied, 50
MQ-9 Reaper, 159
Los muertos (the dead), 107
el mundo (the world), 166; Pentecostal rejection of, 196
Munn, Nancy, on symbolic acts, 139
Music: Adoración (devotional song), 94; Alabanza (song of praise), 94

NAFTA. See North American Free Trade Agreement
Nahuales (human-animal doubles), 82, 106, 210; Elpidio on, 103, 109
Narratives: of Catholicism, 65; of conversion, 31, 53; of Pentecostalism, 30–31, 133; Peterson on, 162; of progress, 29, 65; religious, 162; socio-ontological, 162; use of, 133. See also Migration narratives; Salvation narratives
Native Americans. See Indios
Neoliberalism, social effects of, 93–94
Nepantla (in-betweenness), 207
Neville, Grace, on immigration, 124–25
Ngai, Mae, on illegal alien term, 159–60
Nieto, Raymundo, 40
Night hike, 145. See also Caminata Nocturna
Norget, Kristin, on fiesta system, 60–61
North American Free Trade Agreement (NAFTA), 77; consequences of, 172–73; migration and, 15

Operation Wetback, 77
Organizing. See Collective organizing
Origins, Ramón on, 200
Ornelas, Andrés, 39–41
Otomí communities: El Alberto, 1. See also Sierra Otomí
Otomí language: speakers of, 10. See also Hñähñu

Pachuca, Hidalgo, 10–12, 39
Paper cutting, 108, 110
Parque EcoAlberto, 2, 7, 10–11, 64
Patricia (informant), 147

Patrimonio Indígena del Valle del Mezquital (PIVM), 12, 179; creation of, 32; development by, 48–49; efforts of, 47
Patron saint: function of, 58; San Alberto as, 63–64
Paula (informant): on end times, 202–3; on faith, 134; life vision of, 203–4; on salvation, 204; on Satan, 134–35
Pentecostalism: alcohol and, 34; Bastian on, 94–95; bearing witness in, 65; benefits of, 197–98, 206; Caminata Nocturna and, 25; Catholicism and, 54–55; classification of reality in, 166; as disempowering, 196–97; in El Alberto, 2–4, 8–10, 12–14, 22–23, 30, 207–8; embodiment in, 89–90, 95–96; emergence of, 9, 207–8; as empowering, 197; family emphasis in, 128–29; focus on, 18, 195; on God's protection, 128–29, 132; growth of, 9, 30, 39; indigenous religiosity within, 22; Mexican Dream and, 193–204; migration and, 18, 22–24, 141–42, 193; moral lens of, 30; narratives of, 30–31, 133; oral nature of, 95–96; popularity of, 9; salvation in, 4; La Santa Cruz and, 59–60, 62; separation in, 8; stories of, 33–37; transnational nature of, 9; in Valle del Mezquital, 9; Vásquez on, 117–18; Willems on, 48; worldwide appeal of, 117–18. See also Conversion; Iglesia Cristiana Independiente Pentecostés
Performance: of border enforcement, 158–61; of Caminata Nocturna, 7, 22, 24–25, 162; of comunidad, 179; of indios, 177–78; psychological benefits of, 5–6
Peso collapse, 77, 93
Peterson, Anna, on narratives, 162
Phoenix, AZ: linguistic segregation in, 20; Pentecostal worship in, 83, 97–98; racial segregation in, 20
PIVM. See Patrimonio Indígena del Valle del Mezquital
Play: anti-structural, 166; in Caminata Nocturna, 165–66
Pollero, 210. See also Coyote
Posada Sin Fronteras, 6
Poverty, 23; Catholicism and, 41; Mariz on, 33; migration and, 170–71; prosperity theology and, 100; resources of, 92–93; in Valle del Mezquital, 31–32
Prayer, 6, 96; in action, 137–42; Elpidio on, 128–29; fasting compared to, 97; power

of, 99–100; as protection, 118–21; roles of, 130–31; solidarity and, 89
Predator-B, 159
Prevention through deterrence, 125–26, 152, 176, 192
Productivity, collective labor compared with, 183
Progress: Catholicism on, 66–67; migration and, 66; religious narratives of, 29, 65
Prophecy, 6
Proselytization, 49
Prosperity theology, 23, 31, 90; criticisms of, 100–101; Garrard-Burnett on, 99–100; poverty and, 100
Protection: Pentecostalism on, 128–29, 132; prayer as, 118–21; salvation and, 134–35; of youth, 118–21
Protestant ethic, 30
Protestantism, 96; arrival of, 37; capitalism and, 47–48; denominational differences within, 14; economy and, 49; in El Alberto, 42; Globus Veldman on, 140; growth of, 13; identity and, 13; Martin on, 48; in Mexico, 37–39; transformative effect of, 37–38
Pulque (fermented agave nectar), 34, 43, 107, 175–77, 210

Ramón (informant), 8; *cargo* of, 169; on consumerism, 169–71; on importance of origins, 200; job history of, 172; on migration, 169–70, 189, 199; personal experience of, 171; on survival, 173–74; on true satisfaction, 200
Raúl (informant), on El Alberto, 55–56
Reciprocal exchange, fasting as, 98–99
Reciprocity, Garret Ríos on, 107
Religion: development and, 12–13; Gooren on, 141; harmony and, 66; among hñähñu, 34–35, 57, 106–7; influence of, 20; Levitt on, 3; lived, 22; Long on, 165; Mariz on, 51; Marta on, 75; migration and, 2–10, 75–76, 126–27, 130; migration narratives and, 23, 76, 81; revolution and, 37–38; success and, 30, 89; Tomás on, 47; transnational bond of, 6; Tweed on, 205–6. *See also* Indigenous religiosity; Pentecostalism
Religious conflict, 44
Religious division, Lucita on, 62–63
Religious narratives, 162
Religious transformation: of Alejandro, 122–23, 133; in El Alberto, 13, 39–44, 47; Lucita on, 54; social change and, 47–50; survival and, 52, 94
Retablos (devotional paintings), 6
Revolution, religion and, 37–38
Ritual: border crossing as, 187; Caminata Nocturna as, 166–67; of death, 124–25; fasting as, 137–40; Schechner on, 162; undocumented journey as, 206–7
Ritual specialists (*bādi*), 108, 110, 209
Ritual symbol efficacy, 139
Ritual theory, 5
Roberto (informant): conversion of, 105; employment of, 78–79; as evangelical, 78–79; on migration, 71, 78
Ropa de manta (cotton fabric clothing), 69, 210
Rule of law, 136–37

Sáenz, Moisés, 38
Safety, lack of (*inseguridad*), 113
Salustio (informant), on Caminata Nocturna, 148–49
Salvation, 129; Alejandro on, 135–36; through faith, 198; individual, 4; Paula on, 204; in Pentecostalism, 4; protection and, 134–35; undocumented journey and, 146
Salvation narratives, 46, 50; Smilde on, 49. *See also* Conversion
Sánchez Vásquez, Sergio: on *cangandhos*, 107; on witchcraft, 103
La Santa Cruz, 55–57, 61; Pentecostalism and, 59–60, 62; role of, 58–59
Satan, 23, 101, 195–96; capabilities of, 115; Paula on, 134–35; service to, 111. *See also* Devil
Satanic possession, 134
Schechner, Richard, on ritual, 162
School closing festival (*clausura*), 7–8
Secundaria (middle school), 188, 211
Secure Communities Initiative, 160–61
Semana Santa (Holy Week), 148
Shamans, 106. *See also Bādi*; Dark shamanism
Sierra Otomí, 11; on life force, 108. *See also* Otomí communities
SIL. *See* Summer Institute of Linguistics
Sinaí, Templo, 18
Sirenas (sirens), 106
Smilde, David: on conversion, 133; on salvation narratives, 49

Social change, religious transformation and, 47–50
Social networks, migration and, 2–3
Social network theory, 3
Sorcerer (*hechicero*), 34, 210; witches as distinct from, 108
Sorcery, 106–9; accusations of, 112–13
Spanish fluency, among women, 74
Speaking in tongues (glossolalia), 9
Spiritual cleansings (*limpias*), 108
Spiritual mapping, 115–16
Spiritual nourishment, 96–99
Spiritual warfare, 4, 22–24, 101, 104; geographical origins of, 115–16; global scope of, 117–18
Stereotypes, in Mexican society, 180–81
Summer Institute of Linguistics (SIL), missionary efforts of, 38–39
Survival: *comunidad* and, 187–89; conversion and, 50–53, 61, 193–94; household, 92–93; migration and, 69, 194; Ramón on, 173–74; religious transformation and, 52, 94
Swimming pool area (*balneario*), 10–11. See also Parque EcoAlberto
Symbolic acts, Munn on, 139
Symbolism, 139; of blindfolds, 198–99; of death, 24; evil, 110–12; of torches, 149

Taussig, Michael, on devil references, 112
Temporary contract workers. See *Braceros*
Terrorism, border politics and, 154
Theologizing experience, migration as, 124–26, 131
Theology, of migration, 6
Tithing, 99
Tohono O'odham, 176–77
Tomás (informant): on Catholicism, 36–37; on conversion, 42, 50; recollections of, 33–34; on religion, 47
Tourism, 7; Caminata Nocturna and, 150–58, 165
Traditional greeting, 119
Transnational migration: daily challenges of, 83; religion and, 6, 9, 63. See also Migration
Transnational social field, El Alberto as, 8
Tula River, 10
Turner, Edith and Victor, 163
Tweed, Thomas, on religion, 205–6

Underiner, Tamara, 16
Undocumented immigrants: contradictions experienced by, 172; Inda on, 160; in U.S., 171
Undocumented journey: challenges of, 123–24; faith and, 129; as ritual, 206–7; salvation and, 146
Undocumented migrant: experience of, 1–2, 20, 25; transformation of, 7. See also Migrant
United States (U.S.): agricultural practices of, 172–73; communication to, 88–89; demographic shift in, 80–81; economy of, 171; immigration policies of, 76–77, 80, 136–37, 153–54; labor shortages in, 77; magical appeal of, 82–83; Mexico and, 208; migrant incomes in, 81–82; migration to, 76–81; misconceptions of, 170; undocumented immigrants in, 171. See also U.S. income
Unity, of El Alberto, 55, 64–67
U.S. income: Heriberto on, 81–82; Mateo on, 81

Vásquez, Manuel, on Pentecostalism, 117–18
Vigilias (vigils), 97–98
Vila, Pablo, on boundaries, 135
Violence: in El Alberto, 33–37; gang membership and, 93–94
Virgin of Guadalupe, 63

Wagner, C. Peter, 115–16
Water purification project. See Agua EcoAlberto
Weber, Max, 30, 47–48
Wemas (bones of ancestor giants), 106–7, 211
Whitehead, Neil, on dark shamanism, 108–9
White person (*gringo*), 78–79
Willems, Emilio, on Pentecostalism, 48
Witch (*brujo/bruja*), 34, 118, 209; bloodsucking, 108; sorcerers as distinct from, 108
Witchcraft, 102, 106–9; conversion and, 104–5; Sánchez Vásquez on, 103
Women, 5–6; household role of, 93; migration for, 70–74; Spanish fluency among, 74. See also Migrant women

The world (*el mundo*), 166; Pentecostal rejection of, 196
Wright, Robin, on dark shamanism, 108–9
Wycliffe Bible Translators, 38

Xaltocan, fall of, 11

Yolanda (informant), recollections of, 72

Youth: healing stories of, 118–19; migration effects upon, 146–48; protection of, 118–21; traditional greeting and, 119; vulnerability of, 119–20

Zaki (life force), 108, 211
Zidada, 56, 59, 106
Zinana, 56, 59, 106

ABOUT THE AUTHOR

Leah Sarat is Assistant Professor of Religion in the School of Historical, Philosophical, and Religious Studies at Arizona State University. She lives in Phoenix, Arizona.